PROBE

PETER KREEFT

PROBES

———————

Deep Sea Diving into Saint John's Gospel:
Questions for Individual or Group Study

IGNATIUS PRESS   SAN FRANCISCO

Cover photo © istock/Jay_Zynism

Cover design by Enrique J. Aguilar

© 2019 by Ignatius Press, San Francisco
All rights reserved
ISBN 978-1-62164-156-8
Library of Congress Control Number 2019931773
Printed in the United States of America ∞

Contents

Introduction

We live in a culture in which religion is supposed to be declining. Yet spontaneously arising, lay-organized Bible studies are multiplying like rabbits, in all denominations, especially among Catholics. Here is some rabbit food.

It is digestible by all species of rabbits and would-be rabbits.[1] It is not an agenda for denominational proselytizing or "sheep-stealing". In the course of exploring passages of Scripture that have occasioned disagreements in the past, some of the theological issues that have divided the churches will naturally arise (issues like baptism, the Eucharist, and authority); but this book does not settle them. It is usable by all believing Christians and by interested agnostics, too. (Why not?)

There is no good reason why Catholics, Anglicans, Eastern Orthodox, and Protestants, and different denominations of Protestants, should not study the Bible together. And there are many good reasons why they should. It is their common foundation and source; and returning to that common trunk together is bound to lead to greater mutual understanding and unity among all the different branches of Christendom.

∽

A book should always reveal its assumptions, the point of view from which it is written. Mine is twofold: (1) the truth of the historic Christian faith and (2) the infinite depths and riches of Scripture, which endlessly rewards endless explorations, or "probes".

---

[1] C. S. Lewis would (rightly) find that image insulting. Read his beautiful essay "Man or Rabbit?"—a defense of tough-minded honesty in religion—which concludes: "We are to be re-made. All the rabbit in us is to disappear—the worried, conscientious, ethical rabbit as well as the cowardly and sensual rabbit. We shall bleed and squeal as the handfuls of fur come out; and then, surprisingly, we shall find underneath it all a thing we have never yet imagined: a real Man, an ageless god, a son of God, strong, radiant, wise, beautiful, and drenched in joy."

Because (2) is true, reading and rereading each verse slowly, care-fully, thoughtfully, and prayerfully before trying to answer the ques-tions that make up the content of this book is extremely valuable. It is the essential difference-maker between success and failure in Bible study. If you do this, I guarantee that you will not emerge unchanged from your encounter with the Word of God on paper, any more than anyone ever emerged unchanged from his encounter with the Word of God in the flesh. Scripture calls itself "the sword of the Spirit" (Eph 6:17). Swords make a difference: they cut into you. Scripture is a two-edged sword (Heb 4:12) that actually does something, changes something, cleaves bone from sinew, soul from spirit, head from heart.

This book is nearly worthless in itself. Its whole worth consists in helping you to probe into John's Gospel. Please do not try to read it by itself, as you would read another book. It is a means, not an end; a telescope, not a star; a polishing cloth, not a jewel; an ugly piece of dirty paper money, not the beautiful things you can buy with it. After you read this introduction, do not read another word of this book without having a Bible open. Insofar as this book calls attention to itself, it fails; only insofar as it calls your attention back to the passages in the Bible that it probes and asks questions about does it work.

Do not treat it as a book of puzzles and the Bible as a book of answers to the puzzles. Treat it as a series of loving investigations or probes into the mind of your beloved Lord, a kind of spiritual lovemaking with the Word of God, which is primarily Christ him-self and secondarily his inspired book.

～

The "probes" referred to in my title are questions that you are in-vited actually to raise in dialogue with this greatest of books. For this book is not just a book; it is an instrument of a Person who talks back to you when you read it. The Bible is like a jack-in-the-box, and Jesus is the jack who jumps out. Warning: When you read this book (the Bible, not my book!) in the right way, you might see a Face looking back. Questioning it is really questioning him. (For both Scripture and Christ are called "the Word of God".) And whenever we question him, his answer is usually a question to us in return. It is much more comfortable for us to question than to be questioned, as it is more comfortable to look at someone else than to have someone else look at you. When you read the Bible, you do not look into a mirror, at yourself, or at a famous old painting of a man long dead; you look through a window, where Someone Else is watching you watching him. You don't see the hand of the Spirit who wields this sword or scalpel, but you often feel it, and you feel its sharp effects when it cuts through the skin of your heart and the bones of your mind. Bibles should come with warning labels, seat belts, and life jackets.

This book consists entirely of questions ("probes"). Why?

1. Because asking questions is the primary way to learn. That's one simple and obvious reason why children learn more, and faster, than adults do: because they never stop asking questions.

2. Because figuring out the answer yourself is much better than listening to somebody else (a preacher or teacher) do it for you. What you discover by your own thinking becomes yours more truly and more permanently than what you are given by others.

3. Because questioning yourself and your life is one of the very best things you can ever do. It means that you are being honest and open-minded and in search of truth, which is the food for the soul.

4. Because Jesus never discouraged a question, no matter how foolish.

5. Because whenever God shows up, he asks us a question, or at least gives us a challenge or a command or a task. It forces us to respond, not just to sit and be entertained. Even not-responding is a response. No one was ever allowed to be passive around Jesus. No one should be allowed to be passive in this Bible study, which is about Jesus.

This is not a quiz book or a book of tests, and there are no answer keys. So please do not say to me, "You've written a book of almost 1500 questions; may we please now have a book of the answers?" No, you may not. That is not to say that there are no answers. There are. There is objective truth in religion as much as in science or in common sense (though these three methods for finding truth are different). But many of these questions have not just one right answer, but many. For most of these questions are not merely about "facts" but about understanding. They are stimuli to make your grey matter move; they are "probes". You can't "look up the answers" in another book or on the Internet. You must look for the answers with your own mind.

This is not a work of "scholarship". I deliberately did not read any scholarly commentaries on John's Gospel when writing this book because I did not mean it to be a textbook for a theology course or an original contribution to scholarly biblical theology. I got all these questions from my own Christian experience and thinking, not anyone else's, and you are expected to answer them from your own experience and thinking, not anyone else's.

You are to use both your reason and your faith, both your head and your heart, both your common sense and your imagination, both your experience of this world and your love and longing for God. Don't tie one hand behind your back. If you shouldn't check your faith at the door when you study the great secular classics, then you also shouldn't check your reason at the door when you study the Bible.

Practical Points for Using This Book

1. The book is designed for all Christians, not just for scholars. Its questions are not academic but personal, "existential", life-changing. But the questions are not all easy. (Some are literally labeled "H" for "hard".) If they were all easy, they would be boring. Christ's questions were not all easy, either. But these, like his, are designed for wannabe saints, not for wannabe scholars. (See Mt 5:6.)

2. This book can be used by individuals, but it is best used in groups of two to twelve people who meet regularly (typically once a week for a few hours) for "dialogue" (conversations) about the passages

of Scripture assigned for study each week. Communal study is more powerful than individual study because "iron sharpens iron" (Prov 27:17), as in marriage. Each of us complements each other and sees something unique or from a unique angle. This is as true of reading Scripture as it is of reading life.

3. I do not recommend "meeting" on social media (for example, Twitter or "chat rooms" online) rather than face to face, for two reasons. First, personal contact is the way Jesus worked, and the way we should work too. Jesus didn't even write a book! Second, it's unwieldy because it takes much more time to text and read texts from many people than to talk together in the same room. But I may be wrong; you might try it and find that it does work. But I think it will take much more time to go through the material that way.

4. The most important rule for communal Bible study, and the one we are always tempted to avoid the most, is the need for everyone to participate. No one can be passive. Everyone helps to teach everyone. Bible study is not a college classroom where you sit and listen to a lecture by an expert. No one is the professor. No one gets paid a salary. All of you are rowing the same boat (the text) down the same river (active study) to the same sea, the same goal (more and deeper truth). It's like whitewater rafting: everyone has to row. If a pastor or priest is part of the group, he should be treated exactly like everyone else.

5. But many people are shy and don't want to speak up in public. Well, then, if you are one of them, you can use this Bible study group as a way to overcome your shyness. You are almost certainly not the only shy person in the group. And nobody has all the answers, and therefore nobody expects you to have all the answers. That's why you are studying in a group: what one person can't figure out, somebody else can. There is nothing wrong with saying, "I'm sorry, I just could not figure out the answer to this question" after you honestly give it a fair try. But there is something wrong with not trying.

6. If the group members are not good friends from the beginning, the shyness problem may seriously deter some people from contributing; but that shyness will get less and less as you get to know

each other more and more. No one should pressure anyone else to speak more and overcome his shyness too quickly. If one person's answers are always much too long, and the others always get impatient when he speaks, someone should quietly and respectfully (and privately) ask the long-winded person to try to keep his answers a little shorter to leave more time for others. But leave plenty of room for personal differences, for some people have to ramble and/or speak slowly and take more time to say something (they are God's chosen instruments in training you in patience), while others naturally speak in quick, short sound bites (they are God's instruments in training you in alertness).

7. If it's your turn to answer a question and you just can't, you should be allowed to say simply: "Sorry, I just could not figure that one out", and then someone else in the group (or more than one) will probably speak up and give it a try. In whitewater rafting, when you drop your oar, somebody else rows for you for awhile.

8. After the designated person gives his answer, others should feel free to add to that answer (but do not waste time by just repeating what the first person has already said) or to share a different perspective or angle or to ask another, related question or to disagree and start a friendly argument, if the group as a whole feels it is likely to be profitable. Tangents are okay, but you are there to study the text of Scripture, not to spend most of your time on tangents.

9. Please do not hesitate to give what seems to you to be dumb answers. Often, they are not nearly as dumb as you think they are. And sometimes dumb answers are the best starting point toward a better answer. Every contribution helps. This is not a competition, like a quiz contest. It's a mutual rowing/probing/studying group.

10. However you divide the questions up (I will suggest two ways below), everyone must be made responsible for, and must make himself ready to give an answer to, any and all of the questions, no matter how difficult they may seem and no matter how uncomfortable this responsibility may make you feel. If you get a hard question, remember that no one will judge you. No one gets grades. No one fails, except by not trying. Dumb answers are much better than no answers, just as dumb questions are much better than no questions.

11. Some of the questions have more than one part, labeled A, B, C, and so on. Whoever is answering a multiple-part question should answer all the parts of it.

12. Each participant should understand clearly that he is responsible for thinking through and preparing a brief answer to each question (keep them brief and to the point) before each meeting. These do not have to be written down, though it's okay if some participants like to do this, whether for their own private benefit or to read them out word for word when you meet.

13. How do you divide the questions up? Which ones do you assign to which people? Any way you like, but it has to be random and unpredictable, so that everyone will be ready to answer every question. The simplest way to do this is to use dice (one die if there are six or fewer people, two dice if there are seven to twelve, three dice if there are thirteen to eighteen, four dice if there are nineteen to twenty-four). Give each person a number, then designate one person to roll the dice to determine who will be the answerer for each question.

14. You could also just sit in a circle and take turns with the questions going around the circle. But everyone should sit in a different chair and next to a different person in each meeting, so that no one can predict in advance which numbered questions he will get.

15. No one is the leader. If confusion or tension should develop (though there is no good reason why it would), so that a "facilitator" is needed, that can be done, by consensus; but a "facilitator" is not a "leader", "expert", or teacher. He is not the engine or even the first piston of the engine, but only the oil that helps all the pistons move.

16. When most of the group feels it is time to go on to the next question, do so. This should be an easy and obvious and instinctive group decision most of the time. No one individual should be allowed to trump others by insisting on moving to the next question when most of the others don't want to or by insisting on not moving on when the others do want to. On the other hand, no one individual should be ignored or silenced, either. This is a team effort, even if your personalities bump against each other a bit. After a few meetings (expect the first ones to be a little uncertain and clumsy),

the group will probably begin to feel instinctively and collectively when you are going too slowly and when too fast.

~

How quickly or slowly should you go through the questions? That's up to you. Play it by ear; use whatever schedule works. If you start by trying to discuss thirty questions at each meeting, you may find that you are rushed; or, then again, you may not. If you cover fifteen questions a meeting, you may find that you are dawdling and going off on tangents that prove unprofitable; or you may not. You might even want to go faster than thirty or slower than fifteen. Time is not our master; it is our servant. Do not live by the clock or the calendar. Use them, do not let them use you.

If you covered fifteen questions each meeting, you'd take about one hundred meetings (that is, two years, if you meet weekly) to get through fifteen hundred questions. That's not too slow; we do everything too fast nowadays, and we miss much of life. ("Stop and smell the roses!") Fifteen questions a meeting leaves plenty of time for discussion. Thirty questions a meeting is also a reasonable pace, if you keep your answers short and to the point; and that lets you finish in one year (fifty weekly meetings). The only way you could do justice to fewer than fifty meetings is by omitting many of the questions. (But that's not a sin; my questions, like time, are your servant, not your master.)

There is no one answer to the question of how long it should take to get through all these questions. That's the wrong question, not only because there is no "one size fits all" but also because "getting through" the questions makes it sound like they are your enemies to conquer rather than your friends to enjoy.

If you go through all the questions not in a group but as an individual, I would recommend taking at least two or three times as long to go through this book as you would take in reading an ordinary book, if you ponder each question before you answer it in your mind; and much longer if you pray about them. (Praying and Bible reading work very well together, as two parts of one thing; each part pours new life into the other part.) It will take even longer if you write down your answers after thinking or praying or both. It might take years. So? Is that bad? If a thing is worth doing, isn't it worth doing for a long time?

You will probably think there are far too many questions here. But this is the Bible, and the Bible has an inexhaustible depth of wisdom. It has rewarded thousands of years of exploration by billions of Christians. It is a gold mine. There are not too many "probes" (questions) here but too few.

The fact that most readers will probably think there are too many questions here tells us something about our relationship to time. Our whole culture is dominated by the clock. Only when something very beautiful happens do we stop thinking in terms of how long a time it takes.

Do not rush! This is an absolutely crucial point. You will be tempted to look on this as a game or puzzle with a time limit and try to cover as much Bible territory as you can in a given time. Resist that temptation! There are two reasons for doing so. First, the Bible is inexhaustible. There is always more there than meets the eye. Second, our lives are far too enslaved by clocks. Let us free ourselves from that slavery and experience the exhilaration of emancipation!

When you fish (for fun, as distinct from fishing for profit or for competition), you don't use your watch. You don't calculate, "I caught six fish in twenty minutes." So here: keep fishing in the verse and question you are discussing until the fish stop biting, and then go on to the next verse or question and fish for more. This is not a game with a game clock (it's more like baseball than football in that way) or a business deal that has to be done by closing time or an academic exam that has to be finished before the class period is over.

If you feel very strongly that there are too many questions here for you, and you want to shorten them and skip some, then of course feel free to do so. It's your book and your Bible study. But do not do it to "save time".

And do not skip all the H (hard) questions, because they are usually the most important ones! Don't feel bad, either for yourself, when you are trying to answer a hard question or for others who are doing the same, when you (or they) are stumped by one. The "H" (hard) questions are deliberately designed to be challenging.

I predict that you will soon find even the hard questions easier than they seemed at first. I labeled unusually easy questions with an E to encourage even the least confident people to be confident about answering them, and I labeled unusually hard questions with an H to caution even the most confident people against giving neat little easy answers to them.

I deliberately did not make all the questions of equal difficulty in order to add a little drama and unpredictability to the discussions: you never know ahead of time who will get the easy questions and who will get the hard ones.

~

You can use different Bible translations (since comparisons are often instructive), or you can all decide to use the same one (since your data should not be as questionable as your interpretations of it). My quotations are from the Revised Standard Version, which I recommend as both accurate (literal) and elegant (beautiful). The English Standard Version is also good. The King James Version ("Authorized Version") and the Catholic Douay-Rheims Version are beautiful but archaic, like Shakespeare's English. New versions, with an "N", are usually not faithfully literal but are somewhat skewered in the direction of some kind of contemporary "political correctness" or by an aversion to anything striking, unusual, or poetic in the Greek text and a preference for dumbed-down modern slang.

John 1

Note on the Prologue (1:1–18)

We start very slowly. There are many more questions about this short prologue, these eighteen verses, than about any other part of John's Gospel. You are invited to move slowly and thoughtfully through these first questions, even though you may be tempted to skip some, either because they are difficult and mysterious or because they are not yet part of the exciting narrative of the events of Jesus' life that begin in verse 19. But resist that temptation, for this is perhaps the most profound poem ever written. It is a kind of God's-eye point of view on the person and mission of Jesus Christ; and Christ himself is the essence of Christianity. He is the sharp line drawn in the sand between Christianity and everything else. This line unites all Christians with each other, no matter how many other things divide them from each other, and this line also separates all Christians from everyone else, no matter how many other things they have in common with everyone else. In fact, Christians have many extremely important things in common with everyone else, both on the natural level, as human beings and creatures of God, and on the supernatural level, in common with believers in other religions. But the identity of Christ is an absolute and uncompromisable difference. For all Christians believe what John says about Jesus here: that he is more than a mere man; that he is the eternal, only-begotten Son of God. If you do not believe that, you are not a Christian. And if you do believe that, you are.[1]

---

[1] Like many words, the word "Christian" can be used either usefully or not usefully. It is used usefully when it is used as a description of a belief, a truth-claim. It is used not usefully but confusingly and misleadingly when it is used as an expression of the speaker's subjective personal feelings and attitudes. Many people use the word "Christian" as a personal compliment: "Oh, what a Christian thing you've done!" They mean well, but this is not a compliment if you say it to a Jew, a Muslim, a Hindu, or a Buddhist! In the modern secular media, the word "Christian" is now sometimes used as an insult, meaning "narrow-minded, intolerant, bigoted, Puritanical and Fundamentalist."

In the beginning . . . (1:1)

E1. Who was John, the author of this book?

E2. (A) Why did John write this Gospel (or "good news")? (B) Where do you go to find the answer to that question? (C) Scholars have put forth many theories in answer to the question why John wrote this Gospel; why are all of them superfluous? (Hint: The answer to all three parts of this question is in John 20:31.)

E3. (A) What other book in the Bible begins with the same three words as this one? (B) Can you find at least one other way in which that other book is similar to John's Gospel? (This may take a little thinking, but there are many possible answers available and plenty of time to look for them. In fact, you probably have both more time and more answers than you think. Others in your group should also contribute more answers to this question if they can.)

4. (A) Compare the way John begins with the way the other three Gospels begin. (Read the beginnings of the other three, too.) (B) Matthew, Mark, and Luke are called the "synoptic" Gospels because they are so similar to each other. ("Synoptic" means "seen together" or "similar".) Does the difference between John's "take" on Jesus and that of the synoptics amount to a contradiction between them, or not? (C) How do you know the answer to that question? Why don't you have to be a professional Scripture scholar to know the answer to that question?

H5. If John begins "in the beginning", what is there before "the beginning"? (Warning: This is a trick question! Hint: If all time began "in the beginning", how much time is there "before" the beginning? So is the answer to question 5 [a] nothing at all, [b] a lot more time, [c] infinite time, or [d] something else?)

(That is a word that has also changed its meaning from something theological, objective, and descriptive to something psychological, subjective and evaluative.) It should not be either a compliment or an insult to call someone a Christian because he may be a bad Christian, like Judas, or a good one, like John. And it should not be an insult to call someone a non-Christian, because he may be a bad one, like Stalin, or a good one, like Socrates. To call someone a Christian is simply a description of what he believes to be objectively true about Christ.

E6. If Christ was already there "in the beginning", did Christ himself have a beginning?

H7. (A) What does "eternal" mean? (B) If Christ is God and God is eternal, then Christ is eternal, right? (C) How can the same person (Jesus) be both eternal (because he is divine) and temporal (because he is human)? (This is perhaps the hardest single question in this book.)

H8. In John 8:58, why did Jesus say "Before Abraham was, I am" rather than "Before Abraham was, I was"? (Hint: Read Ex 3:14.)

. . . was the Word. . . . (1:1)

H9. The Greek word translated "word" here is *logos*. It is perhaps the single most profound word in any earthly language. It has three related meanings: (1) word, speech, language, communication, discourse, disclosure, argument, or revelation; (2) mind, thought, idea, knowledge, wisdom, understanding, reason, science, or intelligence, the thing that is spoken or written or revealed or communicated in meaning no. 1; and (3) the objective truth or meaning or order or reality that is known in meaning no. 2 and communicated in meaning no. 1. I put these three meanings in reverse order, for truth must first exist (meaning of *logos* no. 3) before it can be known (meaning of *logos* no. 2), and it must be known before it can be communicated (meaning of *logos* no. 1). John is about to identify Christ as the *Logos* who became flesh (Jn 1:14). So how do all three meanings fit Christ? (Hint: Read Jn 14:6 to start with.)

H10. John 1:1 could have been translated "In the beginning was the Truth" (meaning no. 3 above) or "In the beginning was the Divine Wisdom" (meaning no. 2 above). Why do you think the translators preferred "In the beginning was the Word" (meaning no. 1 above)? This is a very abstract question, but here is a hint to answer it. Ask yourself these two questions: (1) Can there be any words and language (meaning no. 1) without knowledge (meaning no. 2) and without truth (meaning no. 1)? (2) Can there be any truth (meaning no. 1) or knowledge (meaning no. 2) without words (meaning no. 1), any truth that is beyond words? So, in light of your answers to these two questions, which translation of *"logos"* says the most, includes all three meanings? (If this question is still too abstract to you, ask someone else to try to explain it.)

H11. All the sages and philosophers sought the truth, and some claimed to find it and teach it. But Jesus claimed not just to teach the truth but to BE the truth (Jn 14:6). This is a very strange and unique claim, and no other sane human being in history ever said this. This distinguishes Jesus from all the philosophers and sages and saints and prophets. What do you think it could mean? (This is probably the second-hardest question in this entire book.)

. . . and the Word was with God, and the Word was God. (1:1)

H12. Here is another extraordinarily difficult question. (Don't despair; the questions will get a lot easier very soon.) John will identify this "Word" (*logos*) with Christ. How can Christ the *Logos* be both "with" God and also be God? If I am with another person, in a relationship, I am not that other person. And if I am a certain person, I cannot at the same time be with that person, can I? I am myself, but I am not with myself, am I? (Answer that question! Am I?) Here are two hints to answer this very mysterious question. Hint no. 1: The Church, in her early creeds, used the distinction between "person" and "nature" to explain Christianity's two most distinctive and basic beliefs, the Trinity and the Incarnation. The Trinity means that God is three Persons but one nature, one essence or substance or being. And the Incarnation (the eternal Son of God taking on human flesh) means that the incarnate Christ was one person (a divine Person) with two natures (human and divine). Thus the Nicene Creed declares that Christ is "consubstantial" (one in substance, one in nature, one in being) with the Father. Hint no. 2: The word "God" can mean either the one divine nature or the first of the three divine Persons. Now how can these two hints help to answer our question and explain how Christ can both be with God and be God?[2]

---

[2] If you want a clearer account of the classic Christian theology of the Trinity, I recommend the first few chapters of Frank Sheed's *Theology and Sanity*.

H13. (A) Science works by testing all theories, all hypotheses, all explanations, by its data. The theory that explains the most data the most adequately is the best one. This question is about how the classic Christian theology of the Trinity does exactly that with the biblical data about God. This data includes the following: (1) God is one. There is only one God. (2) The Person whom Jesus calls his Father is God. (3) Jesus is God. (4) The Holy Spirit is God. (5) The Father, the Son, and the Spirit are distinct Persons; they are related to each other by commanding and obeying, hearing and telling, sending and being sent, loving and being loved. All five of these points of data are in the Christian Scriptures, the New Testament. Now explain how Christian theology does with this data what science does with its data, that is, it finds a single explanation that will explain all the data. In other words, explain the similarity in method between Christian theology and science; explain how the doctrine of the Trinity is a result of applying the essential principle of the scientific method. (B) Now explain two differences between theology and science: first, in the instruments each uses and, second, in what data each consults.

H14. In trying to explain this verse, let's try the following human analogy. Since one of the meanings of "*logos*" is "mind", we could call Christ "the Mind of God", and you could think of the relation between you and your mind as something like the relation between God and Christ, since you are your mind and you are also with your mind in the sense that there is a distinction between you and your mind, so that you can "make up your mind", you can have an interior dialogue between yourself and your mind: your mind can speak to you, and you can speak to it. (A) How does this human analogy help? (B) How does it break down as inadequate?

15. (A) Is it legitimate to use such human analogies for divine things? (B) Why or why not?

He was in the beginning with God. (1:2)

16. Why do you suppose John repeats, in this verse, two of the things he has already said in verse 1, namely, that Christ was "in the beginning" and that he was "with God"?

All things were made through him, and without him was not anything made that was made. (1:3)

17. Why do you suppose the second half of this verse repeats the first half of it in different words? Why do the Psalms constantly use such "parallelisms" (repetitions in different words)?

18. (A) If this verse applies to all things, it must apply also to mosquitoes, hemorrhoids, and cancer cells, right? (B) If not, why not? If so, what question does this raise, and how would you answer that question?

19. Since "him" in this verse refers to Christ, does this verse identify Christ as the Creator?

H20. If so, why do we usually think of the Father as the Creator instead of the Son?

E21. Find all three Persons of the Trinity in the creation story in Genesis 1:1–3.

22. If "without him was not anything made that was made", then who made Satan?

23. Who made sin?

24. Who made sinners?

In him was life. . . . (1:4)

25. (A) There are two Greek words for "life", *bios* and *zoe*. *Bios* means natural life, or temporal life, life that ends in death. *Zoe* means supernatural life, or eternal life, life that is immortal. Which Greek word do you think is used here? (B) Why?

26. (A) Did Christ have both kinds of life before the Incarnation? (B) Did he have both kinds of life during the Incarnation? (C) Does he have both kinds of life now?

27. Was the Ascension the undoing of the Incarnation, or does Christ have a human body and soul (the two parts of human nature) now in heaven and forever?

. . . and the life was the light of men. (1:4)

28. (A) What is meant by "light" here? What kind of a camera would register it? (B) How is Christ our light, "the light of men"? (C) What are some of the similarities between physical light and spiritual light that make this image appropriate?

29. E(A) Why do you think John used the word "men" here? Does it mean to exclude women or put them in second place? H(B) Why do you think he used "men" instead of "humanity" or "mankind"? (Hint: What's the difference between "a man" and "humanity"? Between "a woman" and "womanhood"? Between "God" and "divinity"?)[3]

30. This is a long question, with many (eight) parts, but they are all so closely connected that the same person should answer all eight parts. (A) In his Gospel and in his first Letter (1 Jn) John's three favorite words to describe God are "light", "life", and "love". These are all analogies from natural things in our experience, things that we all already have in one sense (on the natural level), to help us understand just a little bit the supernatural thing that God offers us through Christ, which we do not all automatically have but need to get, to receive, through faith in Christ. How would you distinguish these two levels (natural and supernatural) for each of these three things (light and life and love)? (B) How much of these three natural things (light and life and love) do we want? (C) How much of these three supernatural things do we want? (D) Do we ever want them to stop? (E) Do we really need them as much as we want them, or do we need them less than we want them, or do we need them more than we want them? (F) What is the difference between wants and needs? (G) Is there anything else that we want as much as we want these three things? (H) Is there anything else that we need as much?

---

[3] All the books that were written before the demands made by modern feminism used "men" to refer to males and females equally. That is simply what the writers meant; that is standard English usage, not necessarily male chauvinist ideology. Like those who first translated the Bible into English, I will use standard English usage in this book because I believe that past injustices to women (and there were many!) are not atoned for by present injustices to language.

31. How does God give us these three things? Which verse in John 1:1–18 is the answer to this question?

32. (A) In light of the answer to a previous question (no. 30), evaluate the following line from a modern hymn: "You can have this whole world, just give me Jesus." (B) Saint Augustine wrote: "He who has God has everything; and he who has everything but God has nothing; and he who has God plus everything else does not have any more than he who has God alone." Is that true? (C) If so, does that mean we don't need food and air? (D) If you had to choose either to go without food and air or to go without God, what would you choose and why?

The light shines in the darkness. . . . (1:5)

E33. Identify some of the darknesses, either general or particular, into which the light of Christ wants to shine. (This question can be endless, so put a time limit on your answer to it here in this group. But do not put a time limit on your answer to it in your life.)

E34. What should you do about your answer to question 33?

. . . and the darkness has not overcome it. (1:5)

E35. (A) What happens when a tiny light shines into an enormous darkness? (B) What happened to the dark pagan world when a few disciples started to tell it the "good news" about Jesus?

36. In what specific ways was the world "dark" before Christ came and "light" afterward? Try to give more than one answer to this question. (Hint: This "darkness" was not just ignorance.)

37. Pope Benedict XVI's friend Rabbi Jacob Neusner asked this question in his book *A Rabbi Talks with Jesus*: How did Jesus change the world? What did he give it that it did not have before him but did have after him? After Jesus came, the world was still full of sin and war and ignorance and hate and pain and disease and death. And the Pope gave this stunningly simple answer: He gave the world God.

Why is that the best possible answer to that question? Why is the question an excellent question?

38. (A) Modern philosophers called their rebellion against the Church "the Enlightenment". Yet the twentieth century was the darkest in history. More Christians were martyred in the twentieth century than in all of the previous nineteen centuries together. Why was this not a defeat? (B) Why can't the world kill Christianity by killing Christians? (C) The world couldn't even kill Christianity by killing Christ; why not?

39. Other lights (truths) can be overcome or put out (by the darkness of forgetting), can't they? Why can't Christ's light ever be put out or overcome?

There was a man sent from God, whose name was John. (1:6)

E40. What is the biblical term for "a man sent from God"?

E41. (A) Which John is this? (B) What did Jesus say about him? (Cf. Lk 7:28.)

He came for testimony, to bear witness to the light. . . . (1:7)

42. What is a "witness" in court?

43. Why do you suppose this is the same Greek word that is translated "martyr"?

44. What is the difference between a martyr and another innocent person who is murdered but who is not a martyr?

45. What is the difference between a martyr and a suicide? (The best answer is in Chesterton's masterpiece *Orthodoxy*.)

. . . that all might believe through him. (1:7)

E46. Does "him" here refer to John the Baptist, John the Evangelist (the writer), or Jesus? (See Jn 1:9.)

47. (A) What other religion in the world sends out missionaries and preachers because it hopes to persuade not just some but all people in the world to believe? (B) Why do Christians send out missionaries? (See Mt 28:19–20.) (C) Why don't Jews send out missionaries?

48. Why is it so important to "believe"? What difference does it make? (This question sounds very formidable, but it ought to be very easy for any believer to answer it from experience. And there are many answers to this question, not only one.)

He was not the light, but came to bear witness to the light. (1:8)

49. How does this verse explain John the Baptist's saying "He must increase, but I must decrease" (Jn 3:30)?

50. (A) Does this "decrease" demean John or exalt him? (B) Why? (See Lk 7:28.)

51. Compare Mary with John here: explain how her "subordination" (Jn 2:5; Lk 1:38) is her glory.

52. How does this principle about Mary fulfill both the Catholic exaltation or glorification of her and the Protestant demand that she never rival or substitute for Christ, like the moon eclipsing the sun? (In the Bible, how many times does she point to herself, and how many times does she point to him?)

The true light that enlightens every man was coming into the world. (1:9)

H53. Christ clearly claimed to be the only Savior from sin, the only "way" to heaven and union with God the Father: "I am the way, and the truth, and the life; no one comes to the Father, but by me" (Jn 14:6). Why does that claim not mean that Jews, Muslims, Hindus, Buddhists, and agnostics have no hope of salvation? How does John 1:9 reconcile John 14:6 with the possible salvation of non-Christians?

E54. Another, equally accurate translation reads: "He was the true light that enlightens every man who comes into the world", i.e., everyone who was ever born. Does "every man" in this verse mean everyone? Or only believers?

H55. If it means everyone, how did Christ "enlighten" (A) Abraham? (See Jn 8:56.) (B) Socrates, the ancient agnostic philosopher? (See Acts 17:22–23.) (C) Buddha, who founded another, very different, religion? (D) Gandhi, who was very holy but very Hindu? (E) Einstein, who knew much about the creation but claimed to know very little about the Creator except that he/it was very intelligent? (F) Judas Iscariot? (G) the fanatically atheistic philosopher Nietzsche, who called himself "the Anti-Christ" and called Christianity the sum of all evils? (H) Hitler?

56. How does John help us to understand the answer to this question (no. 55) by using the word "*logos*" instead of the name "Jesus" (his given name: Mt 1:21) or the title "Christ" (the Jewish "Messiah" or "Promised One")? (For the meaning of "*logos*", review questions 9–11 above.) (Hint: The name "Jesus" would have meant nothing to Abraham, Socrates, or Buddha; they never learned about him or heard the Gospel; so how did Jesus enlighten them?)

57. (A) In light of the answers to the last three questions, what should be our attitude toward unbelievers? (B) When Mother Teresa looked at any person, whether Christian or not, what did she say she saw? (Someone once said to her, "Mother, I wouldn't do what you do for a million dollars!" She replied, "Neither would I.") (C) How was that "seeing" the motivation for her whole life and work? (D) Why did she see this? (E) How might Matthew 25:40 supply the answer? (F) Don't you believe Matthew 25:40? Isn't that the motivation for your life and work as it was for hers? What, then, is the difference between what she saw and what you see in looking at other people?

58. What are some ways of watering down or explaining away or making more comfortable and convenient what Jesus says in Matthew 25:40? What excuses do you use to avoid *living* it? How do you think Christ looks at these excuses? So what will you do about that today?

He was in the world, and the world was made through him, yet the world knew him not. (1:10)

E59. This verse says that the world failed to know him even though it had two good reasons to know him. Explain the two reasons mentioned in this verse. See 1 John 1:1–2 and Romans 1:19–20.

H60. (A) If the world did not know him, how can it be blamed for not accepting him? Isn't ignorance a legitimate excuse? Is it an excuse (a) always, (b) never, or (c) sometimes? If sometimes, which times? (B) How is John 7:17 a hint toward an answer to that question? What is the implied relation in John 7:17 between our mind and our will, or between our knowledge and our choices?

61. (A) If an animal cannot be both outside a cage and inside the cage at the same time, how can God be both the transcendent Creator of the world and also one of the creatures immanent "in the world" at the same time? (B) Here is an analogy to help answer that question: both Alfred Hitchcock and M. Night Shyamalan put themselves into their own movies as one of their characters. (B1) Was that character one person or two? (B2) Did he have one nature or two? That is, was the same single person both the transcendent creator of the whole movie and an immanent creature in it, a part of the whole? (B3) Now compare that to Christ. (C) So what was wrong with the analogy of the animal and the cage? Why was Hitchcock or Shyamalan a better analogy?

H62. (A) In light of both this verse and the next verse (11), is "the world" a space word or a time word? (B) If it is a space word, does it mean the Jewish world ("his own") or the whole planet? If it is a time word ("the world" meaning "the present age or era"), then where (or rather when) are the limits of this age or era?

H63. How could Jesus be sent to the whole world if he was sent, and sent his disciples, only to the Jews (Mt 15:24; 10:6)?

64. John 1:10 repeats the point of John 1:5, because the Greek word translated "overcome" in 1:5 could also be translated "comprehended". In other words, the world did not comprehend or understand Christ. (A) Who did understand him while he was here? Did his own apostles understand him? (B) Why did they begin to

understand him later? And why have later generations of Christians progressed in understanding him, as shown by the progress in understanding throughout the history of the many Christological creeds (first the Apostles' Creed, then the Nicene Creed, the Athanasian Creed, and the Chalcedonian Creed)? Usually, a person's contemporaries and friends know him better than later generations who have never met him. Do you think your great-great-great-grandchildren will know you better than your siblings do? Hint: The answer is in John 16:7, 8, 13, 14.

But to all who received him, who believed in his name, he gave power to become children of God. . . . (1:12)

E65. (A) Shakespeare wrote: "What's in a name? A rose by any other name would smell as sweet." What do you think he meant by that? (B) If you try to cash a million-dollar check in your own name and you have only a hundred dollars in the bank, what happens? (C) What happens when you cash a check your millionaire father signed for you in his name rather than yours? (D) So does "in the name of . . ." in Scripture refer to the letters that make up your name, like a label on the back of a baseball player's uniform, or does it mean "in the reality and authority and power of this person"? (E) So is Shakespeare's speaker wrong? Could he be right about roses and wrong about people?

H66. (A) What happened when God changed Abram's name to Abraham (Gen 17:5)? (B) What happened when God changed Jacob's name to Israel (Gen 32:24–30)? (C) What happened when Jesus changed Simon's name to Peter (Jn 1:42)? (D) What will happen when God changes your name (Rev 2:17)? (E) So in Scripture, what happens when God changes your name?

H67. This is a long question, and a mysterious one, but an important one because it is about the heart of religion as a relationship between ourselves and God. (A) This verse has two verbs expressing the Christian's relation to Christ: "received" and "believed". They are used as synonyms. This is surprising because "believing" seems to be something we choose to do, something psychological, something that happens inside our own minds, something subjective; while "receiving" seems to be something that happens to us from without, like receiving a gift or a message, something that happens between ourselves (as the receivers) and someone else (as the giver), something objective. In other words "believing" is an activity (like pitching a baseball), while "receiving" is a receptivity (like catching a baseball). How can John say our relationship to Christ is both? (B) In Scripture, does "believing" mean essentially the same as "having a belief or opinion in your mind", or does it mean essentially personal trust, like a woman trusting a man in romantic love? (C) Does "receiving" mean something like getting hit with a baseball or something like a woman freely and trustingly choosing to receive a new life (a baby) from a man impregnating her, which is the sexual image that many of the saints and mystics use, based on their allegorical reading of the Song of Solomon? (D) Is the assumption of this allegory or analogy that what happens biologically in sex is a pale image of what happens spiritually in true religion, or vice versa? (E) Now let's use this analogy to help to solve the problem in question A. Is receiving a man's love or God's love or a pitched baseball a passivity or an activity? (F) So if we are speaking of Christian belief (faith) rather than any secular belief (faith), why is "belief" (or "faith") wrongly defined as "thinking a certain idea to be true even though you can't prove it"?

68. How does this sexual analogy (in question 67) cast light on why Judaism, Christianity, and Islam always call God "he" and never "she"?

H69. Critics often say that calling God "he" is male chauvinism. If the analogy above (questions 67 and 68) means that all human souls are like women to God, isn't this female chauvinism? (You might want to take a little time on this question, since there is no one simple, obvious, universally agreed-to answer to it.)

70. How can our believing that Jesus is the Son of God be the cause of our receiving eternal life (*zoe*) from him, as John 20:31 says? This sounds like "If you believe some very strange truths about me, then I will reward you by taking you to heaven, and if you do not believe this, you cannot come." But that is arbitrary, unjust, and cruel. It sounds like we get into heaven by passing a theology exam about these "strange truths", and we go to hell by flunking it. How does

the sexual analogy better explain the cause-and-effect connection between faith (belief) and eternal life? (If you understood question 67, that will help you to answer this one.)

H71. (A) The Greek word translated "power" in this verse is often translated "right" or "authority". "Authority" does not mean merely "power". It means "rightful power" or "moral power" or "power based on right". If "authority" (which is a right) meant simply "power", that would imply that might makes right. In fact, the very idea of "authority" implies the opposite: that right makes might, that right is a kind of moral might. It means the spiritual power of righteousness, not the physical power of force. So how is the "power" that Christ gives us, namely, the power to become children of God (that is, to have *zoe*, divine life, supernatural life, or eternal life, to share God's own divine life in heaven) also a "right" to become children of God? (Hint: John 3:6 might help explain this.)

. . . who were born, not of blood nor of the will of the flesh nor of the will of man, but of God. (1:13)

72. (A) This verse speaks of two kinds of birth. What are they, in your own words? (B) What are some other names for the "second birth", or what we receive in this "second birth", that are terms that come from the New Testament and from Christian theology?

E73. Connect this difference between the two births with the difference between the two kinds of life, *bios* and *zoe*.

74. (A) Does everyone experience both births? (B) If not, why not?

75. (A) What difference does the second "birth" make in this world? (B) What difference does it make after death?

76. The common-sense principle of cause and effect says that effects depend on causes, so you can't get more in the effect than what you have in the cause. Thus the cliché "you can't get blood out of a stone." How does John 1:13 and John 3:6 use this principle to explain why we need God to give us the second birth?

77. If the "second birth" is how you get *zoe*, how do you get the second birth? John seems to give three answers to the question:

water (Jn 3:5), the Spirit (Jn 3:5), and faith (Jn 1:12; 20:31). What is the role of each of these in giving us the second birth and *zoe*?

78. (A) According to the New Testament, do we need all three things mentioned in question 77? (B) If so, why? (C) What does Jesus have to do with all three?

79. (A) How do you know that "water" refers to baptism here? (B) What does the New Testament say that baptism does for us (1 Pet 3:21)? (C) Is the only kind of baptism water baptism? (D) (See CCC 1257–61.) If not, how would 1 Peter 3:21 include more than physical water in its idea of baptism? If so, would God refuse eternal life (*zoe*) to someone who believed in him and loved him but did not receive baptismal water through no fault of his own (e.g., if the church was bombed halfway through the baptism ceremony)?

80. (A) How do Catholics and Protestants agree about baptism? (B) How do they disagree? (C) Do Protestants believe you don't really need baptism because all you need is faith? (D) Do Catholics believe baptism works automatically, like magic, so that you don't necessarily need faith? (E) How do both of those ideas (C and D) seem clearly unscriptural?

81. (A) How do Baptists agree with other Protestants about baptism? (B) How do they disagree?

And the Word became flesh and dwelt among us. . . . (1:14)

H82. (A) What does "flesh" (*sarx*) mean? (I) Does it mean "skin"? (II) Does it mean "meat", like the German word *Fleisch*? (III) Does it mean the same as "body" (*soma*)? If so, why are they two different Greek words? If not, what is the difference? (This is a very important question, and often misunderstood. Look it up, or Google "*sarx*" on a Bible website.) (B) When the Word (*Logos*) became flesh, did he take on (I) a human body, (II) a human soul, (III) both, or (IV) neither?

83. (A) Why is the event described in this verse the most important event that ever happened? What difference did it make? (B) Exactly when did this event happen? (Hint: Catholics celebrate this event on a feast day that occurs on March 25th, not December 25th. Why?)

H84. Christians learned their concept of God, the concept of the nature of God, the divine nature, from Christ's Jewish heritage. This is the most exalted, perfect, and transcendent concept of God in any religion in the world. Islam also inherited this concept of God from Jews and Christians. Yet Christianity also has the most intimate concept of God's personal presence and closeness to us of any religion, for it announces the "good news" that this God became one of us, fully human (except for sin). How can such opposites, such "transcendence" and "immanence", coincide? This verse's juxtaposition, this equation, this event uniting such opposite things as the divine *Logos* and human "flesh" (mortal human nature, body and soul), seems impossible. How can the immortal One become mortal? How can the eternal One, who has no beginning or ending, get a beginning (a birth, in Mary's womb) and an ending (death, on a cross)? How is this possible? Why do over two billion people, most of whom seem quite sane and even wise in other ways, believe that this thing that seems impossible really, literally happened?

H85. This is really a "stretch" question, so you may give it to someone else if you prefer. (A) How is John's equation of "Word" (divine *Logos*) and human "flesh" in some way like Einstein's equation of matter and energy? (B) In a nuclear explosion, matter is transformed into energy and the physical power inherent in the atom is suddenly released. Did something like that happen on the Cross? What power was released then?

86. What does "and dwelt among us" add to "And the Word became flesh"? Suppose Christ had become human flesh but dwelled, not among us, but apart from us, far away; what difference would that make?

. . . full of grace and truth. . . . (1:14)

H87. (A) How can "truth" characterize a person, not just an idea? (Look up the Hebrew word *emeth*.) (B) How are "grace" and "truth" very different concepts? How is "grace" like "mercy" and "truth" like "justice"? (C) How is the relation between grace and truth like the relation between mercy and justice? (D) How did

Christ reconcile and unite mercy and justice in his life? (E) How did he reconcile and unite them in his death on the Cross? (F) How, in Christ, did Truth (or faithfulness) "spring up from the ground" and how did Justice (or righteousness) "look down from heaven" (see Ps 85:11)? (G) How were these two things (heaven and earth) reconciled by Christ's death (same verse)?

88. (A) All of us have some "grace" and "truth", but Jesus was "full of grace and truth". What does this mean? (B) Who else does the Bible say was "full of grace" (Lk 1:28)? (C) In what way was that different from the way Christ was full of grace?

. . . we have beheld his glory, glory as of the only-begotten Son from the Father. (1:14)

H89. (A) In the Old Testament, God said "No man can see my face and live." (Moses was the one exception.) Why does it seem impossible for mortal man actually to behold God's glory? (B) How did Jesus make it possible?

90. In this verse, Jesus is called "the only-begotten Son from the Father". How can we also be sons and daughters of God (1:12) the Father if Jesus is the only-begotten Son? (Hint: Look at each word.)

H91. Jesus consistently calls God his "Father". (A) What does that mean? (B) Suppose Jesus had never used that word; what difference would that make to us today? For instance, Muslims do not use that word for God. What does this word tell us about God that we would not otherwise know, understand, or appreciate? (C) What does it tell us about fathers that we would not otherwise know, understand, or appreciate? (D) In choosing this word for God, what awesome responsibility did Jesus give to human fathers? (E) When we call God our Father, is that only a symbol, image, or analogy? See Ephesians 3:14. If we are made in God's image rather than vice versa, does that make human fatherhood the image or symbol?

John bore witness to him. . . . (1:15)

92. What is a "witness"? What is his task?

93. (A) Which John is this? (B) How was he a "witness"? (C) How are all Christians "witnesses" in the same sense as John was, and how is our "witnessing" different from John's?

. . . and cried: "This was he of whom I said, 'He who comes after me ranks before me, for he was before me.'" (1:15)

94. (A) What did John mean by saying that Jesus was "before me"? Wasn't Jesus six months younger than John, since John's mother, Elizabeth, was already six months pregnant at the time of Jesus' conception (Lk 1:36)? (B) John says that Jesus "ranks" before him. What is "rank"? Are all ranks human inventions, like ranks in the army, or are there also natural, given "ranks"? If there are, what are some examples?

And from his fulness have we all received, grace upon grace. (1:16)

95. Just what "fullness" have we received from Jesus? Fullness of what?

96. How have we received it? Through what?

97. Why does John say "grace upon grace" rather than just saying "grace" once?

H98. (A) Have "all" without exception received the fullness of his grace, or only "we" who believe in him? (B) Why? (C) Is John implying a distinction here between grace and the "fullness" of grace? Or is there a distinction between the fullness of his grace and the grace of his fullness? (If no one can make much sense of this distinction, forget it.) (D) Is "his fullness" something other than "grace", so that "grace" is just the way we receive his fullness (i.e., as a free gift, rather than by working for it and earning it)? If "his fullness" is something more than "grace", what is it?

99. Is there a "common grace" or universal grace for all as well as a particular, special, saving grace? If so, what does that mean? If not, why not?

For the law was given through Moses; grace and truth came through Jesus Christ. (1:17)

100. Why couldn't we receive grace through Moses and the Mosaic law (the Ten Commandments)? (See Rom 3:20.)

101. (A) What is the purpose of this law in relation to Christ? (See Gal 3:23–27.) (B) How is the law in relation to Christ like an X-ray in relation to surgery?

H102. (A) John contrasts Christ with Moses by saying that "grace and truth" came by Christ, not by Moses. Yet the law of Moses (the Ten Commandments) is certainly "true" (Ps 19; Ps 119). Compare how "2 + 2 = 4" or "the sky is blue today" is true (let's call that "Level of Truth no. 1") with how the law is "true" (let's call that "Level of Truth no. 2"). (B) Then compare how Christ is "true" (let's call that "Level of Truth no. 3") with how the law is "true". What kind of "truth" did Christ bring to us that Moses did not?

No one has ever seen God; the only-begotten Son, who is in the bosom of the Father, he has made him known. (1:18)

103. Why is it true that "no man has ever seen God"? One answer, of course, is that God is a spirit, not a body. But we do "see" each other's souls with our souls, not just sense each other's bodies with our bodies and our bodily senses, as animals do. We understand each other's thoughts and feelings, which are not visible to the physical eyes. So what other answers are there to why we cannot "see" God (with our souls) even though we can "see" each other (with our souls)?

H104. Do the great mystics "see" God in their mystical visions? If so, why doesn't that disprove this verse? If not, what do they see? (When you get a hard question like this, don't just give up, even though you don't have a clear answer. Think about it. Try an answer, and if it doesn't work, correct it and improve it. Move! Explore!)

H105. Will we see God in heaven? If so, how? If not, how can we be satisfied without that? (Same comment as above: Try!)

E106. If only Jesus (the Son) makes God (the Father) known, how did the saints of the Old Testament know God? Who made God known to them? (Hint: This is really a very easy question! Look at the words of Jesus.)

107. (A) Jews and Muslims know God, the true God, the God of the Bible. For Jesus was a Jew! And Muhammad learned who God is from the Jews and Christians of his day. He says in the Qur'an that these "people of the Book", Jews and Christians, also received divine revelation from the one true God. In fact all the ninety-nine names of Allah (God) in the Qur'an are in the Bible, too. Yet Jews and Muslims reject Jesus' claim to be the One who makes God known in the unique way Jesus claimed it. How, then, do they know the true God? (B) What answer to that question can we deduce from the following two passages in John's Gospel? The first is that only Jesus makes God known (Jn 1:18), and the second is that Jesus, as the *Logos*, enlightens (makes God known to) every man who comes into the world (Jn 1:9). (C) Why does the first of these two biblical principles seem much too "conservative" for many people and the second one much too "liberal"? (D) What does that tell us about our two favorite categories?

And this is the testimony of John, when the Jews sent priests and Levites from Jerusalem to ask him: "Who are you?" He confessed, he did not deny, but confessed, "I am not the Christ." (1:19–20)

108. (A) What does "Christ" mean? (B) Is it a personal name or a title? (C) Why do Jews call Jesus "Jesus" but not "Christ"? (D) Why do you suppose many of the Jews seemed to think that John the Baptist was the Christ?

H109. (A) What does the question "Who are you?" mean? (B) How is John's Gospel as a whole the answer to that question about Jesus? (C) How does God ask us that question about ourselves every time we make a moral choice?

And they asked him, "What then? Are you Elijah?" He said, "I am not." "Are you the prophet?" And he answered, "No." (1:21)

E110. Why did some of the Jews think John was Elijah? (See Mal 4:5–6, the last thing said by the last prophet of the Old Testament.)

H111. The Jews mentioned three possible identities for John to have: (1) the Messiah, the Christ (both words mean "the anointed one" or "the promised one"), (2) Elijah, or (3) "the prophet". (See v. 25.) Who is "the prophet"? (You may skip this question if no one has an answer to it.)

H112. (A) Jews, like Christians, do not believe in reincarnation. How does Hebrews 9:27 prove that? (B) So what could the prophecy of Elijah's "return" have meant to them? (C) Did Elijah really "return" in Jesus' Transfiguration (Mt 17:1–13)? (D) If so, how was that different from reincarnation? If not, what happened there?

H113. Why do you think it was Moses and Elijah who appeared with Christ at the Transfiguration? How did these two differ from other Old Testament prophets? (Hint: Where are their tombs?)

H114. Jesus said that the coming of John the Baptist was the return of Elijah (Mt 17:10–13); but John said that he was not Elijah (Jn 1:21). Was John mistaken, or did John and Jesus mean two different things here? (Could John have been mistaken? Could Jesus?)

They said to him then, "Who are you? Let us have an answer for those who sent us. What do you say about yourself?" He said, "I am the voice of one crying in the wilderness, 'Make straight the way of the Lord,' as the prophet Isaiah said." (1:22)

115. John the Baptist is quoting Isaiah 40:3–5. Read it. What does "the wilderness" mean here? In what sense does it mean something more than merely a physical place with a lot of sun and sand?

116. What does it mean to "make straight the way of the Lord"?

117. In what ways are we supposed to be doing the same sort of thing John did?

118. How does Isaiah 40:3 show that this prophecy could refer only to Christ? (Hint: The answer to that question is in John 1:18.)

Now they had been sent from the Pharisees. (1:24)

119. Why do you suppose John mentions this fact?

They asked him, "Then why are you baptizing, if you are neither the Christ, nor Elijah, nor the prophet?" John answered them, "I baptize with water; but among you stands one whom you do not know, even he who comes after me, the thong of whose sandal I am not worthy to untie." (1:25–27)

E120. What was the difference between the baptism of John and the baptism of Jesus? (See Mt 3:11.)

H121. (A) What spiritual reality does physical water naturally symbolize? (B) What spiritual act does the act of washing with physical water natural symbolize? (C) How does Christian baptism include (I) literal water, (II) the natural symbolic meaning of water itself, (III) the natural symbolic meaning of the act of washing—all three of which meanings are already in John's baptism—and also (IV) something beyond John's baptism? (For this last question, explain and interpret Matthew 3:11.)

122. In Matthew 11:11, Jesus calls John the greatest of all the prophets. How do the last eleven words in this passage show why John was the greatest prophet? (Hint: Lk 14:11.)

123. (A) How does this verse show how John most resembled Jesus in "job description", i.e., his life, his acts, his work? (Hint: In the ancient world, whose job was it to untie tight sandal latches, remove sandals, and wash dirty feet? Compare Jn 13:5–17.) (B) Does this mean that God, our infinitely perfect and infinitely powerful Creator, freely chooses to be our slave? If so, how astonishing is that? (C) Did Jesus do even more than that? What more could a slave possibly give you than his life's work? (After answering this question in words, try answering it in silent prayer for at least a minute or two.)

This took place in Bethany beyond the Jordan, where John was baptizing.
(1:28)

124. (A) Why do you suppose the Gospels are so full of specific physical, visible, and literal geographical facts like these, that seem to have no deeper spiritual meaning? (For example, Jn 8:6b; why did John put this in?) (B) Contrast the absence of such little eyewitness details in a beautiful fairy tale: what is the famous line that a fairy tale begins with? (C) What does that say about the idea that the Gospels are a fairy tale?

The next day he saw Jesus coming toward him, and said, "Behold, the Lamb of God, who takes away the sin of the world. This is he of whom I said, 'After me comes a man who ranks before me, for he was before me.'" *(1:29–30)*

125. (A) None of Jesus' disciples expected him to be crucified as the sacrificial Passover lamb. Prove this by Matthew 16:21–23. (B) How, then, did John know to call Jesus "the Lamb of God who takes away the sin of the world"? (For a possible clue, see Is 53: 6–7.)

126. (A) Do you think John the Baptist, unlike all of Jesus' other disciples, understood that Jesus had to die on the Cross to take away our sins? If so, how could he have known this, and why didn't he explain it to the others? If not, what do you think he meant by calling Jesus "the Lamb of God who takes away the sin of the world"? (B) Did God mean more than John meant in this verse? (C) Is something like that true in every verse? Does God always mean more than we do, or do our minds and his sometimes completely match?

H127. Why do you suppose God typically (there are many instances throughout the Bible) inspires sayings like this that we do not fully understand at the time but only come to understand later? God certainly could have made his revelation much more simple and clear to everyone; why didn't he? If you were God and wanted to reveal yourself to mankind, wouldn't you do that? (Some clues to a possible answer: Jn 7:17 and Mt 13:10–16.)

128. Explain: "John's job was not to explain but to point."

129. What is meant by the last sentence about "after" and "before"?

"I myself did not know him; but for this I came baptizing with water, that he might be revealed to Israel." (1:31)

130. (A) Why do you think John "did not know him" earlier? (B) Why do you think he knew Jesus now? (How do the next few verses answer that question?)

131. How was it not just John's words but also his baptizing that revealed Jesus?

H132. (A) John seems to be saying here that he (John) revealed him (Jesus) to Israel even before he (John) knew who he (Jesus) was. How could that be? Could Jesus be revealed by John to others even if John did not know Jesus? (B) Do you think non-Christians, who do not know him, could teach us valuable things about Jesus? If so, give a possible example. If not, why not?

And John bore witness, "I saw the Spirit descend as a dove from heaven and remain on him. I myself did not know him; but he who sent me to baptize with water said to me, 'He on whom you see the Spirit descend and remain, this is he who baptizes with the Holy Spirit.' And I have seen and have borne witness that this is the Son of God." (1:32–34)

E133. John here refers to events that have already happened. Where are these events recorded in the other Gospels?

134. (A) Why do you think that all four Gospels begin their account of Jesus' public ministry with his baptism and with John the Baptist? (B) All four Gospels contrast Jesus with John in the same way: John baptizes only with water, but Jesus baptizes with the Holy Spirit. What does this mean? What are these two "baptisms"? (C) Does that contrast mean that Jesus' baptism is NOT with water but ONLY with the Holy Spirit? (D) If water baptism is not the only kind, what is the common meaning of all kinds of "baptism"? What does the word mean literally? (Look it up!)

135. Connect the last two things John says in this passage: How does the fact that Jesus baptizes with the Holy Spirit prove that he is not just another prophet like John but the Son of God?

The next day again John was standing with two of his disciples; and he looked at Jesus as he walked, and said, "Behold, the Lamb of God!" The two disciples heard him say this, and they followed Jesus. (1:35–37)

E136. Who was the first disciple we know of to follow Jesus? (Cf. v. 40.)

137. (A) Who do you think the other one of these two disciples was? (B) Why?

138. Why did these two disciples immediately leave John the Baptist and follow Jesus as soon as they heard John call Jesus "the Lamb of God"? (Hint: Remember John 1:29–34, which is John the Evangelist's account of what had happened the previous day.)

Jesus turned, and saw them following, and said to them, "What do you seek?" (1:38)

(N.B.: A surprisingly large number of questions arise about this one short verse for a very simple reason: because what Jesus says here may be just about the most important question in the world.)

139. These are the first recorded words Jesus said in John's Gospel. Why do you think he began there?

140. Why is this question a test of true discipleship? What kinds of answer(s) would Jesus accept? (This question can go much deeper than the surface!) What kinds of answer(s) would he not accept?

141. What answers to this question did many people who met Jesus give (at least in their hearts), disqualifying them for discipleship? For example, (A) Herod, (B) Pilate, (C) Caiaphas, (D) Judas, (E) many of the Pharisees, (F) the mob who shouted "Crucify him!", and (G) the not-good thief on the cross.

142. (A) How do you think you would have answered this question from Jesus if you had been there then? (B) How do you answer it

today? (C) How did St. Thomas Aquinas answer it near the end of his life when Christ spoke to him from the crucifix? (Look it up.)

E143. What do we all seek? What does everyone seek? Different people seek different things, of course; but how many things (or kinds of things) does every single person in the world seek? If there is more than one answer to this question, give as many as you can.

144. Why is there this deep agreement among all the people in the world about what they want? Where does it come from?

H145. How does this explain why some people go to heaven and some do not? (Hint: What is heaven, really? What does it consist of? Does everyone want what heaven really is? Does everyone get what he most truly wants?)

146. How does what Jesus says here relate to Saint Augustine's famous saying, at the beginning of the *Confessions*, "Thou hast made us for Thyself, and our hearts are restless until they rest in Thee"? In other words, if Augustine's saying is true, how does that explain Jesus' strategy in asking the question he asked?

147. (A) This is the first of many questions Jesus asked. We expect teachers to teach by giving answers, but Jesus teaches first by asking questions. Why? Why does Jesus ask so many questions instead of giving a lot of answers? (B) And why are both the questions and the answers not easy, clear, and simple? (C) Why do we prefer easy, clear, and simple questions, whether from Jesus or from life or from this Bible study? (Or do we, really?)

148. (A) How did God do to Job what Jesus is doing here? (See Job 1:8–11 and 38–41). (B) What result did God get (Job 42:1–6)?

And they said to him, "Rabbi" (which means Teacher), "where are you staying?" (1:38)

E149. How does this verse show that John is writing his Gospel to Gentiles, not just to Jews?

150. Is this half verse (38b) the disciples' answer to Jesus' question (v. 38a) or not? (You could make a good case for either a Yes or a No answer to this question.)

151. What does this question from the disciples indicate or imply or reveal about what is in their hearts?

He said to them, "Come and see." (1:39)

152. (A) Is Jesus' answer an answer, or is it a question? (B) Why? (C) Find another place in the Gospels where Jesus answers a question with another question.

153. (A) Does Jesus' three-word answer imply something more than the obvious literal meaning? (B) If so, with what other part or power of you than your legs do you "come"? (C) With what other part or power of you than your eyes do you "see"? (D) So how do we "come and see" Jesus?

154. (A) Was your answer to 153B something like the will or the heart or the desires or the loves, and was your answer to 153C something like the mind or the understanding? (B) If so, what is the relation between these two powers, namely, (1) the will and the choice to "come" and (2) the intellect and understanding or "seeing", that is implied in Jesus' three words here? Why does he put "come" before "see"? (C) How does John 7:17 imply the same relation between these two things? (This question sounds difficult and abstract, but once you see its point, it is quite obvious.)

155. (A) What is the cause-and-effect relationship between "coming" and "seeing" for physical things? (B) For spiritual things? (C) Why do you think there is this parallel? Where did it come from?

156. How is Jesus' three-word formula the most effective method of evangelism?

E157. Which of Jesus' disciples first learned this method of evangelism?

They came and saw where he was staying; and they stayed with him that day, for it was about the tenth hour. One of the two who heard John speak, and followed him, was Andrew, Simon Peter's brother. He first found his brother Simon, and said to him, "We have found the Messiah" (which means Christ). He brought him to Jesus. (1:39–42)

H158. Why do you think Andrew so quickly came to the belief that Jesus was the Messiah ("the promised one", "the one anointed by God")?

E159. Why do you think Andrew immediately sought out Peter?

H160. Why don't all Christians "evangelize" today as quickly and naturally and immediately as Andrew did?

Jesus looked at him, and said, "So you are Simon the son of John? You shall be called Cephas" (which means Peter). (1:42)

161. (A) How was Jesus' act of changing Simon's name to Peter like his act of forgiving sins? For the answer, see Luke 5:20–21. (Background hint: Religious Jews believe that your name is sacred because God gives you your name; your parents are only his instruments. Your name is also your God-given destiny. Therefore, no religious Jew is allowed to change his name: because our destiny, like our identity, is in God's hands.) (B) How, then, did Abram become Abraham, Sarai become Sarah, and Jacob become Israel?

162. (A) In light of the answer to the above question, why was the Pharisees' hostile attitude to Jesus forgiving sins and changing names a very logical reaction? (B) What is the only other possible logical response to him? (C) Why can't there be a third, middle response? (D) Why do so many people give this third, middle response, then?

163. (A) Will God change your name, too? (B) If so, to what? (See Rev 2:17.)

164. (A) "Peter" means "rock". Yet in the Gospels, Peter is more like sand than rock. He has foot-in-mouth disease, constantly saying the wrong thing. Was Jesus mistaken, then? (B) How is Peter different in Acts 2 than in the four Gospels? (C) What made the difference?

The next day Jesus decided to go to Galilee. And he found Philip and said to him, "Follow me." Now Philip was from Bethsaida, the city of Andrew and Peter. Philip found Nathanael, and said to him, "We have found him of whom Moses in the law and also the prophets wrote, Jesus of Nazareth, the son of Joseph." Nathanael said to him, "Can anything good come out of Nazareth?" Philip said to him, "Come and see." (1:43–46)

165. (A) What do you think Jesus meant by saying "Follow me" to Philip? (B) What do you think he means by saying it to you?

166. How did Philip respond to Jesus in the same way that Andrew did (1:40–41)?

167. (A) What prejudice blocks Nathanael from following Jesus? (B) Are there contemporary parallels to this prejudice? (C) Do you share any of them? If so, which ones? (You need not confess this to your friends, but you do need to confess it to God, for he can do something about it.) (D) Or are you wholly unprejudiced? Or would that be the most deep-seated prejudice of all? (E) Why is it so hard to be genuinely open-minded?

168. (A) How did Philip deal with Nathanael's prejudice? (B) Where did he learn that method? (C) How well did that work?

Jesus saw Nathanael coming to him, and said of him, "Behold, an Israelite indeed, in whom is no guile!" Nathanael said to him, "How do you know me?" Jesus answered him, "Before Philip called you, when you were under the fig tree, I saw you." Nathanael answered him, "Rabbi, you are the Son of God! You are the King of Israel!" Jesus answered him, "Because I said to you, I saw you under the fig tree, do you believe? You shall see greater things than these." And he said to him, "Truly, truly, I say to you, you will see heaven opened, and the angels of God ascending and descending upon the Son of man." (1:47–51)

169. Nathanael says three things in this passage: 1:46, 1:48, and 1:49. (A) What do each of these three verses tell you about Nathanael? (B) Do they fit together into a common personality picture? (C) Does Jesus' characterization of that personality (1:47) fit this pattern?

170. Jews of Jesus' time tend to associate the title 'Son of God' with the Davidic kingship. See, for example, 2 Sam 7:14 and Ps 2:2–7.

Such a title would not be used lightly. Nor was it an Old Testament term for the Messiah. So why did Nathanael call Jesus "the
Son of God"? And what do you think he meant by that term? Evaluate these three possible answers: (I) Perhaps Nathanael was just of
a very passionate, extreme, all-or-nothing personality. (II) Perhaps
Nathanael had heard the rumors that Jesus had already used that
name for himself, and he had not believed it until now. (III) Perhaps he was convinced by Jesus' little miracle (see vv. 48 and 50),
since no mere man can by nature perform a supernatural miracle.

171. What is added by the formula "truly, truly I say to you" (1:51)?

172. (A) Interpret Genesis 28:12 (Jacob's Ladder) in light of what
Jesus says in verse 51 here. What is Jesus claiming to be? (B) What
does this mean?

H173. (A) What does Jesus mean by calling himself "the Son of
man" here? (B) What does this title mean when God uses it repeat-
edly in almost every chapter of Ezekiel in addressing Ezekiel? (C)
What does this title seem to mean in Daniel 7:13? (D) Do you think
Jesus' use of it here is a response to Nathanael calling him "the Son
of God" in verse 49? Why or why not? (E) Do the two titles "Son
of man" and "Son of God" seem to contradict each other? (F) Do
they really contradict each other?

H174. The term "king of Israel" was a title for the Messiah in some
of the Old Testament prophecies, and most of the Jews thought this
meant that the Messiah would be a literal earthly king, like David.
In fact, Jesus' being apolitical was one of the main reasons most of
the Jews were disappointed in him and did not accept him as the
Messiah. (A) So how did Jesus fulfill this Messianic prophecy if he
was apolitical? (B) How does John 19:19–22 answer that question?
(C) Explain the irony of John 19:19–22.

John 2

On the third day there was a marriage at Cana in Galilee, and the mother of Jesus was there; Jesus also was invited to the marriage, with his disciples. When the wine failed, the mother of Jesus said to him, "They have no wine." And Jesus said to her, "O woman, what have you to do with me? My hour has not yet come." His mother said to the servants, "Do whatever he tells you." (2:1–5)

175. Why do you think Jesus chose a marriage as the place for his first miracle?

176. Women appeared in public much less in ancient times, especially in the Near East, than they do today in the modern West. Mary is not present at most of Jesus' miracles, but she is present at this one. Is this accidental, do you think, or part of Jesus' plan? Why?

177. Why do women even today, in our age of so-called gender equality, still concern themselves with marriages and wedding ceremonies much more than men do?

178. Why is the lack of wine such a serious problem?

179. (A) How is Mary's prayer/request to Jesus in 2:3 a model for our prayer? (B) What did Mary NOT say in it that we would expect her to say? (C) What positive thing does this not-saying indicate about Mary? (You might want to read Anne Rice's sensitive and very feminine description of this event in her novel *Christ the Lord: The Road to Cana*. Anne took a vacation from her popular vampire novels to write two very good novels about Jesus' early life; the other one is *Christ the Lord: Out of Egypt*.) (D) Why did Jesus change his plans at his mother's request? (E) Did he ever do this for anyone else?

180. (A) In verse 4, what does Jesus mean by "my hour has not yet come"? (B) How does this explain what he says right before it

in verse 4? (C) Verse 4 is not a personal rebuke and did not appear that way to those who heard it, because it means "What does that have to do with you and me?" In other words, it was not "you" versus "me", Jesus versus Mary, but "that" versus "us". But even so, it seems to be a refusal of Mary's request. Prove that it is not. (This part of the question is really very easy.)

181. (A) How much of the meaning of human life do Mary's words in verse 5 summarize? What needs to be added to this? (Warning: This may be a trick question.) (B) If you were as good a servant as these servants were, and if you obeyed Mary's advice (v. 5) as they did all the time, how would your life change? What would happen? (C) Is this question (B) best answered by thinking about it or by doing it as a kind of laboratory experiment? (D) In light of your answer to question B ("What would happen?"), why don't you perform this "experiment" all the time? (Be passionately honest with your answer!)

Now six stone jars were standing there, for the Jewish rites of purification, each holding twenty or thirty gallons. Jesus said to them, "Fill the jars with water." And they filled them up to the brim. He said to them, "Now draw some out, and take it to the steward of the feast." So they took it. When the steward of the feast tasted the water now become wine, and did not know where it came from (though the servants who had drawn the water knew), the steward of the feast called the bridegroom and said to him, "Every man serves the good wine first; and when men have drunk freely, then the poor wine; but you have kept the good wine until now." This, the first of his signs, Jesus did at Cana in Galilee, and manifested his glory; and his disciples believed in him. (2:6–11)

H182. In light of this miracle and the two others referred to in the following poem, explain Christopher Derrick's poem entitled "The Resurrection of the Body". It goes like this:

> He's a terror, that one—
>   Turns water into wine,
>   Turns wine into blood—
> What on earth does He turn blood into?[1]

---

[1] Christopher Derrick in *New Oxford Review*, October 1981, p. 23.

183. Here is a math problem for you. Assuming (I) that the six jars were twenty-five gallons each (standard size for that time and place), and (II) that there are sixteen glasses of wine in a gallon, and (III) that the wedding lasted ten days (which was common in that time and place), and (IV) that the average person drank six glasses of wine a day during the ten days of festivities (that was also common; most wines then were somewhat less intoxicating than they are now), how many people were probably at this wedding feast?

184. What is the significance of verse 10?

185. Put yourself into this scene as one of the servants. When you see this miracle, what do you feel? What do you think?

186. (A) Why are Jesus' miracles called "signs" (v. 11)? (B) Of what is this one a sign? (C) Is there more than one good answer to that question? If so, suggest a few more.

187. (A) Are miracles a good reason to believe in Jesus (v. 11)? (B) Why or why not? (Different participants may have different answers to this question, all of them good ones. You may want to discuss this for a little while.)

After this he went down to Capernaum, with his mother and his brethren and his disciples; and there they stayed for a few days. (2:12)

188. What do these insignificant domestic details add to the Gospel?

189. The same Hebrew word here translated "brethren" (brothers) also means "cousins" or "close relatives". What reasons are there for thinking that Jesus did nor did not have literal blood brothers?

The Passover of the Jews was at hand, and Jesus went up to Jerusalem. (2:13)

190. (A) How often did the Jews celebrate the Passover? (B) Why did they go to Jerusalem to celebrate it? (C) How often did those who lived far from Jerusalem, e.g., in Nazareth, go? (Cf. Lk 2:41.) (D) What had happened there eighteen years earlier (Lk 2:41–51)?

(E) If Jerusalem is south of Galilee and down lower on the map, why did they speak of going "up" to Jerusalem? (If someone else knows much more cultural and geographical details about first-century Israel than you do, you may give him this question.)

In the temple he found those who were selling oxen and sheep and pigeons, and the money-changers at their business. And making a whip of cords, he drove them all, with the sheep and oxen, out of the temple; and he poured out the coins of the money-changers and overturned their tables. And he told those who sold the pigeons, "Take these things away; you shall not make my Father's house a house of trade." His disciples remembered that it was written, "Zeal for your house will consume me." (2:14–17)

191. Everyone took for granted the presence of these money-making enterprises in the Temple. Why didn't Jesus? What words in verse 16 are a clue to the answer?

192. (A) If you found these things in your city's cathedral, would you do what Jesus did? (B) Why not? (C) So why did Jesus do it?

193. (A) Why don't the people in our culture, including the good and holy people, have the "zeal for your house" that was shown by Jesus and by the prophet who was being quoted here (David, in Ps 69:9)? (B) Where did we ever get our insipid image of "sweet and gentle Jesus"? (C) Compare that Jesus with the Jesus in Eastern Orthodox icons. (D) Compare it with Aslan in C. S. Lewis' *Chronicles of Narnia*. (If you've never read them, ask someone who has.)

194. (A) What does this incident say about the Christian's use of force or violence? (B) How was Jesus' use of violence inspired, not by hate, but by love? (Remember your answer to question 191.) (C) Did his violence actually harm anyone?

The Jews then said to him, "What sign have you to show us for doing this?" Jesus answered them, "Destroy this temple, and in three days I will raise it up." The Jews then said, "It has taken forty-six years to build this temple, and will you raise it up in three days?" But he spoke

of the temple of his body. When therefore he was raised from the dead, his
disciples remembered that he had said this; and they believed the Scripture
and the word which Jesus had spoken. (2:18–22)

195. (A) When John uses the expression "the Jews", does he mean
all Jews? Hint: He himself is a Jew, and so is Jesus. (B) John's Gospel
has been criticized for being "anti-Semitic". Evaluate this criticism.

196. What does the question in 2:18 mean? What is the Jews' challenge to Jesus?

197. How is Jesus' answer to this question (v. 19) the "sign" they
ask for (v. 18)?

198. (A) How is Jesus' body a "temple" (2:21)? (B) How is ours?

H199. To what "Scripture" do you think John is referring in verse
22?

Now when he was in Jerusalem at the Passover feast, many believed in his
name when they saw the signs which he did; but Jesus did not trust himself
to them, because he knew all men and needed no one to bear witness of
man; for he himself knew what was in man. (2:23–25)

200. (A) Would you label Jesus' attitude of not trusting men "cynical" or "realistic"? (B) How are verses 24 and 25 the answer? (C)
Jesus advised us to be "wise as serpents" as well as "innocent as
doves" (Mt 10:16); why are both parts of this advice equally important? What happens if either part is neglected?

201. In light of the above, why do you think the world nearly always classifies Jesus as naïve, idealistic, and unrealistic?

202. (A) If many were willing to believe in him, why would he
not trust himself to them? (Hint: John 4:48 may be part of the answer to that question.) (B) How is Jesus doing the same thing here
—offering the same test or challenge—as he did when he asked
prospective disciples "What do you seek?" (Jn 1:38)?

H203. No one in history ever performed more miracles, or more remarkable miracles, than Jesus. What is the role of miracles ("signs")

for faith? If they are good reasons for faith, why did Jesus not perform more of them? If they are not good reasons for faith, why did Jesus perform them at all? (Hint: Try using the human analogy of courtship. Does Romeo expect Juliet to make a leap in the dark? Or does he bring a battery of lawyers and philosophers to convince her to marry him? What does he do? What "signs" does he give her?)

John 3

Now there was a man of the Pharisees, named Nicodemus, a ruler of the Jews. This man came to Jesus by night and said to him, "Rabbi, we know that you are a teacher come from God; for no one can do these signs that you do, unless God is with him." (3:1–2)

204. How many things can you tell us about the Pharisees?

205. Why did Nicodemus come to Jesus "by night"?

206. (A) Do you think Nicodemus' first sentence praising Jesus is sincere, a skeptical "testing the waters", or a piece of flattering "baloney"? (B) Do you think its reasoning is logical? Does the premise (Jesus' "signs", i.e., miracles) logically entail the conclusion (Jesus is a teacher from God)?

207. (A) What is the question Nicodemus has deep in his heart that he is really asking Jesus? (B) Where does Jesus answer it? (C) How did Jesus know that was his real question?

208. (A) What was the connection between the Jewish Old Testament prophecies about the "Messiah" and the prophecies about the "kingdom of God?" What did the Messiah have to do with the kingdom? (B) How did this connection explain what Jesus said to Nicodemus in verse 3, especially in light of the answer to question 207? (C) Why do you think God left both of these concepts so mysterious in the Jewish prophecies? He certainly could have been more clear and specific! (Hint: Look at the questions about 1:37.)

Jesus answered him, "Truly, truly, I say to you, unless one is born anew, he cannot see the kingdom of God." (3:3)

E209. How is the answer startling?

E210. What is the point of adding "truly, truly, I say to you"?

E211. What is the relationship between "the kingdom of God", "the kingdom of heaven", "heaven", "salvation", "union with God", and "Paradise"?

E212. What is the relationship between being "born anew", "sanctifying grace", "regeneration", "justification", "supernatural life", "divine life", and "eternal life"?

E213. What is the relation between what is common to all the expressions in question 211 and what is common to all the expressions in question 212?

E214. How do verses 4–6 show that Jesus meant "birth" here as an analogy or image or metaphor rather than literally, physically, and biologically?

E215. Jesus used "birth" as an analogy or image or metaphor—for what?

H216. Why do you think he chose this analogy rather than any other, such as waking up (which was Buddha's image for the mystical "Enlightenment" of "Nirvana"), or education (which was Plato's image) or maturing (which is modern psychology's most common image)?

217. Why is birth so radical an event that we celebrate our birthdays and our friends' birthdays each year? What does birth give you that nothing else in life gives you?

Nicodemus said to him, "How can a man be born when he is old? Can he enter a second time into his mother's womb and be born?" (3:4)

218. (A) Do you think Nicodemus meant to ask whether Jesus thought this was literally possible? (B) Why or why not? (C) Do you think he meant to ask whether Jesus was talking about reincarnation, as in Hinduism or Buddhism? (D) Why or why not? (E) So what do you think Nicodemus meant by this question? (Put yourself in Nicodemus' place. Imagine you had never heard this phrase before.)

Jesus answered, "Truly, truly, I say to you, unless one is born of water and the Spirit, he cannot enter the kingdom of God. That which is born of the flesh is flesh, and that which is born of the Spirit is spirit." (3:5–6)

E219. What did Jesus mean by "water" here?

E220. What did Jesus mean by "the Spirit" here?

221. If "water" refers to baptism, is Jesus saying that no one who does not receive water baptism can be saved, so that if a baby dies a second before the water of baptism touches his body, he does not go to heaven, but if he dies a second after, he does? If that is absurd, then is there more than one kind of baptism?

E222. Do "flesh" and "spirit" mean the same as "body" and "soul"? Hint no. 1: the Greek word for "flesh" is *sarx*, and the Greek word for "body" is *soma*. The Greek word for "spirit" is *pneuma*, and the Greek word for "soul" is *psyche*. Hint no. 2: In Galatians 5:19–21, how many of the "works of the flesh" does Paul list? Of these, how many are works of the body, and how many are works of the soul? Hint no. 3: In Galatians 5:17 Paul sees "flesh" and "spirit" as enemies of each other. Are body and soul enemies of each other?

223. So what do "flesh" and "spirit" mean?

224. How does the answer to question 77 (on 1:13) help us to understand 3:6?

"Do not marvel that I said to you, 'You must be born anew.' The wind blows where it wills, and you hear the sound of it, but you do not know where it comes from or where it goes; so it is with every one who is born of the Spirit." (3:7–8)

E225. When Jesus says "do not marvel", is he saying that the new birth is not really so marvelous, or is he saying that there are visible clues in nature that point to this invisible thing and make it more understandable and believable? (Look at the next words; interpret these words in that context.)

H226. In both Greek and Hebrew, the same word can mean both "wind", "breath", and "spirit" (the word is *pneuma* in Greek, *ruah'* in Hebrew). (A) Is this a mere coincidence? (B) If not, why not? (C) Why does the same word mean both something visible and material ("breath") and something invisible and spiritual ("spirit")? Were the ancient Greeks and Jews who invented these words incapable of making the distinction between the material and the spiritual?

227. (A) Would it be correct to say that the parallel or similarity between the wind and the Spirit that Jesus is trying to get across to Nicodemus here is (1) that the Spirit itself is invisible, like the wind, but its effects are visible; or (2) that just as the wind is harder to see than the things it moves (e.g., the trees), so those who are born of and moved by the Spirit are harder to understand than those who are born only of the flesh and moved or motivated only by the flesh? Could it be both? (B) How does 1 Corinthians 2:14–16 explain the cause of (A)(2)? (C) How does John 10–11 explain its effects?

228. (A) Is Jesus talking about God the Holy Spirit when he uses the word "spirit" or about human beings who are born of the Holy Spirit and "have" the Spirit in their souls? (B) Could it be both?

229. The wind is invisible to our eyes, but its effects are not. If the same is true of the Spirit, what are some of the visible effects of the Spirit, some of the visible differences he makes? In other words, what are some of the leaves that the "wind" of the Spirit visibly shakes in our world?

230. This question is added just to make sure you understand that "flesh" does not mean "body" and "spirit" does not mean "soul". (A) Which of the two following things do you think is harder to understand and believe: (I) the physical resurrection of Jesus' body, which was supernaturally effected by the Holy Spirit, or (II) the non-physical thoughts in the natural mind of an unbeliever, e.g., Pontius Pilate, who decided to execute Jesus? (B) Which of these two events was an event of the "flesh"?

Nicodemus said to him, "How can this be?" (3:9)

H231. Nicodemus was not slow or dull of mind. He was a Pharisee, and the Pharisees were very intelligent and learned Jews and experts in the whole of the Jewish Scriptures and history. Why do you think Nicodemus at first found what Jesus said so astonishing and apparently impossible?

232. Must we always understand the "how" of a thing before we can understand it? Give examples.

Jesus answered him, "Are you a teacher of Israel, and yet you do not understand this?" (3:10)

233. Explain the irony, even the humor, in Jesus' question here.

234. (A) Is there a particularly Jewish tone to the humor of Jesus' saying? Speak it aloud as a Jewish comedian would. (B) Why do you think there are so many Jewish comedians as compared to Gentile ones? (C) Was Jesus specifically Jewish, not just generically human? (D) If the answer is Yes, why is that a problem for some people but not others?

235. (A) Would Jesus say the same today to many religious "experts" as he said to Nicodemus? Are there some today who understand almost everything about their religion except "what it's all about"? (B) If so, give their descriptions (not their names). What are they like? What are they "into" instead of "what it's all about"?

"Truly, truly, I say to you, we speak of what we know, and bear witness to what we have seen; but you do not receive our testimony." (3:11)

236. Why does Jesus use the plural ("we") here? Do you think Jesus is talking about himself and the Father? Himself and his disciples? Or is it just a generic "we", a general principle?

237. (A) What makes a "witness" more authentic than an "expert"? (B) How does this apply to religion?

"If I have told you earthly things and you do not believe, how can you believe if I tell you heavenly things?" (3:12)

238. (A) How can Jesus call what he has told Nicodemus about, namely, being "born anew" of the Spirit, "earthly things"? (B) What

would be an example of "heavenly things" that Jesus did not tell him about?

239. Why do you think Jesus spoke much more to us of "earthly things" than of "heavenly things"?

240. (A) What is the right relationship between "earthly things" and "heavenly things" according to Jesus' own directions for our prayers in Matthew 6:10? (B) How does this answer the objection that thinking about "heavenly things" is unrealistic, impractical, and escapist?

"No one has ascended into heaven but he who descended from heaven, the Son of man." (3:13)

241. How is this verse similar to 1:18?

242. The original Greek manuscripts of the New Testament do not have quotation marks. (A) Where do you think the sayings of Jesus end and John's comments on them begin between verses 12 and 22 in this chapter? (B) Do verses 16–21 sound like a continuation of Jesus' talk to Nicodemus? (C) Do you think Jesus is predicting his Ascension in this verse (3:13)?

243. Are Enoch (Gen 5:24) and Elijah (2 Kings 2:11) contradictions or exceptions to what Jesus says here?

"And as Moses lifted up the serpent in the wilderness, so must the Son of man be lifted up, that whoever believes in him may have eternal life." (3:14–15)

244. (A) How many Jews do you think understood the point of the miracle to which Jesus referred here (Num 21:1–9) when they saw it at the time? (B) Why did God perform this miracle if miracles are "signs" and no one could correctly read that "sign" at the time?

245. How many of the following elements in this story (Num 21:1–9) can you explain as divinely designed Messianic symbols in light of the New Testament? (a) the serpent; (b) why it was made of bronze; (c) the pole; (d) being "lifted up"; (e) the deathly sickness

that the serpent healed; (f) looking up at the serpent—why that healed the Jews who did it.

246. Mention one or two (or more than that, if you have the time and the interest) other important events in the Old Testament that became clear only in light of Christ.

For God so loved the world that he gave his only-begotten Son, that whoever believes in him should not perish but have eternal life. (3:16)

E247. This is the verse you often see held up on fans' signs at baseball games. Why? Why is this the most beloved and most quoted verse in the Bible?

H248. How much does God love us? So much that he gave up, to the cruelest torture and death on earth, the most precious thing he had in heaven, his only begotten Son, for the only creatures in the universe who rebelled against him: us. Why? Why did God love us that much? Is he crazy?

249. Is love the motive for everything God does in history?

250. (A) What are some of the things that God does (I) in the Bible, (II) in world history, and (III) in your own life that do not seem to be motivated by love? (B) Why do you believe they are? Or, if not, why do you believe they are not?

251. What is meant by "the world" in this verse?

252. Explain how God's gift to us of his Son, two thousand years ago, is an expression in time of a gift, or a giving, that is the eternal divine life of the Trinity.

H253. What does this "gift of self" mean? How can you give yourself? How can the same self be both the giver and the gift given?

254. What happens when you give yourself away? (Cf. Jn 12:24.)

255. Are there any exceptions to the "whoever" in John 3:16?

256. What is meant by "believes in him"? (Cf. 1:12.)

257. What is meant by "perish"?

258. If Christ is the Father's "only-begotten Son", how can we also be sons and daughters of God? (Hint: Read each word of the verse carefully.)

For God sent the Son into the world, not to condemn the world, but that the world might be saved through him. (3:17)

E259. There have been a number of heresies in the history of the Church that contrasted the just, judging, condemning, punishing God of the Old Testament and of Judaism with the loving, merciful, forgiving God of the New Testament and Christianity. That idea is still fairly common among some Christians today. Is that idea adequately refuted by this verse coupled with the fact that Jesus himself was a Jew and believed all of the Jewish Scriptures and their description of God?

260. If the answer to the previous question is Yes, then God's essential attitude toward the world (of sinners) must have been the same in Old Testament times as it is here described in 3:16–17: love and mercy rather than condemnation. Prove that from the Old Testament. (The answer to this question can be brief, or it can well occupy half a lifetime.)

H261. If all this is true, how do you explain all the many passages in the Old Testament about God's wrath (anger) and judgment and punishment?

He who believes in him is not condemned; he who does not believe is condemned already, because he has not believed in the name of the only-begotten Son of God. (3:18)

262. How do you reconcile verse 17, which says that God did not condemn the world of sinners, with verse 18, which speaks of unbelievers as "condemned"? Who or what is the cause of their condemnation?

H263. How does this answer help to reconcile the infinite love of God with the existence of hell (which Jesus clearly taught in many places)?

H264. (A) Is John saying that all who believe the Christian doctrine about Christ will go to heaven and all who do not believe
it, since they are not Christians, will go to hell? (B) If not, what
does he mean by "believe" here? In answering this question, review
questions 53–58, about John 1:9.

*And this is the judgment, that the light has come into the world, and men
loved darkness rather than light, because their deeds were evil. (3:19)*

265. One translation of this verse begins: "And this is how the
judgment works." What is the agent of judgment, according to this
verse? What is it that judges men as fit for heaven or hell?

266. There are three parts to the answer to question 265 in this
verse: the light, the love, and the deeds. What is the cause-and-effect
relationship among these three things? Which comes first, second,
and third? (Hint: Sometimes one thing is both a cause and an effect
of the other thing.)

267. (A) Explain how "loved" is the key word in this verse that
answers question 265. (B) Connect this with 1:38. (Hint: Remember that to love, to will, and to want are essentially the same thing.)

268. (A) How does this verse answer question 264 by shifting the
locus (place) of decision—the decision that makes the difference
between heaven and hell—from the mind to the will, from the
head to the heart, from doctrine to life? (B) How is that "shifting"
more fair and just than its alternative?

*For every one who does evil hates the light, and does not come to the light,
lest his deeds should be exposed. But he who does what is true comes to
the light, that it may be clearly seen that his deeds have been wrought in
God. (3:20–21)*

269. In light of the psychology in this verse, explain why dishonesty is always part of every other evil.

270. Why is dishonesty (hating the light of truth) more destructive
than any other sin? (Cf. 3:19.)

271. Suppose we were totally, uncompromisingly honest all the
time: What would be the result?

272. Why does John write "he who does what is true"? Shouldn't he say "he who does what is good"?

H273. This question is very important, but it is also very abstract and philosophical, so the person designated to answer this question is allowed to defer to someone else if he wants to. (A) Are truth and goodness both absolute values, or is one relative? (B) If they are both absolute values, how can there be two absolutes? (C) If one is relative to the other, which is relative to which? (D) Can each of them be relative to the other one? (E) If your mind's proper object is truth and your will or heart or love's proper object is goodness, which of these two is the cause, and which is the effect? Does your mind lead your will, like a navigator with a map leading the driver, or does your will command your mind, like the driver commanding his navigator? Or is it both? (Hint: Recall question 266.)

After this Jesus and his disciples went into the land of Judea; there he remained with them and baptized. John was also baptizing at Aenon near Salim, because there was much water there; and people came and were baptized. For John had not yet been put in prison. (3:22–24)

274. (A) Were John and Jesus doing the very same thing when they were baptizing, or were they doing different things? (B) If they were different, how were they different? Is it correct to say that Jesus' baptism included all that was in John's baptism, but John's baptism did not include all that was in Jesus'? Explain.

Now a discussion arose between John's disciples and a Jew over purifying. And they came to John, and said to him, "Rabbi, he who was with you beyond the Jordan, to whom you bore witness, here he is, baptizing, and all are going to him." John answered, "No one can receive anything except what is given him from heaven. You yourselves bear me witness, that I said, I am not the Christ, but I have been sent before him. He who has the bride is the bridegroom; the friend of the bridegroom, who stands and hears him, rejoices greatly at the bridegroom's voice; therefore this joy of mine is now full. He must increase, but I must decrease." (3:25–30)

H275. Why did John receive his "demotion" (v. 30) with joy (v. 29)?

H276. (A) How does 1 Corinthians 4:7 explain John 3:27? (B) What is the gift given from heaven about which John is talking in verse 27, and who is receiving it?

277. About whom is John talking in verse 29? Who is the bridegroom? Who is the friend of the bridegroom? Who is the bride?

He who comes from above is above all; he who is of the earth belongs to the earth, and of the earth he speaks; he who comes from heaven is above all. He bears witness to what he has seen and heard, yet no one receives his testimony; he who receives his testimony sets his seal to this, that God is true. For he whom God has sent utters the words of God, for it is not by measure that he gives the Spirit. (3:31–34)

278. Identify each of the following: (A) "he who comes from above" in verse 31; (B) "he who is of the earth" in verse 31; (C) he who "bears witness to what he has seen and heard" in verse 32; (D) "he who receives his testimony" in verse 33; (E) "he whom God has sent" in verse 34; (F) he who "gives the Spirit" in verse 34.

279. (A) What is meant by "not by measure" in verse 34? Hint: Jesus could have saved the world by shedding just one drop of his divine blood, at his circumcision; yet he poured out all twelve pints of his blood on the Cross. Why? (B) How is there a parallel here between God's gift of his Son and God's gift of his Spirit?

The Father loves the Son, and has given all things into his hand. (3:35)

280. In Matthew 28:18–20, what conclusion does Jesus draw from the fact of which he speaks in this verse?

281. Explain the relation between John 3:35 and John 5:30. Do they say opposite things, or do they fit together?

He who believes in the Son has eternal life; he who does not obey the Son shall not see life, but the wrath of God rests upon him. (3:36)

282. Why can't there be anyone who does not fit into one of these two classes of persons?

283. C. S. Lewis wrote that "there are only two kinds of people in the end: those who say to God, 'Thy will be done,' and those to whom God says, in the end, '*Thy* will be done.'" What, exactly, do you think he meant?

284. Why isn't John confusing things by changing the standard for distinguishing who does and who does not have eternal life when he contrasts "he who *believes* in the Son" with "he who does not *obey* the Son"? Why isn't this contrasting good apples with bad oranges? (Hint: James 2:24, 26.)

H285. Here is another question you may want to omit because it is a very deep theological question that has unfortunately divided Christians for five hundred years even though the solution to it is in the Bible and you yourself are able to see it. The question is: Why do James 2:24–26 and Romans 2:13 (about the importance of good works and justification by good works) not contradict Romans 3:28 and Romans 4:1–3 (about the importance of faith and justification by faith)? (Notice how quickly and easily we are all tempted to focus on only our favorite passages of Scripture and downplay or ignore passages that try to turn our attention to another aspect of the truth. This tempts everyone equally, both Protestants and Catholics, especially when they are arguing with each other.)

H286. What is "the wrath of God"? Isn't God pure love (1 Jn 4:16)? The medieval mystic Lady Julian of Norwich asked God this question and asked him to show her his wrath, and she said he did, and "I saw no wrath but on man's part." What do you think she meant?

John 4

Now when the Lord knew that the Pharisees had heard that Jesus was making and baptizing more disciples than John (although Jesus himself did not baptize, but only his disciples), he left Judea and departed again to Galilee. He had to pass through Samaria. So he came to a city of Samaria, called Sychar, near the field that Jacob gave to his son Joseph. Jacob's well was there, and so Jesus, wearied as he was with his journey, sat down beside the well. It was about the sixth hour.

There came a woman of Samaria to draw water. Jesus said to her, "Give me a drink." For his disciples had gone away into the city to buy food. The Samaritan woman said to him, "How is it that you, a Jew, ask a drink of me, a woman of Samaria?" For Jews have no dealings with Samaritans. (4:1–9)

287. This question is about some relevant factual details as part of the background for this event. One person can be assigned to find the answers to this many-part question if you wish, or the parts can be split up. (A) Why did Jesus and his disciples have to travel through Samaria to go from Judea to Galilee? Look it up on a map. (B) What does the name "Sychar" mean? (C) Where do you find the background story of Jacob's well? (D) Why was well water so important in this country? (E) Is this the only time the Gospels mention Jesus being weary? (F) What time of day is "the sixth hour"? (G) Why was this woman going to the well alone at that hour? Is there a clue in verses 16–19? (H) What was the attitude of the Jews of Jesus' day about a man and an unrelated woman talking to each other alone? (I) Why did the Jews and Samaritans avoid and dislike each other? (One of the reasons is in the Old Testament; the other is in John 4:20.) (J) In light of the last three questions (G, H, and I), what three reasons were there for the disciples' surprise in verse 27?

288. In what way is Jesus' behavior here an example for his disciples (= us) to follow?

289. Ask yourself the same question the Samaritan woman asked Jesus: Why is he asking her for a drink?

Jesus answered her, "If you knew the gift of God, and who it is that is saying to you, 'Give me a drink,' you would have asked him and he would have given you living water." (4:10)

290. What does Jesus mean here by "the gift of God"?

291. How is Jesus reversing the relationship between the two of them here? Who seems to be giving what to whom, and who is really giving what to whom?

The woman said to him, "Sir, you have nothing to draw with, and the well is deep; where do you get that living water? Are you greater than our father Jacob, who gave us the well, and drank from it himself, and his sons, and his cattle?" (4:11–12)

292. (A) What did the woman think "living water" meant? (B) What is the opposite (non-living) kind of water in her mind? (C) What did Jesus mean by "living water"? (D) What is the opposite (non-living) kind of water in his mind? (Hint: John 3:6 answers that question.)

H293. (A) What instrument was used to draw the kind of water the woman was thinking of from its well? (B) What instrument is used to draw the kind of water Jesus was talking about? (C) From what "well" is that kind of water drawn? (D) Jacob made the well from which the woman was drawing water; who made the well (question C) about which Jesus was speaking?

Jesus said to her, "Every one who drinks of this water will thirst again, but whoever drinks of the water that I shall give him will never thirst; the water that I shall give him will become in him a spring of water welling up to eternal life." (4:13–14)

294. How is this passage related to John 1:38?

H295. (A) How is everything in this world related to our desire for happiness in the same way as the woman's well water was related to her thirst? (B) How is Jesus' "living water" different from anything in this world that we can desire? (C) How does the most famous of all quotations from Augustine's *Confessions* say the same thing Jesus says here?

E296. What does Jesus say about this deeper kind of thirst in Matthew 5:6?

H297. Is Jesus talking about something in this life or something in heaven? Can this deeper thirst be quenched in this life or not? Why is that a trick question? Why is its correct answer neither a simple Yes nor a simple No?

298. What were the first two specific things God created, according to Genesis? Why are these two of the best physical images for the spiritual reality about which Jesus is talking?

The woman said to him, "Sir, give me this water, that I may not thirst, nor come here to draw." (4:15)

299. Is the woman understanding what Jesus meant by the "living water" he gives here, or not?

Jesus said to her, "Go, call your husband, and come here." The woman answered him, "I have no husband." Jesus said to her, "You are right in saying, 'I have no husband'; for you have had five husbands, and he whom you now have is not your husband; this you said truly." (4:16– 18)

H300. (A) In verse 16, why didn't Jesus clearly explain himself first and correct her confusion? Why does he instead first give her a task, a test? (B) Why *this* test?

E301. What did Jesus say about divorce? (See Mt 5:31–32; Mt 19:3– 12; Mk 10:2–12; Lk 16:18.) (B) What do you say about it?

302. (A) Does Jesus condemn this woman for her adultery or excuse her? Why is that a trick question? (B) Compare what he did here with what he did in John 8:1–11, especially verse 11.

The woman said to him, "Sir, I perceive that you are a prophet. Our fathers worshiped on this mountain; and you say that in Jerusalem is the place where men ought to worship." Jesus said to her, "Woman, believe me, the hour is coming when neither on this mountain nor in Jerusalem will you worship the Father. You worship what you do not know; we worship what we know, for salvation is from the Jews. But the hour is coming, and now is, when the true worshipers will worship the Father in spirit and truth, for such the Father seeks to worship him. God is spirit, and those who worship him must worship in spirit and truth." (4: 19–24)

303. (A) What did Jesus mean by the "hour" (time) that is "coming" (v. 21) "and now is" (v. 23)? (B) How was Jesus' prophecy here fulfilled more clearly after A.D. 70?

H304. (A) The woman gave Jesus a multiple-choice question in verse 20. How did Jesus answer it? (B) Why does he usually answer our multiple-choice questions in the same way? (C) Can you give some other examples of this in the Gospels?

305. (A) Was Jesus a "hard-line conservative" or a "soft-headed liberal" in addressing the question of the Jewish claim to a special revelation that the Samaritans did not have? (B) Did he win the woman or the argument? (C) Did he win her by ignoring or watering down this Jewish claim, or did he win the argument but lose his audience by being "judgmental"?

306. Does Jesus' answer (v. 24) mean we should not have special church buildings in which to worship? Why or why not?

307. What does it mean to worship "in spirit and in truth"?

H308. What is "spirit"? It's not a body, but what is it?

The woman said to him, "I know that Messiah is coming (he who is called Christ); when he comes, he will show us all things." Jesus said to her, "I who speak to you am he." (4:25–26)

309. (A) The woman is implicitly asking Jesus a question here. What is the question? (B) What made her suspect the answer? (See v. 29.) (C) How was her implicit question like Martha's implicit

question in John 11:22 and 24? (D) How was Jesus' answer to Martha in John 11:25 like his answer to the woman here (Jn 4:24)?

310. (A) What do you think the woman felt when Jesus said verse 26? (B) Compare it with what the congregation must have felt at Jesus' words in Luke 4:16–21.

Just then his disciples came. They marveled that he was talking with a woman, but none said, "What do you wish?" or, "Why are you talking with her?" So the woman left her water jar, and went away into the city, and said to the people, "Come, see a man who told me all that I ever did. Can this be the Christ?" They went out of the city and were coming to him. (4:27–30)

Many Samaritans from that city believed in him because of the woman's testimony, "He told me all that I ever did." So when the Samaritans came to him, they asked him to stay with them; and he stayed there two days. And many more believed because of his word. They said to the woman, "It is no longer because of your words that we believe, for we have heard for ourselves, and we know that this is indeed the Savior of the world." (4:39–42)

311. (A) Why did the disciples "marvel" that Jesus was talking to a woman? (B) Why didn't they ask him about it?

312. Why is it significant that the woman left her water jar at the well?

313. What "method of evangelism" do you see working here?

314. What special talents do you need to have in order to do this sort of evangelism?

315. (A) What two stages of evangelism do we see distinguished in verse 42? (B) How can we today pass from stage 1 to stage 2 if Jesus is no longer here on earth?

Meanwhile the disciples begged him, saying, "Rabbi, eat." But he said to them, "I have food to eat of which you do not know." So the disciples said to one another, "Has any one brought him food?" Jesus said to them,

"My food is to do the will of him who sent me, and to accomplish his work." (4:31–34)

316. Jesus was both tired (v. 6) and hungry (v. 8). What was he doing that energized him so much that he ignored his hunger and thirst (vv. 31–32)?

E317. What is the difference between the kind of food of which the disciples were thinking (vv. 31, 33) and the kind of food of which Jesus spoke (vv. 31, 33)?

E318. How does John 6:27–29 answer this question?

H319. What is the relationship between these two kinds of food?

H320. How is this the same relationship as the relationship between the two kinds of father, or fatherhood, that are mentioned in Ephesians 3:14–15 and in Matthew 23:9?

321. Is the food of which Jesus speaks a figure of speech or metaphor for "real" food? (Cf. Jn 6:55.)

"Do you not say, 'There are yet four months, then comes the harvest'? I tell you, lift up your eyes, and see how the fields are already white for harvest. He who reaps receives wages, and gathers fruit for eternal life, so that sower and reaper may rejoice together. For here the saying holds true, 'One sows and another reaps.' I sent you to reap that for which you did not labor; others have labored, and you have entered into their labor." (4:35–38)

322. Of what "harvest" was Jesus speaking here?

323. How do we see the same relationship between the two meanings of "fields" and of "harvest" in verse 36 as the two meanings of "food" in verses 31–34?

324. Were Jesus' words here addressed just to his time and place, or was he saying it equally to our very different time and place? The next fifteen centuries would show a steady increase in the number of Christians, but the last five hundred years have shown a steady and accelerating decline of Christianity, in both membership and influence, throughout Western civilization (although not through-

out the rest of the world). So are "the fields" (1) more or (2) less or (3) equally "white [ripe] for harvest" today?

325. Is the principle that "one sows and another reaps" true of all human activities? Give examples. How many of the good things that you "reap" in your life were given to you by the "sowing" of previous generations?

After the two days he departed to Galilee. For Jesus himself testified that a prophet has no honor in his own country. So when he came to Galilee, the Galileans welcomed him, having seen all that he had done in Jerusalem at the feast, for they too had gone to the feast. (4:43–45)

H326. Why are prophets honored less in their own home and country?

H327. Isn't there a contradiction in the following? (1) A prophet has no honor in his own country. (2) Jesus' own country was Galilee. (3) Jesus was a prophet. (4) The Galileans welcomed him. (5) Welcome = honor. (Don't spend too much time on this puzzle.)

So he came again to Cana in Galilee, where he had made the water wine. And at Capernaum there was an official whose son was ill. When he heard that Jesus had come from Judea to Galilee, he went and begged him to come down and heal his son, for he was at the point of death. Jesus therefore said to him, "Unless you see signs and wonders you will not believe." The official said to him, "Sir, come down before my child dies." Jesus said to him, "Go; your son will live." The man believed the word that Jesus spoke to him and went his way. As he was going down, his servants met him and told him that his son was living. So he asked them the hour when he began to mend, and they said to him, "Yesterday at the seventh hour the fever left him." The father knew that was the hour when Jesus had said to him, "Your son will live"; and he himself believed, and all his household. This was now the second sign that Jesus did when he had come from Judea to Galilee. (4:46–54)

328. How did Jesus test the official in verse 48? How did the official pass the test in verse 50?

329. Jesus viewed faith, and the eternal life that faith initiates, as far more important than temporal, biological life. How does this relationship between the two kinds of life explain his complaint in verse 48 about the relationship in most people's souls between physical miracles and faith ("unless you see signs and wonders you will not believe")?

330. (A) How many miracles, and how spectacular a miracle, would it take to make someone believe who did not want to believe? (Cf. Lk 16:31.) (B) Is this why God is so "stingy" with his miracles? (C) Could anything else in the world possibly limit or constrain the omnipotent God's actions except our freely chosen attitudes, our refusals to believe? (D) But doesn't it seem clear that many more people would be convinced if God performed many more miracles? (E) Is it reasonable to believe that God knows better than we do exactly how many miracles it would be best for us to have, neither more nor less? (F) Does this mean that we should just stoically accept the fact that miracles are so few and not ask God for more?

E331. (A) Since Jesus said "Your son will live" *before* the official believed (v. 50), Jesus must have responded (with the miracle of healing) to something other than the official's faith, right? (B) If not, why not? If so, what was it?

332. If miracles are "signs", of what was this miracle a sign?

John 5

After this there was a feast of the Jews, and Jesus went up to Jerusalem.
Now there is in Jerusalem by the Sheep Gate a pool, in Hebrew called
Bethzatha, which has five porticoes. In these lay a multitude of invalids,
blind, lame, paralyzed. [For an angel of the Lord went down at certain
seasons into the pool, and troubled the water; whoever stepped in
first after the troubling of the water was healed of whatever disease
he had.] *One man was there, who had been ill for thirty-eight years.*
When Jesus saw him and knew that he had been lying there a long time,
he said to him, "Do you want to be healed?" The sick man answered
him, "Sir, I have no man to put me into the pool when the water is
troubled, and while I am going another steps down before me." Jesus said
to him, "Rise, take up your pallet, and walk." And at once the man was
healed, and he took up his pallet and walked. (5:1–9)

333. Verse 4, about the angel, is not in some of the oldest manuscripts. Many scholars think it was added as an explanation of verse
7. What is your reaction to this verse? Why?

334. Why did Jesus ask the sick man whether he wanted to be
healed? Why wasn't that as stupid a question as it seems?

335. The sick man's plight is a "catch-22", a dilemma that seems
logically impossible to solve. The only reason he could not get his
healing when the angel troubled the water was that he was sick
(probably crippled) and could not move as fast as others, who always got into the pool first, ahead of him. But the only reason he
needed to get into the pool in the first place was because he was
sick! It's like "I can't swim because I can't avoid sinking, and I
can't avoid sinking because I can't swim." This is tragic, but it's
also funny (at least to some people, e.g., fans of Monty Python).
Why?

336. How are we all in the same "catch-22" position as this sick
man on a spiritual level?

337. (A) There is a story in Greek history about Alexander the Great: he alone could undo the Gordian knot that no one else could untie. How did he do it? (Look it up.) (B) How was what Jesus did here the same kind of thing? (C) What instrument did Alexander use? (D) What instrument did Jesus use? Here is a clue: Read Ephesians 6:17, then Hebrews 1:3, then Genesis 1:3.

338. (A) How is this miracle like God's answer to our deepest problem (the one in question 336)? (B) In order to answer this question, you must first answer three others: first, what is our deepest problem; second, why can't we solve it; and third, how does God solve it? (C) Why are all other answers inadequate?

339. (A) Why did Jesus give the sick man a command instead of just healing him? (B) How was it an impossible command for him to obey? (C) How did this man nevertheless obey the impossible command? (D) How is this part of the story also symbolic of, or parallel to, ourselves and our spiritual situation?

Now that day was the sabbath. So the Jews said to the man who was cured, "It is the sabbath, it is not lawful for you to carry your pallet." But he answered them, "The man who healed me said to me, 'Take up your pallet, and walk.'" They asked him, "Who is the man who said to you, 'Take up your pallet, and walk'?" Now the man who had been healed did not know who it was, for Jesus had withdrawn, as there was a crowd in the place. Afterward, Jesus found him in the temple, and said to him, "See, you are well! Sin no more, that nothing worse befall you." The man went away and told the Jews that it was Jesus who had healed him. And this was why the Jews persecuted Jesus, because he did this on the sabbath. But Jesus answered them, "My Father is working still, and I am working." This was why the Jews sought all the more to kill him, because he not only broke the sabbath but also called God his Father, making himself equal with God. (5:9–18)

E340. Why was what this man did a violation of the Sabbath laws of the Jews?

H341. How was the Jews' attitude, which seemed to be defending the Sabbath, really an anti-Sabbath attitude? (See Mk 2:27.)

H342. How was what Jesus said in verse 17 an answer to the Jews' accusation?

H343. To what principle does Jesus implicitly appeal in this verse (17) about the relation between fathers and sons?

H344. How can God both rest (Gen 2:2) and work (Jn 5:17) at the same time (on the Sabbath)?

H345. Is what you are doing now in this Bible study "resting" or "working"? In order to answer that question, first answer the following ones: (A) Is thinking a "work"? (B) Is it an activity? (C) Is all activity "work"? (D) Is "resting" from work an activity or an inactivity, like sleep? (E) Will heaven be "rest" or "work"?

H346. (A) Does what Jesus says to the man after he is healed (v. 14) imply that he was sicker than others because he had committed more sins than others? (B) If not, why is that mistake a natural and apparently reasonable one? (C) Why is "the gospel of prosperity" (if you are good, God will reward you with earthly riches) really judgmental and harmful rather than optimistic and liberating? (D) What is the connection between sin (spiritual sickness) and physical sickness that Jesus is implying here? Is it (I) that for each of us, the more you sin, the more you get sick? Wasn't that the mistake of Job's three friends? Isn't that the "gospel of prosperity" heresy? Don't saints suffer a lot? (E) Is it (II) that there is no connection at all between spiritual evil (sin) and physical evil (sickness and death)? Isn't that refuted by Genesis 3:3, Ezekiel 18:4, and Romans 6:23, and by our "psycho-somatic (soul-body) unity", i.e., by the fact that everything in us has both a physical (body) and spiritual (soul) dimension? (F) So if it's not answer no. I or answer no. II, what is answer no. III? This is a hard question, but it's not hopeless. Use what you know from the Bible to answer it. Start with this question about how individuals are related to each other in the human family: Do we suffer for (because of) each other's sins? If our good (and bad) deeds can help (or harm) others, can our prayers and sufferings (and joys!) also help others or only ourselves?

H347. (A) Jesus called God his Father (v. 18). Why was this a claim of equality with God? (B) In what way are you equal to your human

father? (C) In what way are you not? (D) How is this last answer
(the inequality) reflected in verse 19? (E) Why doesn't this (v. 19)
mean that Jesus is inferior to his Father?

H348. (A) What radical consequences does this fact—that the relationship between Jesus and his Father is one of obedience but not
inequality—have for human relationships of obedience and conformity to another's will and authority (e.g., citizens to rulers, children to parents, and spouses to each other)? (See Eph 5:21—6:9 and
Col 3:18—4:1.) (B) What is the connection between the world's
misunderstanding of Jesus and its misunderstanding of obedience
and submission to another's will as a mark of inferiority? (C) Is
this misunderstanding by "the world" something that we find only
in non-Christians or something that we find in many Christians,
too? (D) Is the proper understanding of obedience something that
we find only in Christians or something that we find in many non-
Christians, too? (E) If your answers to the last two questions was
No, how can that be, if the source of this radical and mysterious
truth about human relationships is Christ and his relationship to
his Father?

349. We also call God "our Father", at Jesus' own command, in
the Lord's Prayer, but we do not claim equality with God. What is
the difference, then, between God's fatherhood to Jesus and God's
fatherhood to us? (Hint: What does it mean to call Christ the "only-
begotten Son of God"?)

H350. God has no biological gender, yet Jesus calls him his "Father", never his "Mother", and he tell us to do the same, in the
Lord's Prayer. Why? Ask yourself what would be the religious consequences of thinking of God as our Mother.

*Jesus said to them, "Truly, truly, I say to you, the Son can do nothing
of his own accord, but only what he sees the Father doing; for whatever
he does, that the Son does likewise. For the Father loves the Son, and
shows him all that he himself is doing; and greater works than these will
he show him, that you may marvel. For as the Father raises the dead and
gives them life, so also the Son gives life to whom he will. The Father
judges no one, but has given all judgment to the Son, that all may honor*

the Son, even as they honor the Father. He who does not honor the Son does not honor the Father who sent him." (5:19–23)

351. Is there any work in this world that only one Person of the Trinity does without the other two?

E352. (A) What does the Father hold back from the Son (v. 20)? (B) So what more is there in the Father than there is in the Son? What is there in the Father that is not in the Son? (See Col 1:19.)

353. So when we go to heaven and see God face to face, what more will there be for us to see in God than there is for us now to see in Jesus? (Hint: The answer to this question logically follows from the answer to the previous question.)

H354. (A) If there is no more in God the Father than there is in Christ the Son, then the only reason why we will see more of God in heaven than we can see now is not that we will see beyond Christ to the Father but because we will have better sight, better eyes, right? (B) If so, what will those eyes be, and where will we get them? (Hint: Which of the Beatitudes in Matthew 5 answers this question?)

355. Why does God and only God have the power to conquer death, to raise the dead to life (v. 21)? (Hint: A commonsense principle of cause and effect is that you cannot give what you do not have.)

H356. Why does John 5:22 not contradict John 3:17?

H357. Jews and Muslims intend to honor God, sincerely and often passionately, but do not believe Jesus is God, and so they do not honor Jesus as God. Why does verse 23 not mean that they do not honor God? To help answer this difficult question, review your answers to questions 53–58, about John 1:9.

"Truly, truly, I say to you, he who hears my word and believes him who sent me, has eternal life; he does not come into judgment, but has passed from death to life." (5:24)

358. How is the giving of eternal life to the soul that is spoken of here a greater thing than the raising of the physical body from the

dead that was spoken of in verse 21? To answer this question, ask how much each of these two resurrections cost God.

359. (A) What "death" is meant in this verse? (Hint: Ask yourself what kind of "life" is meant here.) (B) If there are at least two kinds of death and two kinds of life, does this mean that you can be dead even while you are alive? (C) Is death a punishment for sin? If so, what kind of death? (D) Is sin itself a kind of death? (Cf. Eph 2:1.) (E) Are there then three kinds of death and three kinds of life, two in time and one in eternity? Identify them.

"Truly, truly, I say to you, the hour is coming, and now is, when the dead will hear the voice of the Son of God, and those who hear will live." (5:25)

H360. (A) Is Jesus speaking of the general resurrection of the dead at the end of the world here, as he is in verses 28–29? (B) If so, why does he say that that hour "now is"? If not, of what kind of death and life is he speaking? Is it the kind of which he spoke in verse 24?

"For as the Father has life in himself, so he has granted the Son also to have life in himself . . ." (5:26)

H361. (A) How can Christ's own life be both (1) something received from the Father, "given" to him by the Father, thus apparently subordinating him to the Father, and also (2) something he has "in himself" just as the Father has life in himself, thus making him equal to the Father? How can the Father give to the Son not just life but the privilege of having life "in himself"? (B) Is there a human analogy here? If a human son receives the gift of life from his father, that makes him dependent on his father, right? So how can that gift also be the gift of having life in himself, distinct and independent of his father? Are human sons equal to their fathers or not? (C) How is this the same paradox we found in 1:1: that "[1] the Word was with God, and [2] the Word was God"?

362. If we accept both halves of this paradox as true and revealed by God, as the Church has always done (since both halves are taught

in Scripture), how does this fact about the relationship between the first two divine Persons of the Trinity change our attitude toward human relationships? If it is a fact that Christ, who *receives* from the Father, who teaches only what he has *heard* from the Father (Jn 5:19), and who *conforms* his will to the Father's will (Jn 5:30), is nevertheless equal to the Father—what does this fact say about our assumption that obeying a command that we have received is less perfect than commanding, that receiving is less perfect than giving? Women, e.g., receive something physical from men in sexual inter- course, and children receive many things from parents, both phys- ical (first of all, life itself, then food) and spiritual (like love and education); does this mean that the receivers are inferior rather than equal? (Hint: Does "equal" necessarily mean "the same" when used outside of a mathematical equation just as it does in a mathematical equation?)

". . . and has given him authority to execute judgment, because he is the Son of man." (5:26)

363. (A) How does Christ being the Son of man as well as the Son of God give him the rightful authority to judge man? (Hint: Would cats have the authority to judge dogs?) (B) How does this principle explain why Paul in 1 Corinthians 6:1–8 is scandalized by Christians accepting the authority of pagans to judge them in law courts? (C) What does that passage tell us about what the early Christians thought conversion was, what difference becoming a Christian made to the kind of being we have, even to the spiritual species to which we belong? (Is Paul saying that the difference be- tween pagans and Christians is like the difference between cats and dogs rather than the difference between bad dogs and good dogs?)

"Do not marvel at this; for the hour is coming when all who are in the tombs will hear his voice and come forth, those who have done good, to the resurrection of life, and those who have done evil, to the resurrection of judgment." (5:28–29)

E364. (A) What percentage of human beings eventually become "the dead"? (B) What percentage of human beings, then, will hear

Christ's voice in the resurrection from the dead, either to eternal life or eternal death, at the Last Judgment? (C) If all who die hear Christ's voice in the resurrection and the Last Judgment, will there be anyone who hears Christ's voice at the resurrection and the Last Judgment who has not died? (See 1 Cor 15:51.)

365. (A) Will those who never heard of Christ during their lifetime on earth also hear Christ's voice when they rise from the dead? (B) How will they know him? (Hint: Remember John 1:9.)

366. (A) Does verse 29 prove salvation by works instead of salvation by faith? (B) If not, why not?

367. What does the rest of Scripture say about this? Does it say we are saved by faith or not? Does it say we will be judged by our works or not?

H368. (A) Verse 29 contrasts the resurrection to life with the resurrection to judgment. "Judgment", or "justice", sometimes means something more general, namely, (I) judgment as to whether the person judged is good or evil, guilty or innocent; and it sometimes means something more specific , namely, (II) just punishment for guilt. Which meaning is used here? (B) What difference does it make whether we think of hell as eternal life with pain while heaven is also eternal life but with joy, or whether we think of hell as eternal death while heaven is eternal life? (C) Is life something more, and more important, than joy and freedom from pain? If it is not, wouldn't that make euthanasia a good thing?

"I can do nothing on my own authority; as I hear, I judge; and my judgment is just, because I seek not my own will but the will of him who sent me." (5:30)

369. (A) Why doesn't this make Christ a limp wimp, a weak, passive doormat? (B) Compare those who do only their own will (like the great tyrants) with those who do God's will (the saints): Which are weak and brittle? Which are strong and fearless? H(C) Why does it work that way?

"If I bear witness to myself, my testimony is not true; there is another who bears witness to me, and I know that the testimony which he bears to me is true." (5:31–32)

370. How is this principle accepted also in secular law and common sense?

371. (A) Is the "other" about whom Jesus is talking here his Father or John the Baptist? (B) Why?

372. Jesus says not just that "the testimony which he bears to me is true" but that "I know that the testimony which he bears to me is true." How does Jesus know this? (This is really an easier question than it may seem.)

"You sent to John, and he has borne witness to the truth. Not that the testimony which I receive is from man; but I say this that you may be saved." (5:33–34)

H373. (A) Why is Jesus not minimizing or dismissing the testimony that John the Baptist gave to him here (with his words "not that the testimony which I receive is from man") but in fact maximizing it? (B) On another occasion, when Jesus demanded that the Pharisees answer the question whether the baptism of John the Baptist was from man or from God, they refused to answer, because if they said "from man", the people would scorn them, because they knew John was a prophet, and if they said "from God", Jesus would reply, "Why then did you not believe him [especially when he pointed to Jesus as the Messiah]?" (Mt 21:24–27). How is Jesus saying the same thing here? (C) Why does Jesus note that "you sent to John"? (D) Why does he add, "I say this that you may be saved"? Who can save us? Can we be saved by a prophet like John? If not, why does Jesus mention salvation here?

"He was a burning and shining lamp, and you were willing to rejoice for a while in his light." (5:35)

374. (A) What physical thing(s) are both "burning" and "shining"? (B) What two spiritual powers or abilities of the soul do these two

physical powers (to burn and to shine) naturally symbolize? (C) Why does a prophet need both? Why can't a prophet "burn" without "shining", and why can't he "shine" without "burning"?

H375. (A) Why do we find it so hard to reconcile and unite these two spiritual powers in ourselves and our own lives? (B) Why did John do it so well that Jesus praises him for it? What was his secret?

"But the testimony which I have is greater than that of John; for the works which the Father has granted me to accomplish, those very works which I am doing, bear me witness that the Father has sent me." (5:36)

376. (A) To which "works" is Christ referring here? (B) How do they bear witness that God has sent him? (C) If the "works" to which Jesus is referring are his miracles, do miracles prove that God is behind them? Can any natural creature perform real supernatural miracles? (Cf. Jn 3:2.) (D) Can demons perform real miracles? (E) Can they perform fake miracles, apparent miracles?

377. (A) Has anyone else in history ever performed more miracles, or more remarkable miracles, than Jesus? (B) How reasonable is it to believe in Christ because of his miracles? (C) How unreasonable is it to disbelieve in him even though he performed so many miracles? (D) Why didn't Jesus perform even more miracles? If someone literally saw Christ perform a miracle, wouldn't he then have to believe in him? (Cf. Lk 16:19–31, especially v. 31.) H(E) If Luke 16:31 is true, what makes the difference, then, between belief and unbelief? Why do some believe and some not?

"And the Father who sent me has himself borne witness to me." (5:37)

H378. Jesus puts an "and" between this statement and the previous one, which referred to his miracles (his "works"), so this "witness" refers to something else. What other "witness" from God the Father do you think he is talking about here?

"His voice you have never heard, his form you have never seen; and you do not have his word abiding in you, for you do not believe him whom he has sent." (5:37–38)

E379. There are four statements here, four sentences. Which of the four are true of all people and which only of some?

H380. (A) In what sense can we "hear" God's "voice"? (B) Do all people hear God's voice in that sense, or only some? (C) Is there any sense in which we can "see his form"?

"You search the Scriptures, because you think that in them you have eternal life; and it is they that bear witness to me; yet you refuse to come to me that you may have life." (5:39–40)

381. How is this so ironic that it is funny, even though it is tragic? Imagine Romeo "mooning" over Juliet's picture in his room. Juliet knocks on his door: "Romeo, Romeo, wherefore art thou, Romeo? Open your door and come to me!" Romeo replies, "Go away and be quiet; I'm looking at my beloved Juliet." How are the Jews to whom Jesus is talking here doing the same thing Romeo is doing?

382. How is it easy and common also for us Christians to do the same thing the Jews were doing here?

H383. (A) Christ focuses on "life" in these two verses. In what sense can a book be alive? (B) In what sense can we get "life" from the Bible? (C) How does Hebrews 4:12 answer that question? Interpret that verse.

384. (A) Explain how Christ's words and his miracles are both signs. (B) What is the practical purpose of a sign? For example, suppose you are starving and you see a sign, "Free food this way". Can you eat the sign? (C) How were Jesus' unbelieving audience eating their signs? (D) How can we be that stupid?

385. What, then, is the proper use of Scripture and of Bible studies like this one?

"I do not receive glory from men. But I know that you have not the love of God within you. I have come in my Father's name, and you do not receive me; if another comes in his own name, him you will receive. How can you believe, who receive glory from one another and do not seek the glory that comes from the only God?" (5:41–44)

386. (A) Distinguish three kinds of glory in this passage: it may come from God, self, or others; i.e., from above, from within, or from outside the one who receives it. Of which kind should we be the most suspicious, and to which should we pay the least attention? (B) To which kind do we typically pay the most attention? (C) Why do we do that? (Perhaps if we diagnose the disease, we can work on a cure.)

387. (A) Why does the fact that the people Jesus was addressing did not love him show that they did not love God? (B) They did not think that was true! They thought they loved God. How can you be mistaken about your own love? How can you think you love God when you really don't? (C) How can you know whether you do or do not love God? What is the touchstone? (D) Can you make the same mistake toward other human beings, too? (E) If so, how can you correct that mistake?

388. (A) Is Christ here speaking to all Jews, some Jews, all people, or some people? (B) Your answer probably comes from common sense, but prove your answer from Scripture also: find examples of (I) Jews who loved God, (II) Jews who did not, (III) Gentiles who loved God, and (IV) Gentiles who did not.

"Do not think that I shall accuse you to the Father; it is Moses who accuses you, on whom you set your hope. If you believed Moses, you would believe me, for he wrote of me. But if you do not believe his writings, how will you believe my words?" (5:45–47)

389. Why is it just that Moses rather than Jesus judges the unbelieving Jews?

H390. Where did Moses write of Christ?

391. (A) Can we say that all those who met Christ in the Gospels believed in him if they believed in Moses? (B) If not, doesn't that prove Jesus was wrong in verse 46? (C) What sort of "believing in Moses" do you think Christ meant here? (D) What does this say about conducting good Jewish-Christian dialogue today? (E) How do "Messianic Jews", or Jews who become Christians today, answer these questions?

John 6

After this Jesus went to the other side of the Sea of Galilee, which is the Sea of Tiberias. And a multitude followed him, because they saw the signs which he did on those who were diseased. (6:1–2)

392. (A) Is this (his healing miracles) a good reason for following Jesus? (B) If not, why did he encourage it by doing miracles? If so, why is it? (C) Distinguish two or three degrees of "following" Jesus. How far into these can miracles lead us? What else do we need?

Jesus went up into the hills, and there sat down with his disciples. (6:3)

393. (A) Why do you think Jesus went up into the hills? (B) Why do high places feel closer to God if they are not literally any closer to God since God is not in the sky any more than he is on the earth?

394. Why does John mention that Jesus "sat down"? What does posture reveal about human relationships? Give examples.

Now the Passover, the feast of the Jews, was at hand. (6:4)

395. How does this verse show that John was writing primarily not to Jews but to Gentiles?

Lifting up his eyes, then, and seeing that a multitude was coming to him, Jesus said to Philip, "How are we to buy bread, so that these people may eat?" This he said to test him, for he himself knew what he would do. (6:5–6)

396. (A) Do you think Jesus just forgot to bring bread, or do you think this was deliberate? If it was deliberate, why? (B) If Jesus was perfect man as well as perfect God, do you think that fact means

he could never have forgotten anything? Why or why not? (C) In the Gospels does he ever confess ignorance? (Cf. Mt 24:36.) (D) If he does, why doesn't this prove that he was not divine? (Hint: When he was born, did he come out of Mary's womb speaking perfect adult Hebrew?) (E) Did he ever confess moral faults? (Cf. Jn 8:46.) (F) Was there any other occasion where he remembered food while everyone else forgot it? (Cf. Lk 8:55.) (G) How does God's providence sometimes appear to forget important things that we need? (H) Might God do this for the same reason Jesus "forgot" to bring food?

Philip answered him, "Two hundred denarii would not buy enough bread for each of them to get a little." One of his disciples, Andrew, Simon Peter's brother, said to him, "There is a lad here who has five barley loaves and two fish; but what are they among so many?" (6:7–9)

397. Compare the responses of Philip and Andrew here. Contrast what each focused on.

398. What did the "lad" focus on?

Jesus said, "Make the people sit down." Now there was much grass in the place; so the men sat down, in number about five thousand. Jesus then took the loaves, and when he had given thanks, he distributed them to those who were seated; so also the fish, as much as they wanted. (6:10–11)

399. (A) How did Jesus do this miracle? (B) Is that question a bad question? If not, answer it. If so, is it a bad question because it's too easy or too hard to answer? Might it be both?

400. (A) Is there anything in your life that Christ multiplies when you give it to him, as he did these loaves and fishes? (B) If time is one of those things, why don't you give him more of it? For instance, on a morning when you have twice as many things to do as there is time in the day to do them, why don't you take more time to pray rather than less? (C) If you've never done that, why not? If you have, then you know by experience that it really works

—or, rather, that he really works. So that's even more reason to do it again and again; so why don't you? (Question B again.)

401. (A) How does the grassiness of the place show something about divine providence? (B) Is that (your answer to question A) an exception, or is it true of all places and circumstances, including those that seem to be exactly the opposite? (For example, suppose the place had had no grass, only rocks. Would that disprove divine providence?)

402. (A) Can you identify any occasions or circumstances where we too have to "sit down" first before God will give us his gifts? (I) Literally? (II) Metaphorically? (B) Do you see a connection between this point and folding our hands when we pray?

E403. (A) Why did Christ give thanks before multiplying and distributing the loaves and fishes? (B) Why did he do the same at the Last Supper? (C) Why do we say grace before meals?

404. Why do you think this is one of the few miracles recorded by all four Gospel writers?

405. Of the four evangelists, only John mentions that the loaves and fishes were from a little boy. Why do you think this is so? Here is a hint: John died much later than any of the other apostles.

And when they had eaten their fill, he told his disciples, "Gather up the fragments left over, that nothing may be lost." So they gathered them up and filled twelve baskets with fragments from the five barley loaves, left by those who had eaten. (6:12–13)

406. ". . . they had eaten their fill"—what does this phrase say about the relationship between God's gifts and our desires?

407. (A) Why did Jesus do this miracle? Was he teaching anything besides keeping the environment clean and not wasting food? (B) What was he teaching when he reminded his disciples of this miracle later in Matthew 16:9–10?

E408. Why did they collect the leftovers from the loaves but not from the fish?

When the people saw the sign which he had done, they said, "This is indeed the prophet who is to come into the world!"

Perceiving then that they were about to come and take him by force to make him king, Jesus withdrew again to the hills by himself. (6:14–15)

409. Why did this miracle lead the people to the conclusion that Jesus was the promised Messiah?

410. (A) Why did they want to make Jesus their king? (B) Why did he so much not want that that he fled away (v. 15)?

411. (A) If Jesus ran for president, would he win? (B) Why wouldn't he run? Doesn't he want to be the president of everyone's life?

When evening came, his disciples went down to the sea, got into a boat, and started across the sea to Capernaum. It was now dark, and Jesus had not yet come to them. The sea rose because a strong wind was blowing. When they had rowed about three or four miles, they saw Jesus walking on the sea and drawing near to the boat. They were frightened, but he said to them, "It is I; do not be afraid." Then they were glad to take him into the boat, and immediately the boat was at the land to which they were going. (6:16–21)

412. It's night. Jesus is not there. It's stormy. These are three reasons for fear. Yet when Jesus comes and removes the second of these two reasons for fear, they fear more. Why? Why would you be afraid if you saw what they saw?

413. (A) "It is I; do not be afraid." Does he still speak these words about everything we are afraid of? Is there anything to which these words do not apply? (B) How can we contrive to hear them?

414. Is there a spiritual or allegorical dimension to the last verse? If so, what do the boat and the land symbolize?

415. (A) Is it right to interpret a passage (especially, but not only, a passage about a miracle) both literally (physically) and allegorically (spiritually)? (B) Why? (C) Apply this to Jesus' greatest miracle, his Resurrection. (D) The Greek word for "miracle" (*sēmeion*) means "sign". When you see a sign, whether it is a word or a street sign or someone else's "body language", you both look *at it* and *along*

it toward the thing to which it points. How does this fact explain the answer to question (A)?

On the next day the people who remained on the other side of the sea saw that there had been only one boat there, and that Jesus had not entered the boat with his disciples, but that his disciples had gone away alone. However, boats from Tiberias came near the place where they ate the bread after the Lord had given thanks. So when the people saw that Jesus was not there, nor his disciples, they themselves got into the boats and went to Capernaum, seeking Jesus.

When they found him on the other side of the sea, they said to him, "Rabbi, when did you come here?" (6:22–25)

416. (A) Explain the reason for the tone of surprise in the people's question. (B) How had Jesus come there?

Jesus answered them, "Truly, truly, I say to you, you seek me, not because you saw signs, but because you ate your fill of the loaves. Do not labor for the food which perishes, but for the food which endures to eternal life, which the Son of man will give to you; for on him has God the Father set his seal." (6:26–27)

H417. (A) Distinguish three levels of motives for following Jesus that are implied in this passage. (B) What is the best one? Why? What is the worst one? Why? What is the middle one? (C) What is a "seal"? (D) What is God's "seal" on Christ?

Then they said to him, "What must we do, to be doing the works of God?" Jesus answered them, "This is the work of God, that you believe in him whom he has sent." (6:28–29)

418. How is Jesus' answer here a surprise?

H419. (A) Does Jesus answer the question they asked him here or another one? (B) What does his answer say about faith and works? (C) Is faith itself a work? (D) Is it a "work of God"? (E) If it is a work of God, how can it also be a work of man, so that it is our free choice and we are responsible for it?

So they said to him, "Then what sign do you do, that we may see, and believe you? What work do you perform? Our fathers ate the manna in the wilderness; as it is written, 'He gave them bread from heaven to eat.'" Jesus then said to them, "Truly, truly, I say to you, it was not Moses who gave you the bread from heaven; my Father gives you the true bread from heaven. For the bread of God is that which comes down from heaven, and gives life to the world." (6:30–33)

420. (A) Is their question a good question or not? (B) If the people had just seen Jesus perform the miraculous work of feeding the five thousand, why are they asking him for another "sign" (miracle)? (C) Why did they mention the miracle of the manna when they asked him the question: "What sign do you do that we may believe you? What work do you perform?"

E421. The word "manna" literally means "What is that?" because when God gave the Jews the manna they did not understand it. They had never seen anything like this before. (See Ex 16:15, 31.) How is Jesus like manna in this way?

422. State at least two other ways in which Jesus is like the manna.

H423. Why is it more accurate to say that the manna was like Jesus than that Jesus is like the manna?

H424. (A) How can bread be a person or a person be bread? Isn't that a logical impossibility? (B) If so, how can it be true to say that Jesus himself is our bread (or manna)? (C) How can it be true to say that the *bread* of the Eucharist *is Jesus*? (D) Why do Protestants and Catholics agree that Jesus is our bread (B) but not that the Eucharistic bread is Jesus (C)? (E) Do Catholics believe that the Eucharistic bread is both bread and Jesus or that it is not bread at all, even though it looks and tastes like bread?

425. (A) How is this equation (of Jesus himself with bread) shocking in the same way John 1:14 is shocking? (B) How is it the same kind of shock as John 14:6?

426. (A) Jesus frequently says "I am . . ." in John's Gospel. Find at least three other examples. (B) How does this relate to Exodus 3:14? (C) What is Jesus here revealing about his identity and his relation with God the Father?

427. (A) How much of this theology do you think was understood by the wisest person in his audience (perhaps John himself) at the time? (B) If no one understood it adequately, why did Jesus teach it? (C) Why did John understand it so much better later when he wrote his Gospel?

428. (A) What kind of life did the manna give? What kind of life does Jesus give? (B) Jesus both identifies himself with the manna and also distinguishes himself from it. How can he do both?

429. (A) Did Jesus mean, in verse 32, that the manna was not literally bread at all? (B) Was the manna literal or symbolic? (C) Is that a bad question? Why or why not?

They said to him, "Lord, give us this bread always." (6:34)

430. (A) Do you think this was a sincere question or not? (B) What do you think they meant by "this bread"?

Jesus said to them, "I am the bread of life; he who comes to me shall not hunger, and he who believes in me shall never thirst." (6:35)

H431. (A) They said, "Give us this bread." Jesus replied, "I am the bread." Does that reply mean that they were really asking for Jesus but didn't know it? (B) If so, is that true not just for the few people to whom Jesus was talking here but for everyone in the world? (C) And if that is true, what are the consequences of that fact for evangelism? (Take just a little more time to think about this question than you would otherwise do; you may very well discover something surprising and important.)

H432. John 1:38 implies that we need to choose what our heart most deeply seeks and is most deeply in love with: either Christ or something else. But if everyone is really seeking Jesus even if they don't know it, because they are really seeking what Jesus really is, namely, "the bread of life", as the previous question seemed to imply, then how can there be any alternatives to Jesus and salvation; how can there be a choice between Jesus and anything else if everyone is seeking Jesus?

H433. Of what desire is Jesus promising to be the always-sufficient satisfaction when he calls himself "the bread of life"? (Hint: What do we mean when we say "It's a matter of life or death"? Mere biological survival?)

H434. (A) Does the first part of Jesus' sentence refer to predestination and the second part to free will? If not, why not? (B) (I) If so, how do you reconcile these two things? (II) If you cannot reconcile these two things, which of them do you see as prior or primary, that is, more important for us, clearer, more necessary for us to believe, and more obviously true? Why?

"For I have come down from heaven, not to do my own will, but the will of him who sent me." (6:38)

H435. (A) Why does this subordination of his will to the Father's not make Jesus inferior to the Father? (B) How does what Jesus says in Mark 10:42–45, about the difference between the way the world works and the way the Church ("the people of God") works, logically follow from this verse (Jn 6:38)? (C) How does it follow from the essential nature of the internal life of the eternal Trinity? (D) How does it apply to the most important, most intimate, and most complete of all human relationships, namely, marriage (Eph 5:21)?

436. (A) Is this (previous question) what *agape* (love, charity) means? (B) Is there anything else to becoming a saint, i.e., becoming holy, besides this one thing? (C) Does Jesus (I) *say* this or (II) *do* this, or (III) *is* he this? (See Jn 2:4.) If all three, what is the relationship between these three things? (D) Is this the essential meaning of becoming a saint? (E) Is becoming a saint the essential meaning of becoming a success in life? (F) Is it OK to get A's in all your courses but to flunk Life? (G) If you are not yet a saint, is this because you do not *know* the meaning of life or because you do not choose to do it? (H) Explain Jesus' surprising reversal of the relationship between these two things in John 7:17.

"And this is the will of him who sent me, that I should lose nothing of all that he has given me, but raise it up at the last day. For this is the will

of my Father, that every one who sees the Son and believes in him should have eternal life; and I will raise him up at the last day." (6:39–40)

E437. (A) Is there any conceivable or possible "good news" that is better than this: that God—who is all-good (and therefore wills your best good), all-wise (and therefore knows exactly what is best for you), and all-powerful (and therefore is able to accomplish everything that he wills)—loves you? (B) Does Romans 8:28 logically follow from this? (C) Is there any more essential definition of love than this, to will the good of the beloved? (D) Is there any greater love conceivable than this love, namely, God's will to give you the gift of his own eternal life?

The Jews then murmured at him, because he said, "I am the bread which came down from heaven." They said, "Is not this Jesus, the son of Joseph, whose father and mother we know? How does he now say, 'I have come down from heaven'?" (6:41–42)

438. (A) Was Joseph Jesus' biological father? (B) Did Jesus, then, come from heaven rather than from earth? (C) Was Mary his biological mother? (D) Did Jesus, then, come from earth rather than from heaven? (E) If he came from heaven, he has a heavenly divine nature; and if he comes from earth, he has an earthly, human nature; can a single person have two different natures?

439. (A) The question asked by the Jews who "murmured at him" seems reasonable. But there are two false assumptions behind this question. One of these assumptions is a false general principle, which the correct answer to question 438E corrects. What is it? (B) The other false assumption is factual (a specific fact) and is stated in so many words by them as part of their question. What is it?

Jesus answered them, "Do not murmur among yourselves. No one can come to me unless the Father who sent me draws him; and I will raise him up at the last day. It is written in the prophets, 'And they shall all be taught by God.' Every one who has heard and learned from the Father

comes to me. Not that any one has seen the Father except him who is
from God; he has seen the Father." (6:43–46)

H440. (A) Why does verse 44 seem to be an excuse for those who
do not believe in Jesus? (B) Why isn't it? Why can't the unbeliever
blame not himself but God for not "drawing" him, i.e., not giving
him the grace to believe?

441. If free will and predestination are both true, which one comes
first, according to verse 44?

H442. (A) Why does this answer seem to contradict your answer
to question 434? (B) Why doesn't it? In other words, if predestination is prior in objective fact and causality, and free will is prior in
subjective experience and in our knowledge, why does that seem to
be a contradiction and why is it not really a contradiction? (C) If
this question is too abstract for you, here's an easier one that gives
you the same result: If "grace perfects nature", and if predestination is grace while free will is (human) nature, what, then, is the
relationship between predestination and free will?

443. (A) Does verse 45 mean that we cannot be taught by each
other but only by God? (B) If so, why are we doing this Bible
study together? If not, why not? (C) What is the relation between
being taught by God and being taught by good human teachers?
(Hint: Remember that "grace uses and perfects nature.")

H444. If, as verse 46 (and also Jn 1:18) says, no one "has seen the
Father except him who is from God" (Christ), how can *we* have
"heard and learned from the Father" (v. 45)? (Hint no. 1: Look at
the words carefully. Hint no. 2: What is the distinction in Job 42:5?
How might that apply here?)

"Truly, truly, I say to you, he who believes has eternal life. I am the
bread of life. Your fathers ate the manna in the wilderness, and they died.
This is the bread which comes down from heaven, that a man may eat
of it, and not die. I am the living bread which came down from heaven;
if any one eats of this bread, he will live for ever; and the bread which I
shall give for the life of the world is my flesh." (6:47–51)

H445. In verses 49 and 50, Christ says that those who ate the manna died but those who "eat" him (i.e., believe in him: verse 47) will never die. Why isn't this proved false by the fact that Christians die just as the Jews who ate the manna died? If the answer is that believers will live forever after death, isn't this also true of unbelievers, since all human souls are immortal? (Hint: Does the Bible ever describe hell as "eternal *life*"?)

446. (A) Here is a controversial question that divides Catholics and most Protestants: Does "eating" Christ the "bread of (eternal) life" mean believing in him (v. 47), or does it mean eating his body and blood (vv. 52–58), which seems to refer to the Eucharist? (B) Here are three easy factual questions that may help begin to bridge this great divide. The questions are about the relation between the sacrament and its effect, which is eternal life—not just life after death in the future but the eternal life of Christ in our souls, which begins in the present. Question no. 1: According to Catholic theology, do those who receive the Eucharist but do not believe receive eternal life from it? Question no. 2: According to Catholic theology, are Protestants who believe in Christ but who do not believe in or receive the Eucharist denied eternal life? Is that how Catholics interpret 6:53? Question no. 3: According to Catholic theology, is it in objective fact the same Christ who (a) is received materially in the Eucharist as well as believed in spiritually by Catholics and who (b) is only believed in spiritually but not received materially in this sacrament by Protestants? Are the Catholic Christ and the Protestant Christ two Christs?

H447. (A) What is the relationship between Christ the "bread of (eternal) life" giving us his flesh to eat on the Cross and Christ giving us his flesh to eat when he says "this is my body" as he institutes this sacrament (the Eucharist, or the Lord's Supper) on the evening before his death? (B) The easy answer is the intuitive one, which naturally occurs to anyone who sees this scene in Mel Gibson's movie *The Passion of the Christ*. How does your intuitive mind see this relation? (C) The hard answer is the more abstract theological one. How does your theology explain this? (D) Did Christ institute the easy answer or the hard one? Did he say "Take and understand" or "Take and eat"?

H448. In biblical terminology, "flesh" means, not "skin" or "meat" (as *Fleisch* does in German), but "mortal body". The resurrection body, in contrast, is not made of "flesh" and is immortal, even though it is physical and touchable, as Christ's resurrection body was. Why does Christ use the word "flesh" here (*sarx*) instead of the word "body" (*soma*)? (Hint: Your answer to question 447A should lead you to the answer to this one.)

H449. (A) How does the principle "You are what you eat" apply to this passage? (Cf. Jn 3:3, 6.) (B) Saint Augustine wrote: "When we eat the Body of Christ, we become the Body of Christ." What is the relationship here between the Eucharist and the Church? (C) If the Eucharist and the Church are both "the Body of Christ", if the same special term is used for both, then why do we think of these two things as very different things? We think, not of the Eucharist, but of the Church as a worldwide community of believers; and we think, not of the Church, but of the Eucharist as a sacrament that we receive as individuals. Is the "not" part of this wrong? Is the Church much more intimately individual, and the Eucharist much more globally communal, than we habitually think? Is it wrong to think of the Eucharist as a "salvation pill" and of the Church as "Jesus People Incorporated"?

450. (A) When we eat ordinary bread, we do not turn into bread, but the bread turns into us in our bodies. When we "eat" Christ's body (whether you interpret this in the Catholic way, as literal, in the Eucharist, or whether you interpret it in the usual Protestant way, "eating" being symbolic of faith and the Eucharistic bread being only a *symbol* of Christ), does the same thing happen? (B) If so, what is that same thing? If not, what does happen?

The Jews then disputed among themselves, saying, "How can this man give us his flesh to eat?" (6:52)

451. (A) Why does this seem to be a very good question? (B) Why isn't it? (Hint: What word in their question is the most questionable?)

452. In the first few Christian centuries, one of the standard pagan arguments against Christianity was that Christians were cannibals.

(A) Why did this objection naturally arise? (B) How did all Christians answer it in the first few centuries? (B1) Did any of them deny that Christ's presence in the Eucharist was literally real rather than only symbolic? (B2) If not, does that mean his presence is only literal and *not* symbolic? (B3) Did any of them use the theological term "transubstantiation" that Catholic theology has used since the Middle Ages? (B4) If not, does that mean this term is not true? (Hint: How many times does the Bible use the term "Trinity"?)

453. The previous question was mainly objective and factual; this one is highly subjective and personal and can be skipped if it generates any personal rancor and argumentation, if it leads to too long a tangent, or if it is judged to be simply too hard to answer. The question is: What conclusion do you draw from the factual answers to question 452B above?

454. (A) How do different churches and denominations give different answers to this question today? (You may want to do a little research on this, but don't get stuck on it for long.) (B) What did Saint Paul say about denominationalism and denominational disagreements in 1 Corinthians 1–2?

So Jesus said to them, "Truly, truly, I say to you, unless you eat the flesh of the Son of man and drink his blood, you have no life in you; he who eats my flesh and drinks my blood has eternal life, and I will raise him up at the last day." (6:53–54)

455. E(A) Again, for the umpteenth time, Jesus uses the Rabbinic formula "Truly, truly, I say to you". What does this formula mean? (Hint: It tells us how to interpret the words that follow it.) H(B) Now apply your answer to the things Jesus says that follow this formula.

H456. Jesus' words are so shocking here that we learn in the next few verses that most of his disciples leave him, scandalized. If taken literally, it sounds like cannibalism. Protestants and Catholics interpret these words very differently, but here are two equally hard questions for both. If you are a Protestant, here is a "hard question" for you: Why do you think these words were so shocking if they were not meant literally but only symbolically? And why didn't Jesus call back these disciples who were scandalized, gently reprimanding them for misunderstanding his words by taking them literally? If you are a Catholic, here is an equally "hard question" for you: If Jesus is really, truly, literally, personally, and totally present in the Eucharist, why do Catholics receive him so casually? Why do you? A Muslim once said to me: "If I believed what you say you believe about the Eucharist, that that is really not bread and wine but Jesus himself and that Jesus is God himself become incarnate—of course I do not believe that, but if I did believe that—I don't see how I could ever get up off my knees again for the rest of my life." Why do you find it so easy to believe it, and why do you find it so easy to get up off your knees? Why do you exit the church as soon as you can after Holy Communion?

457. "Hermeneutics" is a technical term for "the science of interpretation". How does the principle of hermeneutics to which Jesus appeals in John 7:17 help us to interpret this "hard saying"?

458. Why does Jesus add "drink my blood" to "eat my flesh"? (Hint: What did "blood" mean to the Jews? Why were they forbidden to drink the blood of animals?)

459. In the Eucharist (whether you interpret it literally or only symbolically), the wine, which is and/or symbolizes Christ's blood, is separate from the bread, which is and/or symbolizes his body. Why? (You do not have to be a Catholic to figure this one out.)

460. In terms of what Christ says here, in what way was the feeding of the five thousand a Eucharistic symbol, and in what way was it not?

"For my flesh is food indeed, and my blood is drink indeed." (6:55)

461. (A) "Indeed " is a translation of a word that means "real", "authentic", or "true", as real money is not counterfeit, or a child in a Halloween costume is not a "real" witch or devil, or as a portrait is not a real person but only a picture of a real person. The picture is only a symbol of the real person. Now whether you believe the Eucharist is only symbolic or something more, it is at least symbolic; and we naturally interpret this symbolism "up" rather than "down",

that is, we interpret physical, natural bread or food as literal and the "food" or "bread of life" that Christ speaks of here as symbolic. How does Christ turn this natural interpretation upside down and interpret it "down" rather than "up"? Which of the two is a symbol of the other in his mind? Which is "the real thing", and which is a picture or image or symbol of it? (B) Why, then, are we usually upside down in our thinking?

462. How does Paul do the same thing with the word "father" in Ephesians 3:14-15?

463. How does Jesus do the same thing with "food" (or "meat" or "bread") in John 4:31-34, John 6:27, and John 6:55?

H464. (A) What do all these biblical examples say about the relation between matter and spirit? How does it change our usual, natural view of both? (B) How does it challenge and change our natural view of spirit? (Hint: In the movies, when souls leave bodies at death, they often look like thin, wispy fogs; what's wrong with that image?) (C) And how does it correct our natural view of matter? How do matter and material bodies mean more in this view (Jesus' view) rather than less?

"He who eats my flesh and drinks my blood abides in me, and I in him. As the living Father sent me, and I live because of the Father, so he who eats me will live because of me." (6:56-57)

E465. What does it mean to "abide"? Does it mean to live, to inhabit, to remain, or all three?

H466. How can a person "abide" in another person? Are there any human approximations or analogies for this?

H467. How can it be true both that we are "in" Christ and that Christ is "in" us?

H468. (A) How is verse 57 an answer to the previous question about verse 56? (B) Question 466 asked for a purely human analogy for the relationship between Christ and ourselves. In verse 57, Christ gives a purely divine analogy for this relationship. What is common to both; what makes both work?

"This is the bread which came down from heaven, not such as the fathers ate and died; he who eats this bread will live for ever." This he said in the synagogue, as he taught at Capernaum. (6:58–59)

E469. (A) Everything in verse 58 is repeated from other verses. Why does Christ so often use repetition? Why does it work as a teaching device? (B) He does not repeat everything; in fact he repeats only a few things. Why does he repeat this one?

470. How does the fact that Christ said these scandalous words in the synagogue add to their weight?

Many of his disciples, when they heard it, said, "This is a hard saying; who can listen to it?" (6:60)

471. What does "listen to" mean here more than just "hear and pay attention to"?

472. Why was this such a "hard saying" even for those who had already become Jesus' disciples?

But Jesus, knowing in himself that his disciples murmured at it, said to them, "Do you take offense at this? Then what if you were to see the Son of man ascending where he was before? It is the Spirit that gives life, the flesh is of no avail; the words that I have spoken to you are Spirit and life. But there are some of you that do not believe." For Jesus knew from the first who those were that did not believe, and who it was that would betray him. And he said, "This is why I told you that no one can come to me unless it is granted him by the Father."
   After this many of his disciples drew back and no longer walked with him. (6:61–66)

473. Compare 6:61–62 to 3:12. Do you think 6:61–62 means (I) that the Ascension will be even harder to accept than these words, (II) that only after Jesus ascends to heaven and sends the Holy Spirit to them will they understand it, or (III) something else?

474. (A) Does "spirit" in verse 63 mean "the inspiration of the Holy Spirit" or "the spiritual, or symbolic rather than the physical, or literal sense of these words"? (B) Give a reason for your answer.

H475. In light of verses 65–66, why is it not a good excuse for an unbeliever to say that he does not believe because God has not given him the grace to believe? (Here is a hint that will make the question either clearer and easier to answer or perhaps more confusing [if so, ignore it]: Can you distinguish two meanings of "because"? The word actually has three meanings: one event can cause [make] another event; a motive can cause [motivate] a choice; or a reason can cause [justify] a conclusion or belief.)

476. Jesus could have said many other things in answer to his disciples' objections in order to lessen the scandal and keep them from leaving him. Why didn't he?

Jesus said to the Twelve, "Will you also go away?" Simon Peter answered him, "Lord, to whom shall we go? You have the words of eternal life; and we have believed, and have come to know, that you are the Holy One of God." (6:67–69)

477. If you had to play the part of Jesus in a play, what emotional tone of voice would you use for the line "Will you also go away?"

478. Asked why he was a Christian, Walker Percy answered, "What else is there?" In light of Simon Peter's answer to Jesus, is this a good answer?

479. When Percy gave that answer, the interviewer said something like: "Well, there's atheism and agnosticism and secular humanism, and Islamic jihad and Hindu mysticism and Zen Buddhism and Social Darwinism and Utilitarianism and hedonism and pragmatism and Marxism and the New Age Movement. . . ." Percy replied, "That's what I mean." Compare his answer with Peter's.

480. (A) Can words save us from death? (B) If not, then how can words be "the words of eternal life" (v. 68)? (C) What is the literal meaning of the word "gospel"? (D) Is news made of words or of real events? (E) What is the role of words, then, in teaching and learning news? (This is the answer to question B, the hard one.) (F) Are any human words "magic" words? (G) Are any of God's words "magic" words? (See Gen 1:3 and Jn 11:43.)

481. In Peter's answer in verse 69, what is the relation between believing and knowing?

Jesus answered them, "Did I not choose you, the Twelve, and one of you is a devil?" He spoke of Judas the son of Simon Iscariot, for he, one of the Twelve, was to betray him. (6:70–71)

482. Jesus often surprises us by harsh words when we expect praise. (See Mt 16:21–23, immediately following Mt 16:11–12.) Why does he do that?

483. Jesus clearly labeled Judas as an unbeliever (v. 64); yet Judas did not leave Jesus when many of his other disciples did, but remained with "the Twelve". What do you think his motives were for remaining? (There is no one certain answer to this question.)

484. (A) Why did Jesus call Judas a "devil"? Was he exaggerating? (B) Is betrayal an unforgivable sin? Didn't Jesus offer Judas forgiveness when he called him "friend" even as he was in the act of betraying him (Mt 26:50)? (C) Why is he so harsh to him here, after Judas decided to remain faithfully with Jesus, and so merciful to him when Judas was in the act of unfaithfully betraying him?

John 7

After this Jesus went about in Galilee; he would not go about in Judea, because the Jews sought to kill him. (7:1)

485. Jesus seems to be deliberately avoiding death here. Why? Didn't he come to earth to die?

Now the Jews' feast of Tabernacles was at hand. So his brethren said to him, "Leave here and go to Judea, that your disciples may see the works you are doing. For no man works in secret if he seeks to be known openly. If you do these things, show yourself to the world." For even his brethren did not believe in him. (7:2-5)

486. The Hebrew word here for "brethren" ("brothers") can mean either (a) literal biological brothers or (b) any blood relatives, family members such as cousins. Which do you think is meant here? Why?

487. In light of verse 1 and verse 5, why do Jesus' brethren want him to go to Judea?

H488. In Jesus' day, only a few believed in him. If Jesus had indeed "shown himself to the world" by performing many more public miracles, as his brethren told him to do, wouldn't nearly everyone have believed in him? And isn't that why he came to earth, since he commanded us to "make disciples of all nations" (Mt 28:19)? Why wouldn't many more miracles have accomplished his purpose better? Who would doubt him if he had made the sky rip apart or the mountains literally dance?

Jesus said to them, "My time has not yet come, but your time is always here." (7:6)

489. (A) What did he mean by that? (B) How does it help answer question 488?

"The world cannot hate you, but it hates me because I testify of it that its works are evil." (7:7)

H490. (A) Why do so many people feel sure that if they had lived two thousand years ago and had met Jesus, they would never have hated him and shouted "Crucify him!"? (B) Why did Jesus make so many enemies? Wasn't he a "nice guy"? (C) Why are false prophets often loved and followed and true prophets often hated and even killed? (D) Why do many people feel more threatened by great saints than by great sinners?

491. Does verse 7 mean that Jesus was "judgmental"? (Hint: It might be useful to use the reasonable but bothersome logical technique of defining our terms here!)

492. (A) Just how did Jesus testify to the world of its evil? Did he use the same method on (I) hard-hearted unbelievers like the Pharisees, (II) the masses, and (III) his disciples? (B) If different methods were used, how were they different? (C) Is this a model for us his disciples to follow in addressing the world's problems? (D) In evangelism? (E) If so, why do we usually use a "one size fits all" approach instead?

493. (A) What do you think is the most needed specific application today of "testifying to the world that its works are evil"? (B) Why do you think this is the most necessary? (This question obviously opens up a large can of worms for discussion; don't spend all your time arguing about it.)

"Go to the feast yourselves; I am not going up to this feast, for my time has not yet fully come." So saying, he remained in Galilee.

But after his brethren had gone up to the feast, then he also went up, not publicly but in private. (7:8–10)

H494. Did Jesus lie to his brethren here? If not, why not?

E495. (A) What did Jesus mean by saying that his "time" had not yet come? (B) Most languages (but not English) have two words for "time" rather than just one. One means impersonal, physical, or cosmic time, which we measure by the sun and with clocks. (*"Kronos"* in Greek.) The other word means spiritual or personal time, which we measure by meanings and purposes. ("*Kairos*" in Greek.) Which word do you think Jesus used here?

496. (A) Compare what Jesus said about his "time" to his brethren here with what he said about this to Mary at Cana (Jn 2:4). (B) Even more than the other three Gospel writers, John introduces the theme of Jesus' enemies and his forthcoming death almost from the beginning, and references to it hover over even his early ministry like a dark cloud. Why do you think he did that? (C) Fulton Sheen famously said that the life of Jesus was "the only life in the world that was ever lived backward" when it came to the relationship between death and life. What do you think he meant by that?

The Jews were looking for him at the feast, and saying, "Where is he?" And there was much muttering about him among the people. While some said, "He is a good man," others said, "No, he is leading the people astray." Yet for fear of the Jews no one spoke openly of him. (7:11–13)

497. Why did Jesus' enemies think he was "leading the people astray"?

E498. There were, in Jesus' time, and still are, in our time, three opinions about Jesus. (I) Most of those who said "He is a good man" did not also say "He is the Son of God." They were like most of the non-Christian world today. (II) His enemies among the Jews, like today's "new atheists", thought he was not a good man, that he was bad for the world, that he did harm, that he was "leading the people astray". (III). His disciples believed not only that he was a good man but also that he was the Son of God. Explain how group II, his enemies who said, "No, he is not a good man for he is leading the people astray", were more logical and consistent than group I, his friends who said that he was a good man but only a good man. (Hint: Is a man who claims to be divine, but isn't, a good man or a bad man?)

499. (A) Are these the only three possible attitudes toward Jesus? (B) If so, why? If not, what is another one?

500. Prove by verse 13 that when John writes "the Jews", he does not mean "all Jews".

501. (A) Today we do not fear the religious authorities, as many of the Jews did in Jesus' day (v. 13). Why not, do you think? (B) Yet we, too, fear to speak honestly if we are "politically incorrect". Why, do you think? (C) What do we fear the most to talk about in public? (D) Why?

About the middle of the feast Jesus went up into the temple and taught. The Jews marveled at it, saying, "How is it that this man has learning, when he has never studied?" (7:14-15)

502. What is the answer to their question?

503. The Greek word used most frequently in the Gospels to describe the immediate reaction of everyone who met Jesus—his enemies as well as his friends and neutrals or agnostics—is "wonder" or "amazement" (*thaumadzein* in Greek). Even unbelievers, even his enemies, even those who plot to kill him, were amazed at him and his words. Why?

So Jesus answered them, "My teaching is not mine, but his who sent me." (7:16)

504. (A) How is this (v. 16) the true answer to their question (v. 15)? (B) How does this apply to us if we are teachers?

505. Jesus is saying here that he is not "original", that the origin of his teaching is not himself, his own mind and will, but that of his Father. If so, how come he is the most original, creative, unique, and unpredictable human being who ever lived?

H506. (A) Great fiction has been written about every other historical character, but never about Jesus. Most Jesus fiction is embarrassingly shallow. Why? (Hint: How is this related to his "originality"?) (B) Do you know any exceptions to this general principle, any good fiction about Jesus?

H507. (A) Jesus here claims to be totally submissive to the Father in his mind and in his teaching. Elsewhere he says the same thing about his will, that he came into the world not to do his own will but the will of the Father. Why isn't Jesus' total submission or surrender in both mind and will to his Father incompatible with his full deity or divinity, his equality with the Father? (B) What are the radical social consequences of this theological principle about the relation of the Persons in the Trinity? Big hint: In pre-Christian societies, there was authority and obedience but not equality; in modern post-Christian society, there is equality but not authority and obedience (or at least not much of it). In Christian society, there is both. Why? Hint to the hint: Saint Paul, in his epistles (Eph 5:21—6:9 and Col 3:18–23), when dealing with the three most important human relationships in all times, places, and cultures, namely, the relationships between husband and wife, parent and child, and ruler and servant or citizen, affirms both (1) the equality of the two parties, as well as mutual and reciprocal duties, in each of these three relationships and also (2) the demand for submission or obedience in all three relationships. This obedience is obviously different in the different relationships, and the submission or surrender is to be a mutual submission, explicitly in the case of husbands and wives and implicitly in the other two cases, too. How is all this rooted in the nature of ultimate reality, namely, the Trinity?

"If any man's will is to do his will, he shall know whether the teaching is from God or whether I am speaking on my own authority." (7:17)

508. How is this the secret of interpreting the Bible?

509. How is it also the secret of personal discernment of God's will? We usually think that rightly discerning God's will for ourselves, especially regarding difficult decisions, is essentially a problem in our minds; why is it rather essentially a problem in our will?

510. How is it also the secret of effective religious teaching (evangelism, edification, and catechesis)?

511. How does it explain how Mother Teresa never lost an argument? (Typical example: "Mother, you shouldn't be against population control; there are too many people." "Too many people? That's like saying there are too many flowers.")

H512. (A) Is Jesus saying here that all who love God, and want to do his will, will (at least eventually) believe that Jesus and his teach-

ing are truly from God? (B) If so, why do so many good God-loving
Jews and Muslims not believe this? If not, why does that *seem* to be
what he is saying?

*"He who speaks on his own authority seeks his own glory; but he who
seeks the glory of him who sent him is true, and in him there is no false-
hood." (7:18)*

513. (A) Explain this principle. What is Jesus saying here? (B) How
do we use this principle in the secular world, too? Give an example.
(C) What eventually happens, in the "real world", to people who
seek their own glory? Give examples.

*"Did not Moses give you the law? Yet none of you keeps the law. Why
do you seek to kill me?" The people answered, "You have a demon! Who
is seeking to kill you?" (7:19–20)*

514. (A) Is Jesus accusing everyone here or only the Pharisees? (B)
Most of the Pharisees kept the Mosaic law to the letter, so how can
Jesus say they are not keeping the law? (Matthew's Gospel gives
you detailed answers to this question.)

515. Why was Jesus so harsh here? What did he hope to accomplish? Was his motive love?

516. (A) Why did they respond even more harshly? (B) Would it
have been better if Jesus had spoken in a more conciliatory way
and evoked a conciliatory response? (C) If not, why not? If so, why
didn't he?

*Jesus answered them, "I did one deed, and you all marvel at it. Moses
gave you circumcision (not that it is from Moses, but from the fathers),
and you circumcise a man upon the sabbath. If on the sabbath a man
receives circumcision, so that the law of Moses may not be broken, are
you angry with me because on the sabbath I made a man's whole body
well? Do not judge by appearances, but judge with right judgment."
(7:21–24)*

517. Explain the logic of Jesus' argument in verse 23.

518. (A) In light of verse 24, evaluate advertising's most famous slogan, "image is everything." (B) Who invented advertising, when, and where? (See Genesis 3 for the answer.) (C) Does that make it the world's oldest profession?

Some of the people of Jerusalem therefore said, "Is not this the man whom they seek to kill? And here he is, speaking openly, and they say nothing to him! Can it be that the authorities really know that this is the Christ? Yet we know where this man comes from; and when the Christ appears, no one will know where he comes from." So Jesus proclaimed, as he taught in the temple, "You know me, and you know where I come from? But I have not come of my own accord; he who sent me is true, and him you do not know. I know him, for I come from him, and he sent me." So they sought to arrest him; but no one laid hands on him, because his hour had not yet come. Yet many of the people believed in him; they said, "When the Christ appears, will he do more signs than this man has done?" (7:25–31)

519. Why didn't Jesus' enemies kill him earlier?

520. (A) What two reasons led some people to think that Jesus was the promised Messiah? (See vv. 25–26 and v. 31.) (B) How good were these two reasons?

521. (A) What reason led some people to think that Jesus was not the Messiah? (See v. 27.) (B) How good a reason was it? (C) What was wrong with it?

522. How did Jesus answer it in the next verse?

523. (A) What does Jesus mean by "know" in this verse? (B) What do the people mean by it?

H524. (A) Can anyone "know" Christ as he uses the word "know" and still reject him? (B) Why or why not?

525. Is it possible that some of the people both did (in one sense) and did not (in another sense) know who Jesus was and where he came from?

526. Why does where Christ came from show who he was? How does our origin determine our nature?

527. If we come merely from primordial slime by random chance and accident, as a purely materialistic evolutionism says, what does that say about what we will be as well as what we are, about our destiny as well as our nature? (Anti-Darwinist bumper sticker: "My ancestors were all humans: sorry to hear about yours.")

528. Is there a sense in which we, too, like Christ, can say what he says in verse 29? (Cf. Jn 3:3, 6.)

529. Why did Christ's words in verse 29 anger some people so much that they wanted to kill him?

H530. What kind of "because" is the explanation in verse 30 for why they did not kill him?

531. (A) Why was it the religious authorities and the Pharisees, the ones who were the most passionate about God and keeping God's law, who hated and feared Jesus the most? (B) Didn't he say, many times and in many ways, that knowing the Father and knowing the Son constituted a "package deal", that no one could know either one without knowing the other? How, then, could many of the Jews (and, later, Muslims) believe in and obey the Father yet reject the Son? (C) Does this question have two very different answers for two different kinds of believing and practicing Jews who did not believe in Jesus: those who wanted to kill him (like most of the Pharisees) and those who did not (like Nicodemus, who was also a Pharisee)? (D) Does your answer to question 512 also answer this question?

The Pharisees heard the crowd thus muttering about him, and the chief priests and Pharisees sent officers to arrest him. Jesus then said, "I shall be with you a little longer, and then I go to him who sent me; you will seek me and you will not find me; where I am you cannot come." The Jews said to one another, "Where does this man intend to go that we shall not find him? Does he intend to go to the Dispersion among the Greeks and teach the Greeks? What does he mean by saying, 'You will seek me and you will not find me,' and, 'Where I am you cannot come'?" (7:32–36)

532. What did Jesus mean by saying this?

533. Why did the Jews so badly misunderstand him?

534. (A) When the Gospel was preached to the Gentiles ("Greeks"), e.g., by Paul (cf. Acts 17), did Jesus then go to the Gentiles? (B) Did he go there physically? (C) Was it just information about him that went there when Paul preached there? (D) If the answer to A is Yes and the answer to both B and C is No, then, was Jesus' presence among the Gentiles something between these two things? If so, what kind of presence was it?

On the last day of the feast, the great day, Jesus stood up and proclaimed, "If any one thirst, let him come to me and drink. He who believes in me, as the Scripture has said, 'Out of his heart shall flow rivers of living water.'" Now this he said about the Spirit, which those who believed in him were to receive; for as yet the Spirit had not been given, because Jesus was not yet glorified. (7:37–39)

535. To what "thirst" was Jesus referring in verse 37? Connect this to John 1:38.

536. (A) Imagine a preacher saying this today in some public assembly. What would the majority reaction probably be? (B) Why would that be the reaction? (C) Is that the same reaction Jesus got from the majority of his audience then? (D) If so, are most people so stupid that they can't tell the difference between the real Messiah and fake ones? If not, was the difference between then and now a difference in the audiences or in the speakers or both?

537. Why isn't what Jesus said here the most arrogant and dangerous egotism in history? Buddha never said "come to me." He said, "Look not to me, look to my teaching." All great philosophers, prophets, saints, and sages said the same. But Jesus said "come to me." While Buddha said, "Be lights unto yourselves", Jesus said "I am the light of the world." Why isn't that egotistic?

538. Where else did Jesus speak of the Spirit as "living water"?

539. Think (and feel) through that image. (Take a breath! Take some time!) Why is it a most appropriate one?

540. (A) Why is this same image used in Jesus' last message to us (Rev 22:17)? How is this the essence of the startling "good news"

of the Gospel? (B) How does it presuppose an equally startling "bad news"?

541. (A) Why does this "living water" come from the "heart"? (B) What does the Bible mean by the "heart"? (C) How is it different from what Hollywood, Hallmark greeting cards, and popular songs mean by the "heart"? (D) Does it come from the heart as its first cause or as its conduit, its instrument, its landing field?

H542. What did John mean by saying that the Spirit had not yet been given because Jesus was not yet "glorified"? Was this "glorification" (I) the sending of the Holy Spirit at Pentecost, (II) Jesus' Resurrection, or (III) Jesus' crucifixion? If it is (I), how was it Jesus who was glorified when it was the Holy Spirit who was sent? If it is (II), where does the Bible say the Spirit was sent or released at the time of the Resurrection? If it is (III), how could a crucifixion and death be a "glorification"? And where does the Bible say the Spirit was given then? Was the Spirit something like the energy released when an atom is split—when the Son was forsaken by the Father (Mt 27:46)? How is that analogy a bad one, and how is it a good one?

When they heard these words, some of the people said, "This is really the prophet." Others said, "This is the Christ." But some said, "Is the Christ to come from Galilee? Has not the Scripture said that Christ is descended from David, and comes from Bethlehem, the village where David was?" So there was a division among the people over him. Some of them wanted to arrest him, but no one laid hands on him. (7:40–44)

H543. (A) What was there about Jesus or about his words that led some people to believe that he was the promised Messiah ("Christ") or at least his prophet? This sounds like a difficult question, but perhaps its answer is really very easy. Imagine you are a pious Jew of Jesus' time, knowing the Old Testament Scriptures but knowing nothing of what you now know of Christian theology, and you met Jesus. Why might you believe in him? (B) Why might you not?

H544. Here is a "stretch" question, but it may help answer the previous one. When you meet a saint, how do you know he is a saint? How do you know someone is not a saint? What kind of "knowing" is this?

545. (A) Evaluate the mistake of the unbelievers. As far as they knew, Jesus was born in Nazareth; but the Messiah was to be born in Bethlehem. Therefore Jesus could not be the Messiah. That's a valid logical argument. Yet it is mistaken. How could they have corrected their mistake?

H546. Why did some good and reasonable people believe his claim even if they knew the Bethlehem prophecy and believed that Jesus had been born in Nazareth instead of Bethlehem? Does the answer to question 544 help answer this one?

The officers then went back to the chief priests and Pharisees, who said to them, "Why did you not bring him?" The officers answered, "No man ever spoke like this man!" The Pharisees answered them, "Are you led astray, you also? Have any of the authorities or of the Pharisees believed in him? But this crowd, who do not know the law, are accursed." Nicodemus, who had gone to him before, and who was one of them, said to them, "Does our law judge a man without first giving him a hearing and learning what he does?" They replied, "Are you from Galilee too? Search and you will see that no prophet is to rise from Galilee." They went each to his own house, but Jesus went to the Mount of Olives. (7:45—8:1)

547. (A) Why did tough, worldly, practical, commonsensical police officers find Jesus so impressive that they refused to arrest him, while pious religious authorities wanted to kill him? (B) Was it his words? But if anyone else had spoken these same words, the effect would not have been present, right? (C) What was it, then, what did Jesus have, what was there about him, that was almost like a physical force? Compare 18:4–6. How could spiritual power have such physical effects? (D) The Chinese have a word for this: *Te*. It means "spiritual power" or "personal moral authority". It is a hard thing to define or explain (the soldiers could not explain it very well to the Pharisees), but it is an easy thing to recognize when you meet it in some people. Which people? Who has it? (E) And where does it come from?

548. What does the Pharisees' argument in verses 47–48 reveal about Jesus? How much does it reveal about *them*?

549. (A) What is the essential contrast between the character of Nicodemus and that of the other Pharisees that explains why he was led to faith in Christ while most of the others rejected Christ? What crucial virtue did Nicodemus have? (B) How does his meeting with Jesus in chapter 3 show this character trait? (C) Where else is Nicodemus mentioned in the Gospels, and what does that mention show about his character?

550. Imagine yourself in Nicodemus' place in the scene here. (A) Why do you feel uncomfortable? (B) What else do you feel?

H551. (A) If at least part of the answer to question 549A is open-minded honesty and fairness, do you think that this virtue always leads to faith, as it did for Nicodemus? (B) Why or why not? (C) If your answer is Yes, why do you think there are so many apparently honest, fair, and open-minded unbelievers? If your answer is No, what other human qualities or virtues are needed to lead one to faith? (D) Do you think arrogance, pride, and closed mindedness always lead away from faith? (E) Why or why not? (F) If your answer is Yes, how do you account for the conversion of Paul of Tarsus? (See Acts 9.) If your answer is No, what else is needed? What makes the crucial difference between belief and unbelief?

552. How would you characterize the Pharisees' prejudice (vv. 48–49)? Are there contemporary examples of it?

553. (A) Do you think that if the Pharisees had known that Jesus was born in Bethlehem, thus fulfilling that Messianic prophecy, they would have believed in him? (B) If not, why did they offer that as their reason for not believing in him?

John 8

Early in the morning he came again to the temple; all the people came to him, and he sat down and taught them. The scribes and the Pharisees brought a woman who had been caught in adultery, and placing her in their midst they said to him, "Teacher, this woman has been caught in the act of adultery. Now in the law Moses commanded us to stone such. What do you say about her?" This they said to test him, that they might have some charge to bring against him. (8:2–6)

554. They seem to have Jesus infallibly caught in a trap. Mosaic law mandated death by stoning as the penalty for adultery. Roman law, on the other hand, did not allow the Jews the right of capital punishment. Jesus has either to answer this question or not. If he does not answer it, he admits defeat. If he answers it Yes, he violates Roman law. If he answers it No, he violates Mosaic law. What would the Pharisees have said and done to him in each of these three cases?

H555. How is it possible for anyone to escape such an inescapable logical dilemma?

556. (A) Compare this story with the one about Solomon and the two women in 1 Kings 3:16–28. (B) How does the last verse of the Solomon story (v. 28) answer question 555? (There is actually a book, *Ben Israel*, by Arthur Katz, about an actual example of the conversion of a Jewish agnostic to Christ because of this passage in John 8. You might look it up.)

Jesus bent down and wrote with his finger on the ground. (8:6)

557. John does not tell us what he wrote. Nothing comes of this detail. Why is it there? What does it show?

558. If you had to guess, what would you say Jesus wrote?

559. This is the only time Jesus is ever recorded as having written anything, and it was quickly erased forever by the wind. Why do you think he never wrote a book? (You might look up Saint Thomas Aquinas' answer to that question in his *Summa Theologiae* III, 42, 4.)

560. (A) A little research project: Next to Jesus, the two most influential and important teachers of all time were probably Socrates and Buddha. How many words do we have of their writings? (B) What do you think is the reason for this? Is the reason similar in the case of Jesus? (See Aquinas' answer to that question regarding Socrates, whom he mentions in the passage referred to above.)

And as they continued to ask him, he stood up and said to them, "Let him who is without sin among you be the first to throw a stone at her." (8:7)

561. The story is familiar, so we are not shocked by his answer. But everyone there certainly was. Why?

562. What do you think the woman felt when she heard his answer?

563. What do you think the Pharisees felt?

564. What do you think Jesus' disciples felt?

565. What do you think Judas felt?

566. What do you think most of the people, who had not yet become his disciples, felt?

H567. What do you think Jesus felt? (He was fully human, so he had fully human emotions, too.)

H568. (A) What was Jesus doing to the Mosaic law here? Compare Matthew 5 (the whole chapter). (B) Why wasn't Jesus implying that the Mosaic law was wrong or not really God's will, if it was not to be enforced on the woman?

569. Give a contemporary instance, a real or imagined specific case, of following Jesus' example here.

570. (A) Does Jesus' treatment of this woman show that he did not take sexual morality as seriously as other areas of morality? (B) Why or why not? (C) If not, why do most people today interpret him that way? If so, why did he label even lust as a kind of adultery (Mt 5:28)?

And once more he bent down and wrote with his finger on the ground. (8:8)

571. What do you think is going on here? What is he doing? What is everyone thinking?

And as they continued to ask him, he stood up and said to them, "Let him who is without sin among you be the first to throw a stone at her." And once more he bent down and wrote with his finger on the ground. But when they heard it, they went away, one by one, beginning with the eldest, and Jesus was left alone with the woman standing before him. Jesus looked up and said to her, "Woman, where are they? Has no one condemned you?" She said, "No one, Lord." And Jesus said, "Neither do I condemn you; go, and do not sin again." (8:7–11)

572. Why does Jesus seem to behave so casually here, as if their question were a distraction?

573. (A) Why did they all go away? (B) Why did the oldest go away first?

574. Did the Pharisees go away, too? If so, what do you think they were thinking, what do you think was in their hearts as they went away?

575. What is the importance of Jesus being alone with the woman before he forgives her? What's the difference between (I) being guilty and standing before human judges who are charged with enforcing the law, whether this is human law or divine law, and (II) being guilty and standing before Jesus alone?

H576. (A) If Jesus offers more mercy than human judges do, does that mean he offers less justice? (B) If not, why not? If so, how could he compromise justice? (C) What is the relation between mercy and justice in our actions? (D) What is the relation between mercy and justice in God's actions? (E) How is this question answered by Psalm 85:10, even though neither the word "justice" nor the word "mercy" is used? (F) How is Psalm 85:10 explained by Psalm 85:11? (G) Which is prior, justice or mercy, and why? (See Aquinas' surprising answer to this question in *Summa Theologiae* I, 21, 3–4.)

H577. It is obvious how mercy was done in this case, but how was justice done?

578. Why did Jesus "look up" at the woman only now? What was he doing before?

579. Do you think this woman sinned again by committing adultery after this or not? Why or why not?

Again Jesus spoke to them, saying, "I am the light of the world; he who follows me will not walk in darkness, but will have the light of life." The Pharisees then said to him, "You are bearing witness to yourself; your testimony is not true." Jesus answered, "Even if I do bear witness to myself, my testimony is true, for I know where I have come from and where I am going, but you do not know where I come from or where I am going. You judge according to the flesh, I judge no one. Yet even if I do judge, my judgment is true, for it is not I alone that judge, but I and he who sent me. In your law it is written that the testimony of two men is true; I bear witness to myself, and the Father who sent me bears witness to me." They said to him therefore, "Where is your Father?" Jesus answered, "You know neither me nor my Father; if you knew me, you would know my Father also." These words he spoke in the treasury, as he taught in the temple; but no one arrested him, because his hour had not yet come. (8:12–20)

580. (A) Why did Jesus say "I am the light of the world" rather than "I reveal the light of the world", or "I teach the light of the world"? (B) Did any other great teacher ever claim this?

581. (A) What is "the light of life"? Does it just mean "advice for living"? Hint: Is "life" *bios* or *zoe*? (See question 25.) (B) When we have *zoe*, what "light" or understanding do we have that we did not have before, when we had only *bios*? (Hint: Question 556A points to the answer.)

582. Explain verse 14. (A) Where does Jesus come from? (B) Where do the Pharisees think he came from? (C) Where is he going? (D) Where do the Pharisees think he is going? (E) Where did you come from? (F) Where are you going?

583. What does it mean to "judge according to the flesh"? Remember that "flesh" (*sarx*) means, not "meat" or "skin" or even "body", but *bios*, which includes soul as well as body (see question 25).

H584. (A) We confess in the Apostles' Creed that "he will come again to judge the living and the dead." In what sense does Jesus judge no one (as v. 15 says), and in what sense does he judge everyone (as the Creed says)? (B) Who are "the living", and who are "the dead" here?

H585. It is clear how Jesus bears witness to his Father: he reveals the Father and his nature, his character, especially his love and mercy. But how does the Father bear witness to the Son (v. 18)?

586. (A) Why does Jesus say "if you knew me, you would know my Father also" (v. 19)? Hint: Read John 14:8-9. (B) What was Philip's mistake there? (C) How did Jesus correct him? (D) How does verse 19 make the same point?

H587. Among human beings, to know a son is not necessarily to know his father. For instance, Socrates' sons were not particularly wise, like their father; and in the Old Testament, the pious priest Eli had two very wicked sons. Since Jesus said, "He who has seen me has seen the Father", this disconnect and difference is not true in the Trinity. Why not? Why must there be equality, not inequality, in the Trinity between Father and Son?

Again he said to them, "I go away, and you will seek me and die in your sin; where I am going, you cannot come." Then said the Jews, "Will he kill himself, since he says, 'Where I am going, you cannot come'?" (8:21–22)

588. Why did the Jews so bizarrely misunderstand Jesus that they thought he would kill himself?

589. Since Jesus could have saved himself from death in various ways, either natural (stay away from Jerusalem) or miraculous (call down twelve legions of angels), and either morally legitimate and sinless (don't go out of your way to antagonize your enemies) or immoral and sinful (tell lies), but he didn't use any of these ways, why wasn't his death a suicide?

590. Jesus was headed for martyrdom, not suicide. Why are those two not similar but radical opposites?

He said to them, "You are from below, I am from above; you are of this world, I am not of this world. I told you that you would die in your sins, for you will die in your sins unless you believe that I am he." They said to him, "Who are you?" Jesus said to them, "Even what I have told you from the beginning. I have much to say about you and much to judge; but he who sent me is true, and I declare to the world what I have heard from him." They did not understand that he spoke to them of the Father. So Jesus said, "When you have lifted up the Son of man, then you will know that I am he, and that I do nothing on my own authority but speak thus as the Father taught me. And he who sent me is with me; he has not left me alone, for I always do what is pleasing to him." As he spoke thus, many believed in him. (8:23–30)

H591. Why does Jesus say simply that "I am he" rather than using a more specific predicate (v. 24)? When they ask him "Who are you?", why does he again avoid being more specific and clear (v. 25)? Might Exodus 3:14 be a clue?

592. The great philosopher Plato, who always sought clear and adequate definitions of the nature of things, devoted every one of his

dialogues to a "what" question (e.g., "what is justice?" or "what is love?"), but the Gospels focus on the "who" question of verse 25, like a "whodunit" detective story or like the old *Lone Ranger* radio and TV series, in which a typical episode ended with the Lone Ranger riding away and leaving people saying, "Who was that masked man, anyway?" Why this difference?

H593. How could the Jews miss the point that seems so obvious to us: that "he spoke to them of the Father" (v. 27)?

594. In verse 28 Jesus appeals to his submission to his Father as the source of his authority. How does that work? Cf. the centurion in Matthew 8:5–13. (A) To whom was the centurion submissive? (B) What authority, authority over whom, flowed from this submission? (C) To whom was Jesus submissive? (D) What authority, authority over what, flowed from this submission? (E) What is the relationship between authority and submission?

595. E(A) What does Jesus mean by "lifted up the Son of man" (v. 27)? H(B) Why does he use the phrase "lifted up" if he means his crucifixion, which is the opposite of what it seems to mean (honor and glory)?

596. Verse 29: (A) Did the Father ever leave the Son alone, abandon him, or forsake him? (B) Did Jesus ever feel forsaken or abandoned? (C) What is the obvious practical application of those two facts for us?

597. (A) Jesus says that the Father "has not left me alone for I always do what is pleasing to him" (v. 29). Does this mean that when we sin, i.e., do what is not pleasing to him, God really does leave us alone? (B) If your answer is Yes, then why did God do the exact opposite of that in response to our sin when he sent his Son to us? If your answer is No, then it is sin that makes us feel alone and abandoned by God; so does that mean that when we feel alone and abandoned by God, it is always because we sinned? If so, why did the sinless Christ feel abandoned on the Cross, and why do all the saints (in the biblical sense, all believers are saints) go through a "dark night of the soul", when they feel alone and abandoned? What is God doing to them?

Jesus then said to the Jews who had believed in him, "If you continue in my word, you are truly my disciples, and you will know the truth, and the truth will make you free." They answered him, "We are descendants of Abraham, and have never been in bondage to any one. How is it that you say, 'You will be made free'?"

Jesus answered them, "Truly, truly, I say to you, every one who commits sin is a slave to sin. The slave does not continue in the house for ever; the son continues for ever. So if the Son makes you free, you will be free indeed." (8:31–36)

H598. Jesus here addresses believers, and he defines our discipleship as not just initial belief but "continuing" in his word. (A) Is it possible for a believer to fall away from faith and, therefore, from salvation? (B) If not, why does Christ warn against that here? If so, why do many Christians (especially Fundamentalists and Calvinists) believe "once saved, always saved"? Is there a half-truth here, or a truth from one point of view but not another? (C) How does this problem relate to the problem of the relationship between predestination and free will?

599. How can Christ say that the truth will make us free? Doesn't truth limit freedom? For instance, doesn't the truth that we are human beings and not Superman limit our ability to leap tall buildings at a single bound? Give a concrete example from ordinary secular life where the truth does not limit our freedom but makes us free.

600. What truth is Christ talking about here? (Connect v. 32 and v. 36.)

H601. Many people believe, or think they believe, that truth is subjective ("That's your truth but not my truth"), especially about good and evil ("There is nothing good or bad, but thinking makes it so"). Why are such people less free than people who know that there is objective truth?

602. How is the belief that truth is subjective, that there is really no such thing as objective truth, illogical, self-contradictory, and self-refuting?

603. The Jews Jesus spoke to here were believers (v. 31); yet their reply to him in verse 33 apparently shows that they felt threatened or insulted by what he said to them. Why?

604. (A) Of what kind of freedom were they thinking? Freedom from what? (B) Of what kind of freedom was Christ thinking? Freedom from what? (C) Why do most people think and worry more about the first kind of freedom than about the second?

E605. A murderer avoided capture for many years, then was caught, convicted, and imprisoned for life. In prison he found faith in Christ and said "I thank God for this prison, because now I'm free. I was really in prison out there." How does verse 34 explain that paradox?

606. (A) How is all sin, then, like cocaine? (B) Why does that work psychologically? Why is it so powerful? (C) Why won't that work in heaven?

607. According to the Old Testament prophecies, the Messiah would free the Jews from their enemies. When Jesus came, some Jews believed in him, and some did not. Explain how those who believed in him understood who their true enemies were, while those who did not believe in him wrongly identified their "enemies". (Hint: Why did the angel tell Joseph to call Mary's child "Jesus", which means "Savior"? Savior from what?) (Second hint: Jesus did not free the Jews from their Roman oppressors, who were almost as cruel as Nazis. This was a major reason why many Jews did not believe in him.)

608. (A) God could have inspired his Old Testament prophets to be more clear and specific when they said that the Messiah would free the Jews from their enemies. Why do you think he didn't? (B) After you have given your answer to question A, look at John 1:38. How does that verse answer that question?

609. When speaking to these Jewish believers, Jesus first assumes that they do believe in him but then adds that they must "continue" in his word (i.e., continue to believe and live according to his word) in order to be his disciples. What does this say about the relation between faith and good works? (Hint: Did the angel say that his

name should be "Jesus" ["Savior"] because he would save his people only from the *punishment* for their sins, from damnation?)

610. Prove from the text that Jesus was not speaking about the same people in verse 37 as in verse 31.

"I speak of what I have seen with my Father, and you do what you have heard from your father."

They answered him, "Abraham is our father." Jesus said to them, "If you were Abraham's children, you would do what Abraham did, but now you seek to kill me, a man who has told you the truth which I heard from God; this is not what Abraham did. You do the works of your father." They said to him, "We were not born of fornication; we have one Father, even God." Jesus said to them, "If God were your Father, you would love me, for I proceeded and came forth from God; I came not of my own accord, but he sent me. Why do you not understand what I say? It is because you cannot bear to hear my word. You are of your father the devil, and your will is to do your father's desires. He was a murderer from the beginning, and has nothing to do with the truth, because there is no truth in him. When he lies, he speaks according to his own nature, for he is a liar and the father of lies. But, because I tell the truth, you do not believe me. Which of you convicts me of sin? If I tell the truth, why do you not believe me? He who is of God hears the words of God; the reason why you do not hear them is that you are not of God." (8:38–47)

611. How does verse 38 illustrate the principle that one's actions reveal one's nature and one's nature reveals one's origin?

612. How does verse 42 illustrate the principle "like father, like son"? Review question 586 again here.

613. How does verse 44 also illustrate that principle?

614. How is 8:43 explained by 7:17? What's the psychology here? What's going on inside their souls? Is their mind moving their will, or is their will ("bear to hear") moving their mind ("understand")?

615. (A) Is Jesus exaggerating in verse 44? Is he merely saying that they are sinners (44a)? But we're all sinners, right? If that's all he meant, why does he exaggerate so much as to bring in the devil?

(B) If he is not exaggerating, is he saying that these people were all actually demon-possessed and needed exorcism? If so, why didn't he exorcise them? (C) Does he mean what he says about the devil being their father only as a kind of metaphor or figure of speech rather than literally? (D) If he meant it literally, does that mean physically, biologically? (E) Why couldn't it possibly be meant physically?

H616. What does it mean, then, to have Satan rather than God as your father, if not any of the four answers above, neither A (exaggeration) nor B (demon possession) nor C (mere figure of speech) nor D (biological)?

617. Why are we moderns so skeptical about the devil?

E618. Why must a Christian believe the devil is real? (This question is much easier than you may think.)

619. H(A) Verse 44 identifies the devil as the source of both lies and murder. What is the connection between these two things? How is every lie a kind of murder, and how is every murder a kind of lie? (B) What is the most total opposite of a lie? (C) What is the most total opposite of murder, of hating someone so much that you murder them? (D) The answer to question A was a connection between two bad things; what is the connection between the two opposite good things, the connection between the answer to question B and the answer to question C? (E) If lies and murders come ultimately from Satan, where do the two total opposites of these two things (answers B and C) ultimately come from?

H620. We expect Jesus to say: "Although I tell you the truth, you do not believe me." Instead, he says: "Because I tell [you] the truth, you do not believe me" (v. 45). Why does he say that?

621. (A) Has anyone else in history ever truly said what Jesus said in verse 46, namely, that no one can convict him of any sin? (B) If what he says here is not true, what logically follows? What attitude should we have toward Jesus in that case? (C) What is the difference between a sinner who admits he is a sinner and a sinner who says he is sinless?

622. Jesus is about to claim divinity in the most uncompromising and explicit way, in verse 58, by claiming the unique divine name

"I Am". But he already had claimed to be sinless (v. 46) and to forgive other people's sins (on many occasions in the other three Gospels and here in 8:11). As the Jews rightly perceived, these were two implicit claims to divinity. Why?

H623. In verse 47, "hears" implies not just "hears" but "heeds", "accepts", or "believes". So what if someone reads verse 47 and says "I've heard Jesus' words, but I cannot believe in Jesus because I am just not one of those people who Jesus says is 'of God'. Don't blame me for not believing; God just did not predestine me to believe, and there is nothing I can do about that." Why isn't that a good excuse for unbelief?

The Jews answered him, "Are we not right in saying that you are a Samaritan and have a demon?" (8:48)

624. What does the additional insult of "you are a Samaritan" tell you about Jesus' accusers?

625. Did you ever hear anybody accuse anybody of having a demon? Why not? If nearly everyone today thinks this charge is ridiculous, excessive, "over the top", or fanatical, why didn't everyone think that then?

626. (A) What do we mean today by "demonizing" our enemies? (B) Why is that so easy to do? (C) Do you know any modern examples?

627. How is this charge ironic? (Hint: Where are the demons, really, in this scene?)

Jesus answered, "I have not a demon; but I honor my Father, and you dishonor me. Yet I do not seek my own glory; there is One who seeks it and he will be the judge." (8:49–50)

628. Explain how the rest of Jesus' answer is evidence for the truth of the first part, that "I have not a demon."

E629. How can a man who is about to claim that he is God, in as uncompromising, direct, and literal a way as possible (verse 58), say that "I do not seek my own glory"? If you told your friends that you were God, that would be seeking divine glory, wouldn't it? So why isn't it that when Jesus says it?

630. Whose glory, then, does Jesus seek? And who seeks *his* glory?

631. How does this (the answer to question 630) define or express the eternal life of the Trinity?

"Truly, truly, I say to you, if any one keeps my word, he will never see death." (8:51)

632. Jesus' claims are now becoming more and more extreme. How is this an implicit claim to divinity?

633. About what kind of death is Jesus talking here? Everybody dies, don't they?

The Jews said to him "Now we know that you have a demon. Abraham died, as did the prophets; and you say, 'If any one keeps my word, he will never taste death.' Are you greater than our father Abraham, who died? And the prophets died! Who do you claim to be?" (8:52–53)

634. Why do the Jews see what Jesus just said, not just as false, ridiculous, unbelievable, gross exaggeration, or even insanity, but as proof that he has a demon? Is there some real, and even reasonable, principle behind their reaction?

635. Why is the fact that "Abraham died, as did the prophets" apparent proof that Jesus could not be speaking the truth when he says "If any one keeps my word, he will never taste death"?

636. (A) Why doesn't Jesus answer their question "Who do you claim to be?" by saying: "I am the Second Person of the eternal Trinity"? (B) Why doesn't he answer their question directly here at all? Why doesn't he say "I am . . ." or "I claim to be . . ."? And then fill in the blank.

Jesus answered, "If I glorify myself, my glory is nothing; it is my Father who glorifies me, of whom you say that he is your God. But you have not known him; I know him. If I said, I do not know him, I should be a liar like you; but I do know him and I keep his word." (8:54–55)

637. Why is Jesus' answer here better than any of the immediate, direct answers that begin "I am . . ." or "I claim to be . . ."? What does it accomplish?

638. How does what Jesus says in verse 54 answer the Jews' argument in verse 53?

639. (A) Is Jesus implying, in verses 54 and 55, that his Father is not the Jews' God, as they claim? (B) If so, who is their God? (C) Which commandment is Jesus accusing them of disobeying? (D) Which commandment are they accusing him of disobeying?

640. What do you think Jesus was trying to accomplish in insulting the Jews so directly in verse 55?

641. (A) What did Jesus mean by "knowing" God in verse 55? (B) In what sense can we "know" God as Jesus did, and in what sense can we not? (C) In what sense can an unbeliever "know" what a believer means by "God", and in what sense can he not?

642. This question is for anyone who knows either French or German (or old Scots, which is similar to German here): What are the two words for "know" in these languages, and how do they mean very different things?

"Your father Abraham rejoiced that he was to see my day; he saw it and was glad." (8:56)

643. What would you think if you heard someone say this?

644. How does Jesus here increase the tension and the offense?

645. Explain how this is an implicit claim to divinity. What divine attribute is Jesus implicitly claiming?

646. How did Abraham in fact see Jesus? When and where?

The Jews then said to him, "You are not yet fifty years old, and have you seen Abraham?" Jesus said to them, "Truly, truly, I say to you, before Abraham was, I am." So they took up stones to throw at him; but Jesus hid himself, and went out of the temple. (8:57–59)

647. How is verse 58 an even more explicit and offensive answer to their question in verse 57 than a simple "Yes"?

E648. (A) About how many times have you already heard Jesus using the formula "Truly, truly, I say to you"? (B) Why is the word "truly" said twice instead of just once? (C) This was a Rabbinic formula for rightly interpreting the words that follow it. Which of the following does this formula mean? (I) What I am about to say is true. (II) What I am about to say is very important. (III) I am not exaggerating when I say this. (IV) I mean this literally, not just figuratively. (V) I am choosing my words very carefully. (VI) Do not water this down; interpret it in the strongest sense, not the weakest sense. (VII) All of the above.

E649. Where in the Bible do you find the two words "I AM" as a personal name?

650. When the speaker uttered these words (I refer to the answer to the previous question), why did he not add another name, like "I am Zeus" or "I am Buddy"?

651. You may have to do some research on this question. Why do Jews never pronounce, in Hebrew, the words "I AM"? (Hint: It is not merely out of intense love and respect, as a romantic lover might so revere the name of his beloved that he would not pronounce her name because it is so holy to him. It is that, but it is more than that.) If God had said "I am Oscar", it would not necessarily be blasphemous to utter the word "Oscar", since you could say "Oscar, I adore you", or "Oscar is great." Why is "I AM" different from all other names in this way? (If you understand grammar, and the difference between first-, second-, and third-person pronouns, you will get the answer easily.)

652. How many times in the Bible does God give us his own absolute, eternal, essential name, rather than names for what he is in historical relation to us, like Creator, Lord, Redeemer, etc.?

653. (A) In light of the answers to the previous questions, now imagine you are a first-century religious Jew. You hear Jesus utter this word. What do you immediately and instinctively feel? (B) What do you think?

E654. Under Mosaic law, what was the penalty for public blasphemy before witnesses? (You can look it up, or you can guess it from verse 59.)

655. Why was the reaction of the Jews who tried to kill Jesus more logical than the reaction of those who didn't want him either dead or worshipped?

656. About how many people in the world, out of about 7.5 billion, believe each of the following ideas: (I) Jesus is God; (II) Jesus is a wicked, blaspheming liar or an insanely egotistic idiot; (III) Jesus is neither; he is just a good man?

657. Are there any other logical options than these three?

658. (A) In light of the answers to the above three questions (655–57), how logical is the belief that almost all non-Christians have about Jesus (option III in question 656)? (B) Why is that much more *comfortable* than either option I or option II? (C) So why do non-Christians typically think that Christianity is believed not because it is logical but because it is comforting? Is *that* believed because it is logical or because it is comforting and convenient?

E659. Let's assume that Jesus never said these words, that John made it up, that Jesus was just a nice guy who never claimed to be God; in fact, that Matthew, Mark, Luke, and John all made up the whole story of the divinity-claiming, miracle-working, virgin-born, resurrecting, sin-saving Son of God. In other words, they were the liars, not Jesus. (A) What could have motivated them to tell this lie, which was so highly offensive to their Jewish countrymen, and to die for it as martyrs? (B) What other made-up fiction has ever been as compelling a story, as interesting a story, as life-changing a story, as influential a story, and as misunderstood a story (misunderstood by 2 billion Christians as true when in fact it was all an invented fiction according to this assumption) as this one? (C) And why has no one ever invented anything like it since then? (D) And how did four first-century peasants have such great literary art that they invented a whole new genre, realistic fantasy, two thousand years before Tolkien? (E) Why can contemporary fiction writers improve on any of the past stories of any historical figure who ever lived except this one, Jesus? Why is all "Jesus fiction" ever written so pitifully shallow compared with the four Gospels, if they too were just fiction? H(F) Why is this question (E659) so easy for you but so hard for half the world that it ignores the question?

John 9

As he passed by, he saw a man blind from his birth. And his disciples asked him, "Rabbi, who sinned, this man or his parents, that he was born blind?" Jesus answered, "It was not that this man sinned, or his parents, but that the works of God might be made manifest in him." (9:1–3)

E660. (A) Apparently open-minded questions often have hidden assumptions. What are the disciples assuming in asking this question? (B) Why do you think they are assuming that?

H661. The "problem of evil" (more accurately, the mystery of evil) is one of the great puzzles of life: Why do bad things happen to good people? How does this incident, especially Jesus' answer to his disciples' question in verse 3, help to solve the problem of evil?

662. Does Jesus give us the solution to the problem of evil here (if so, what is it?) or does he show us why we cannot solve it (if so, why is that?)?

"We must work the works of him who sent me, while it is day; night comes, when no one can work. As long as I am in the world, I am the light of the world." (9:4–5)

H663. Why does Jesus insert this remark here? What does it have to do with this healing miracle?

664. What does Jesus mean by "day" and "night" here?

As he said this, he spat on the ground and made clay of the spittle and anointed the man's eyes with the clay, saying to him, "Go, wash in the pool of Siloam" (which means Sent). So he went and washed and came back seeing. (9:6–7)

H665. (A) Jesus could have healed this man instantly, and without using any material intermediary means. Why do you think he used spit and clay instead? (B) Why do you think he postponed the cure until the man went and washed?

666. (A) Interpretation is not the same as belief. Therefore it is bad literary science to say "I interpret this passage according to my own sincerely held beliefs." Interpretation means figuring out what the writer believed and meant, not what the reader believes. Why is it, therefore, bad literary science to interpret Jesus' miracles as mere fables, parables, myths, fictions, or symbols for abstract, invisible, universal truths? (B) What does the literary style of eyewitness description have to do with your answer? (C) Even though Jesus' miracles literally happened in this visible world, they also often symbolize our future heavenly destiny. If that is true of this miracle, what does it symbolize?

667. (A) Was it an accident, a coincidence, or divine providence that when this pool was named, centuries ago, it was named "Sent"? (B) Do you think anyone understood the real meaning of the name then (centuries ago)?

668. H(A) Compare this not-understanding with what the disciples did not understand in their question about the man born blind in verses 2–3. E(B) Why can't we understand God's plans until he reveals them?

The neighbors and those who had seen him before as a beggar, said, "Is not this the man who used to sit and beg?" Some said, "It is he"; others said, "No, but he is like him." He said, "I am the man." They said to him, "Then how were your eyes opened?" He answered, "The man called Jesus made clay and anointed my eyes and said to me, 'Go to Siloam and wash'; so I went and washed and received my sight." They said to him, "Where is he?" He said, "I do not know."

They brought to the Pharisees the man who had formerly been blind. Now it was a sabbath day when Jesus made the clay and opened his eyes. The Pharisees again asked him how he had received his sight. And he said to them, "He put clay on my eyes, and I washed, and I see." Some of the Pharisees said, "This man is not from God, for he does not keep the sabbath." But others said, "How can a man who is a sinner do such signs?" There was a division among them. (9:8–16)

669. How does verse 32 explain the people's hesitation to identify the blind beggar in verses 8–9?

670. How does verse 14 explain the Pharisees' detective-like prosecution of the case? Why is the word "again" significant?

671. Why, in their minds, did there seem to be a contradiction between these two facts (that for the first time in history a man born blind was healed and that Jesus did it on a Sabbath day)?

672. (A) What is the assumption of those who said, "This man is not from God, for he does not keep the sabbath"? (B) What is the assumption of those who said, "How can a man who is a sinner do such signs"? (C) Evaluate these two assumptions.

So they again said to the blind man, "What do you say about him, since he has opened your eyes?" He said, "He is a prophet."
    The Jews did not believe that he had been blind and had received his sight, until they called the parents of the man who had received his sight, and asked them, "Is this your son, who you say was born blind? How then does he now see?" His parents answered, "We know that this is our son, and that he was born blind; but how he now sees we do not know, nor do we know who opened his eyes. Ask him; he is of age, he will speak for himself." His parents said this because they feared the Jews, for the Jews had already agreed that if any one should confess him to be Christ, he was to be put out of the synagogue. Therefore his parents said, "He is of age, ask him."
    So for the second time they called the man who had been blind, and said to him, "Give God the praise; we know that this man is a sinner." He answered, "Whether he is a sinner, I do not know; one thing I know, that though I was blind, now I see." (9:17–25)

673. (A) The Pharisees say Jesus is a sinner and not the Christ (Messiah). The blind man's answer to the Pharisees' question "Who is this man?" is "a prophet". That sounds halfway between the two

other answers. But is that closer to "the Christ" or to "a sinner" (i.e., a notorious sinner, a public sinner, a habitual sinner)? (B) To answer that question, ask two more: (B1) Can prophets be such sinners? (B2) Is the Messiah *also* a prophet?

674. Give your evaluation of the moral character of the blind man's parents. What does their answer reveal about their relationship to their son?

675. The Pharisees thought that their authoritative judgment that "this man is a sinner" resolved the issue (v. 24). How did the blind man's reply in verse 25 answer their argument? (Hint: What is the relation between facts and opinions? Which ought to determine the other?)

676. In what sense can every Christian say what this blind man said, that "Though I was blind, now I see" (v. 25)?

They said to him, "What did he do to you? How did he open your eyes?" He answered them, "I have told you already, and you would not listen. Why do you want to hear it again? Do you too want to become his disciples?" And they reviled him, saying, "You are his disciple, but we are disciples of Moses. We know that God has spoken to Moses, but as for this man, we do not know where he comes from." The man answered, "Why, this is a marvel! You do not know where he comes from, and yet he opened my eyes. We know that God does not listen to sinners, but if any one is a worshiper of God and does his will, God listens to him. Never since the world began has it been heard that any one opened the eyes of a man born blind. If this man were not from God, he could do nothing." They answered him, "You were born in utter sin, and would you teach us?" And they cast him out. (9:26–34)

677. This is the fourth time they have asked this question (vv. 10, 15, 19, 26)! What weakness does that reveal? How does verse 27 show that the blind man perceived this weakness?

678. Was the blind man in fact, as the Pharisees accused him, a disciple of Jesus? If so, what verse first reveals this?

679. Explain why verse 30, in its context, is humorous (sarcastic and ironic).

680. (A) What is the blind man's argument in verses 31–33, in your own words? (B) Evaluate it.

681. How do the Pharisees answer his argument? How is it an *ad hominem*? (Look it up!)

682. What do you think emboldened the blind man to talk so directly and fearlessly to the Pharisees that they cast him out?

Jesus heard that they had cast him out, and having found him he said, "Do you believe in the Son of man?" He answered, "And who is he, sir, that I may believe in him?" Jesus said to him, "You have seen him, and it is he who speaks to you." He said, "Lord, I believe"; and he worshiped him. (9:35–38)

683. What is the significance of the fact that Jesus sought and found this man rather than vice versa?

684. How much do you think the blind man understood about who Jesus was when he "worshiped" Jesus?

685. Why do you think the blind man called Jesus "Lord" in verse 38 rather than just "sir" as in verse 36?

Jesus said, "For judgment I came into this world, that those who do not see may see, and that those who see may become blind." (9:39)

686. (A) Do you think Jesus means here (I) that he will make the blind see and the sighted blind, or (II) that many of those who do not see literally already do see spiritually, while those who do see literally are often blind spiritually? (B) Why?

687. (A) Why does Jesus call this "judgment"? (B) How is it different from "the Last Judgment"?

688. (A) How is Jesus' presence in the world the "judgment"? (B) Why do (I) the blind see and (II) the sighted become blind only in the presence of Jesus?

689. Socrates divided all mankind into fools, who thought they were wise, and the wise, who knew they were fools. Compare this to Jesus' implicit division and "judgment" of mankind here.

690. Pascal also divided mankind into two classes: sinners who see themselves as saints and saints who see themselves as sinners. Compare this division with Jesus' division. Compare it with Socrates' division.

Some of the Pharisees near him heard this, and they said to him, "Are we also blind?" Jesus said to them, "If you were blind, you would have no guilt; but now that you say, 'We see,' your guilt remains." (9:40–41)

691. (A) Jesus has just condemned the Pharisees for being (spiritually) blind (v. 39); now he condemns them for *not* being blind. This seems to be a contradiction, but it isn't. Why not? What does he mean here (v. 41), and what did he mean earlier (v. 39)? (B) How should we distinguish (I) physical, (II) mental or intellectual, and (III) spiritual sight or blindness here? Do we have three kinds of eyes?

692. There is a commonsense principle of morality that says that one's guilt is proportionate to one's knowledge, because guilt presupposes responsibility, and responsibility presupposes knowledge. (A) Why is this reasonable? Give examples. (B) Explain how this is implied in what Jesus is saying here.

693. Is Jesus saying that the Pharisees are guilty because they do see or because they think they do when they do not?

"Truly, truly, I say to you, he who does not enter the sheepfold by the door but climbs in by another way, that man is a thief and a robber; but he who enters by the door is the shepherd of the sheep. To him the gatekeeper opens; the sheep hear his voice, and he calls his own sheep by name and leads them out. When he has brought out all his own, he goes before them, and the sheep follow him, for they know his voice. A stranger they will not follow, but they will flee from him, for they do not know the voice of strangers." (10:1–5)

694. If Jesus is the door and heaven is the sheepfold, is he saying here that no non-Christian can go to heaven? That would be very severe and unfair, wouldn't it? If he's not saying that, are there other doors to heaven besides him? That would be very relativistic and wishy-washy, wouldn't it? Is there a third alternative? The issue came up before (question 53, on 1:9) and will come up again (on 14:6), and it's important and controversial enough to review it again.

695. To go back one more time to this all-important question: According to John's Gospel, what is a Christian? How did Jesus in chapter 3 give Nicodemus a better answer to that question than an answer that tells us only what a Christian believes or what a Christian does?

H696. (A) Is Jesus implying in verse 1 that some people sneak into heaven by other means than through Jesus the door? (B) If that's impossible, who are these sneaks?

H697. If the sheep are Christians, how do they "hear his voice"? How do you hear Jesus' voice? Describe his voice. Is this a subjective feeling or emotion? Is it the words of Jesus in the Gospels (often printed in red)? Or is it something else?

H698. Jesus says the sheep "know his voice". How do you "know his voice"? How do you know it's Jesus and not "the voice of strangers"? How is his voice distinctive?

699. (A) How does he "call them by name"? (B) What is the difference between being called by name and being called in a group? (N.B.: answering question B does not yet answer question A.)

700. (A) According to the Bible, are we also called in a group, community, or body, or is that something we add to Christ's call, organizing ourselves into a body after he calls us individually? (B) Do Protestants and Catholics give opposite answers to this question or not?

701. (A) When does Christ call you by name? Is it in the past, the present, the future, or all three? Explain. (B) Compare Revelation 2:17.

702. When the Shepherd "leads them out", what does he lead them out from?

703. (A) If you've ever seen shepherds (or sheepdogs, too, for that matter) work with sheep, in real life or in movies, there is one striking difference between that and Jesus' picture of himself as the shepherd. Can you find it? (Hint: Look at verse 4 carefully.) (B) How does this picture make the sheep less "sheepish"? (What do we usually mean by "sheepish"?)

This figure Jesus used with them, but they did not understand what he was saying to them.

So Jesus again said to them, "Truly, truly, I say to you, I am the door of the sheep. All who came before me are thieves and robbers; but the sheep did not heed them. I am the door; if any one enters by me, he will be saved, and will go in and out and find pasture. The thief comes only to steal and kill and destroy; I came that they may have life, and have it abundantly. I am the good shepherd. The good shepherd lays down his life for the sheep. He who is a hireling and not a shepherd, whose own the sheep are not, sees the wolf coming and leaves the sheep and flees; and the wolf snatches them and scatters them. He flees because he is a

hireling and cares nothing for the sheep. I am the good shepherd; I know
my own and my own know me, as the Father knows me and I know the
Father; and I lay down my life for the sheep." (10:6–15)

704. Why do you think the disciples were so slow to understand
Jesus' parable of the good shepherd?

705. To whom is Jesus referring in verse 8?

706. What does Jesus mean by "pasture" in verse 9? What is the
"pasture" his sheep find; what "pasture" do they enter through him
as the door?

707. Who is the wolf? What does the wolf seek?

708. Who are the "hirelings"?

E709. (A) What does Jesus mean by "I lay down my life for the
sheep"? (B) Do you think the disciples understood that answer at
the time? (C) If not, why not? (D) Why do you understand it better
than they did?

H710. There seems to be a connection, in Jesus' mind, in verse
15, between his relation to his Father and his relation to his sheep.
What is it?

H711. Here is a surprising answer to question 698: Jesus says we
know him as he knows his Father! (A) Could that possibly mean
"as adequately as" or "as much as"? (B) If it does not refer to the
same degree or adequacy of knowledge, does it refer to the same
kind of knowledge, though to an infinitely lesser degree of it? (C)
To test whether your answer to question B is right or not, ask:
(I) What kind of knowledge is there between Jesus and his Father?
(Remember the question about the distinction between what the
Germans call *kennen* vs. *wissen* and what the French call *connaître* vs.
savoir), and then ask: (II) What kind of knowledge is there between
Jesus and you?

"And I have other sheep, that are not of this fold; I must bring them also,
and they will heed my voice. So there shall be one flock, one shepherd."
(10:16)

H712. (A) Do you think Jesus means by "other sheep" (I) all future believers in him, (II) Gentile as well as Jewish Christians, (III) people in other religions than Christianity, or (IV) people who do not seem to believe in any religion at all? Give reasons for your opinion. (B) If it's III or IV, how could Jesus say that non-Christians, too, "heed my voice"? (You might want to go back one more time to question 695 ["What is a Christian?"] to help answer this question.)

H713. When and where do you think this "one flock" exists? If it is here and now on earth, what could this "one flock" be? We (and our shepherds) look pretty badly divided. If it is only in the future in heaven, isn't that so obvious (that there are no religious wars or spiritual arguments and divisions in heaven) that it's hardly worth saying?

"For this reason the Father loves me, because I lay down my life, that I may take it again. No one takes it from me, but I lay it down of my own accord. I have power to lay it down, and I have power to take it again; this charge I have received from my Father." (10:17–18)

H714. (A) Does the Father love the Son more because he lays down his life for his sheep, for God's dearly beloved kids? (B) Does he love us more if we do the same (lay down our life, give ourselves out of love) than if we don't? Or does God love every person the same no matter what he does? (C) Why? Hint: You could rephrase the question this way: Does God love you more if you are more lovable? The answer is not obvious. Both answers seem to be true. For, on the one hand, there is more sunlight reflected in a large mirror than in a small one, so we can contain more of God's love the more saintly we are; and, on the other hand, God gives us love, not because we deserve it, but because we need it. In fact, the shepherd spends more of his time on the one wandering "black sheep" that is lost than on the ninety-nine good sheep who stay home.

E715. This question may help you to answer the previous question. (A) Is there anything wrong with the following argument? The more God loves you, the more joy and meaning you have in your life. The more God can love you, the more he does love you. The more he finds in you to love, the more he can love you. The more lovable you are, the more God finds to love in you. The more loving and self-giving you are, the more lovable you are. Therefore, the more loving and self-giving you are, the more joy and meaning you have in your life. (B) Is the conclusion of this argument provable not just by logically valid argument but also by experience, in fact by active experiment? Explain.

H716. What difference does verse 17 make?

E717. Jesus had more than one good reason for giving up his life for us, but what was his ultimate reason according to his own words in verse 18?

718. (A) Of course he also did it because he loved us and because he wanted to save us, but does it surprise you that his ultimate reason is something different from that? (B) Does it disappoint you? Would you rather he had put his first reason (v. 18) second and our salvation first? (C) Why or why not?

H719. Here is a longer and deeper version of question 718. When Jesus was tempted in the wilderness by Satan (Lk 4), one of the temptations was this: "The devil took him up, and showed him all the kingdoms of the world in a moment of time, and said to him, 'To you I will give all this authority and their glory; for it has been delivered to me, and I give it to whom I will. If you, then, will worship me, it shall all be yours.' And Jesus answered him, 'It is written, "You shall worship the Lord your God, and him only shall you serve."'" What was this temptation? One reasonable interpretation of its meaning is this: the tempting thing could not have been worldly power, riches, and political authority for two reasons. For one thing, the devil did not have authority over "all the kingdoms of the world", for Saint Paul wrote: "Let every person be subject to the governing authorities. For there is no authority except from God, and those that exist have been instituted by God. Therefore he who resists the authorities resists what God has appointed" (Rom 13:1–2). A second and even more obvious reason is that Jesus would never have been tempted in the least by political power, and certainly not enough to commit idolatry and apostasy and to worship Satan instead of his Father. Why, even you are wise enough not to be moved by that stupid temptation! Are you better than Jesus? Rather, when the devil said he would give Christ "all the kingdoms of the world", that probably meant souls, people—all the souls in the hell from which Christ had come to save mankind. Satan would open the doors of hell and free all human souls; for he did have rightful authority over all those souls who had chosen him and hell over God and heaven. If Jesus only did his job of salvation Satan's way, it would be 100 percent successful, not one of those children would be eternally lost whom God loved so much that he sent his Son into the world to die to save them (Jn 3:16). But if Jesus did not do things Satan's way, many souls would be lost forever. Jesus' mission of salvation would not be 100 percent successful. The price of universal salvation was only one act of idolatry. Now if you were Jesus, wouldn't you be tempted by that? So was Jesus right to say No to this temptation simply because he knew it was wrong and forbidden by the Father, even though he knew that it meant that some of his beloved children would go to hell forever? Christ answered this question by his choice, his refusal, and also by his teaching that summarized the whole of God's law and will and commandments by saying that "the first and greatest commandment" was not to love other human beings as you love yourself (that is "the second" commandment) but to love God with your whole heart, soul, mind, and strength (that is, in an unlimited and unmeasured way). Are you surprised by Jesus' prioritizing? Do you disagree with it? Why or why not?

There was again a division among the Jews because of these words. Many of them said, "He has a demon, and he is mad; why listen to him?" Others said, "These are not the sayings of one who has a demon. Can a demon open the eyes of the blind?" (10:19–21)

E720. Why did none of the Jews take a middle position and say Jesus was neither insane and demon-possessed nor the miracle-working Messiah and Lord, but just a good man? The rest of the world (the non-Christian world) believes that middle position; were the Jews who wanted to kill him because he was demon-possessed and mad more reasonable than the rest of the world?

721. E(A) How important was the role of Christ's miracles in these Jewish believers' argument (v. 21)? H(B) The unbelieving Jews saw the miracles, too, but interpreted them as demonic rather than

divine. Why? (N.B.: Demons can work apparent miracles, as did Pharaoh's magicians in Egypt at the time of the Exodus.)

It was the feast of the Dedication at Jerusalem; it was winter, and Jesus was walking in the temple, in the portico of Solomon. So the Jews gathered round him and said to him, "How long will you keep us in suspense? If you are the Christ, tell us plainly." Jesus answered them, "I told you, and you do not believe. The works that I do in my Father's name, they bear witness to me; but you do not believe, because you do not belong to my sheep. My sheep hear my voice, and I know them, and they follow me; and I give them eternal life, and they shall never perish, and no one shall snatch them out of my hand. My Father, who has given them to me, is greater than all, and no one is able to snatch them out of the Father's hand. I and the Father are one." (10:22–30)

E722. Why do you think John put in the details about time and place in verse 22? Compare myths and fairy tales, which take place "once upon a time" or "in a galaxy far away".

H723. (A) Isn't the Jews' question in verse 24 a fair one? (B) Why didn't Jesus answer it plainly and directly with a simple "Yes"? (C) Why, instead, does he appeal to his "works" (miracles)?

H724. Jesus explains in verse 26 that the reason they do not believe in him is that they are not his "sheep". Suppose they replied that the reason they were not his "sheep" (disciples) was that they did not believe him: Why is his explanation any better than theirs?

H725. Let's transpose this argument (question 724) into theological terms. Jesus is saying that they do not believe because they are not his "sheep" who "hear his voice", i.e., they do not have God's life in them, which they get through God's grace. Why isn't that a good excuse?—"I can't believe because God hasn't given me the grace to believe."

EH726. E(A) Why can no one snatch Jesus' "sheep" out of his hand (v. 28)? H(B) Why can't I slip through his fingers? When Corrie Ten Boom was asked that question, she answered: "Because I am one of his fingers." What do you think she meant by that? H(C) To find out, read 1 Corinthians 1:12–27 and think through the biblical phrase "You are the body of Christ" (1 Cor 12:27). How do the "members" of your body (v. 27) mean something different from the "members" of a club? In what way are they more "one", more unified? E(D) Does that mean that the Christian's union with Christ is closer than a human lover's union with his human beloved?

727. The doctrine that God is omnipotent (all-powerful) is often thought of as a piece of abstract, logical, objective, eternal theological truth but not immediately relevant to the very personal and practical issue of my salvation. How does verse 29 overcome this disconnect? What psychological, emotional difference would it make to you if you did not believe in God's omnipotence?

E728. "One" is a many-layered word. There are many ways we can be "one" with each other. How does the Jews' reaction (in v. 31) to Jesus statement that "I and the Father (God) are one" (v. 30) show us that Jesus did not mean by this "oneness" merely that he and the Father agreed, understood, and loved each other?

The Jews took up stones again to stone him. Jesus answered them, "I have shown you many good works from the Father; for which of these do you stone me?" The Jews answered him, "We stone you for no good work but for blasphemy; because you, being a man, make yourself God." (10:31–33)

729. Why did they want to stone Jesus instead of killing him in some other way? (Hint: Look up the word "stone" [the verb, not the noun] in the Old Testament in a concordance.)

730. How do the Jews' words seem more clear and logical than Jesus' words here?

H731. How can a man be God? God is infinite, immortal, invisible, and eternal; every man is finite, mortal, visible, and temporal. Why isn't the essential Christian doctrine about Christ—that he is both God and man—simply self-contradictory, like a round square? (Hint: The early creeds answered that question by distinguishing his "person" from his "nature". One is single; the other double.)

H732. The same distinction, between "person" and "nature", also helped explain why the doctrine of the Trinity (that God is both one and three) is not a self-contradiction; how?

Jesus answered them, "Is it not written in your law, 'I said, you are gods'? If he called them gods to whom the word of God came (and Scripture cannot be nullified), do you say of him whom the Father consecrated and sent into the world, 'You are blaspheming,' because I said, 'I am the Son of God'?" (10:34–36)

N.B.: Questions 733 and 734 are hard for different reasons: 733 is about theology, and 734 is about psychology.

H733. (A) Christ never said the simple words "I am God", but he said "I am the Son of God", right? (B) How different are these two things? (Hint: The son of a dog is a dog, and the son of a lion is a lion, so the son of God is . . . what?) (C) How does the distinction between (I) "God" as the proper name of a single Person (the Father) and (II) "God" as the name of a nature common to three divine Persons answer the question why Jesus said "I am the Son of God" rather than simply "I am God"?

H734. Surely the way in which Christ is God is not the same as the way in which those addressed in Scripture (human lords and rulers) are called "gods". Is Christ committing the logical fallacy of equivocation or ambiguity here? If not, is he playing with his audience, making what is almost a pun on words? What effect did he hope his words might have on them? (Hint: Remember who his audience is: they hate him and want to stone him on the spot for blasphemy.)

"If I am not doing the works of my Father, then do not believe me; but if I do them, even though you do not believe me, believe the works, that you may know and understand that the Father is in me and I am in the Father." (10:37–38)

H735. How would you explain both (a) the power and (b) the limits of Jesus' miracles as reasons for faith in him? (A) Were they good reasons for faith? (B) Why or why not? (C) Were they the best reasons? (D) Why or why not? (E) If not, what would be better reasons?

736. What is the relation between (1) "believe the works" and (2) "know and understand that the Father is in me and I am in the Father"? (A) Does the first (the works, the miracles) logically prove the second (Christ's oneness with the Father)? (B) If so, how? If not, how can the first at least lead to the second in one's journey to deeper faith?

Again they tried to arrest him, but he escaped from their hands.

He went away again across the Jordan to the place where John at first baptized, and there he remained. And many came to him; and they said, "John did no sign, but everything that John said about this man was true." And many believed in him there. (10:39–42)

E737. How many times now has Jesus just barely escaped being killed? What does that fact do for the narrative arc of John's Gospel?

H738. Why do you think Jesus both (I) deliberately goes from Galilee to Judea and Jerusalem, where he knows the Jews are who want to kill him, and also (II) escapes and hides (as he does here) to avoid being killed? Does he change his mind? Or does he have a plan?

E739. (A) Why is it significant that those "many" who "believed in him there" (v. 43) were those who "came to him" (v. 41) rather than those who merely saw him come to them, like the scribes and Pharisees in Jerusalem? (B) How do 1:39 and 1:46 answer this question?

John 11

Now a certain man was ill, Lazarus of Bethany, the village of Mary and her sister Martha. It was Mary who anointed the Lord with ointment and wiped his feet with her hair, whose brother Lazarus was ill. So the sisters sent to him, saying, "Lord, he whom you love is ill." But when Jesus heard it he said, "This illness is not unto death; it is for the glory of God, so that the Son of God may be glorified by means of it."

Now Jesus loved Martha and her sister and Lazarus. So when he heard that he was ill, he stayed two days longer in the place where he was. (11:1–6)

740. There are at least four Marys in the Gospels. Can you distinguish them? (Hint: Three of them are around the Cross.)

741. (A) From the insight into Mary's character that you get from the description of Mary's and Martha's words and behavior in this chapter and also in Luke 10:38–42, why is it fitting and predictable that it was Mary rather than Martha who anointed Jesus' feet with the expensive ointment and wiped them with her hair, as referred to in verse 2 and as later described in detail in chapter 12? (B) Was this Mary (Mary of Bethany) the same Mary as Mary Magdalene? Wasn't Mary Magdalene the "sinful woman" (prostitute) who anointed Jesus' feet with her hair in Luke 7:36–50?

The New Testament seems to mention no fewer than *seven* Marys. Which of these might have been identical with one of the others?

1. Mary the mother of Jesus (Mt 1)
2. Mary Magdalene (Mt 27:56)
3. Mary the mother of James and John (Mt 27:56)
4. Mary the wife of Cleophas (Jn 19:25)
5. Mary of Bethany, Lazarus' sister (Jn 11)
6. Mary the mother of John Mark (Acts 12:12)
7. Mary who lived in Rome (Rom 16:6)

E742. (A) Compare the sisters' petition to Jesus in verse 3 with another Mary's petition at the wedding at Cana (2:3). How are they similar? (B) How do they express more faith than a longer petition would do?

743. Why does Jesus deliberately speak ambiguously in verse 4?

744. This is a long six-part question, but an important one, and the answers are clear. (A) John says that "Jesus loved Martha and her sister and Lazarus so when he heard that he was ill, he stayed two days longer in the place where he was" so that Lazarus would die. Does that look like love, to let a friend die when you can prevent it? (B) Does God do the same to us? Does he let us die when he can prevent it? (C) If so, does he do that to us for the same reason he did that to Mary and Martha: not because he does not love us but because he does? (D) Let's think logically about it. As I write this, a very dear friend is dying of cancer. All our prayers for her recovery were answered with a No. There are only five possible explanations: (I) There is no God, just random chance that governs the world. (II) God exists but lacks the power to do this good thing, this miraculous cure. (III) God lacks the wisdom to know that this miracle would be a good thing for her. (IV) God lacks the love to care enough about her to do a miracle for her. (V) God lacks neither power nor wisdom nor love; he denies her and us this cure precisely because he is all-powerful, all-wise, and, most important of all, all-loving. Now which is more likely: that God lacks existence (answer I) or power (answer II) or wisdom (answer III) or love (answer IV) or that it is we who lack them (answer V)? (E) In light of this answer, should we thank God for his Nos as well as his Yeses? (F) Is that hard? Does it take faith to do that? (Remember your answer to question A.)

Then after this he said to the disciples, "Let us go into Judea again." The disciples said to him, "Rabbi, the Jews were but now seeking to stone you, and are you going there again?" Jesus answered, "Are there not twelve hours in the day? If any one walks in the day, he does not stumble, because he sees the light of this world. But if any one walks in the night, he stumbles, because the light is not in him." (11:7–10)

H745. (A) Why do you think Jesus gave an obscure and indirect answer (vv. 9–10) to his disciples' very clear and direct warning

(v. 8)? (B) Can you figure out what he means by that answer and
how it relates to Lazarus?

*Thus he spoke, and then he said to them, "Our friend Lazarus has fallen
asleep, but I go to awake him out of sleep." The disciples said to him,
"Lord, if he has fallen asleep, he will recover." Now Jesus had spoken of
his death, but they thought that he meant taking rest in sleep. Then Jesus
told them plainly, "Lazarus is dead; and for your sake I am glad that I
was not there, so that you may believe. But let us go to him." Thomas,
called the Twin, said to his fellow disciples, "Let us also go, that we may
die with him." (11:11–16)*

746. (A) Verse 11 is clearer than verses 9–10, but not yet as clear as
verse 14. Why do you think Jesus spoke on three levels of decreas-
ing ambiguity and increasing clarity here? (B) How did he do the
same thing in general and overall in his three-year public ministry?
What became clearer and clearer to his disciples about him between
the first and last chapters of John's Gospel?

747. (A) What do you think of Thomas' reply in verse 16? (B)
What virtue is present in it, and what virtue is missing? (C) This
is "Doubting Thomas" (20:24–29). Do you see any character trait
common to this saying and Thomas' refusal to believe in Jesus' Resurrection until he touched his wounds?

*Now when Jesus came, he found that Lazarus had already been in the
tomb four days. Bethany was near Jerusalem, about two miles off, and
many of the Jews had come to Martha and Mary to console them concerning their brother. When Martha heard that Jesus was coming, she went
and met him, while Mary sat in the house. (11:17–20)*

748. (A) Jesus waited two days, but he came not two days but four
days too late. Do you think he would have performed the same
miracle of resurrecting Lazarus, and would it have had the same
effect, if he had had modern technologies of nearly instant travel
and instant communications? (B) If not, can you think of any other
modern technological "advantages" that would also have been dis-
advantages to him? For example, how would Jesus fare among mod-

ern media? The *New York Times* slogan is: "All the news that's fit
to print." Would they report the "good news" of Christ? (C) If
more modern technologies would have impeded his work, would
a more technologically primitive age also have impeded his work?
If so, how? (D) Did he come to earth at just the right time, then?

749. (A) How do Mary's and Martha's opposite reactions to the
news that Jesus was coming show their different personalities? (B)
How do they both show faith? (C) Which has the deeper faith and
why? (D) How are the answers to all three of these questions also
applicable to the Mary and Martha story in Luke 10:38–42?

*Martha said to Jesus, "Lord, if you had been here, my brother would not
have died." (11:21)*

750. (A) Is this an expression of faith or of despair? (B) Why? (C)
Is it an impolite complaint to Jesus and a negative judgment about
his delay, or is it a polite question to him about why he delayed?

*"And even now I know that whatever you ask from God, God will give
you." (11:22)*

751. How does this sentence express more faith than the previous
one?

Jesus said to her, "Your brother will rise again." (11:23)

752. Jesus uses a deliberate ambiguity here: it's not clear whether
by "rise again" he means the same thing Martha means, namely, the
general resurrection (v. 24), or whether he means that he will do a
special miracle (as he eventually does). How does he use this ambiguity as a test, to tease out of Martha a deeper faith or a stronger
confession of faith?

*Martha said to him, "I know that he will rise again in the resurrection
at the last day." (11:24)*

753. Jesus was testing Martha by the last thing he said (question
752); do you think Martha is testing Jesus here, hoping that his

response will go beyond her faith in the general resurrection to a special miracle, or is she simply confessing the lesser level of faith that she has (in the general resurrection)? (The text does not answer this question; you have to guess. What's the reason for your guess?)

Jesus said to her, "I am the resurrection and the life; he who believes in me, though he die, yet shall he live, and whoever lives and believes in me shall never die. Do you believe this?" (11:25–26)

754. (A) Jesus asks Martha, "Do you believe this?" How is this "this" a greater thing for Martha to believe than what she already believed? In other words, how does Jesus redirect Martha's faith from x to y, from a lesser object of faith to a greater one? (B) Why is y greater than x? (754B is a harder question than 754A and will help the next person to answer the even harder and more mysterious next question, 755.)

H755. When Jesus says "I am the resurrection", how can he identify something general (the resurrection) with something particular (himself)? He did the same thing in John 14:6 ("I am the way, and the truth, and the life"), and Saint Paul did the same thing in 1 Corinthians 1:30 ("Jesus, whom God made our wisdom, our righteousness and sanctification and redemption"). Resurrection, the way, the truth, life, wisdom, righteousness, sanctification, and redemption—these are all abstract, general concepts; how can they be a concrete, particular person (Jesus)? How can Jesus not only *give* us these things but *be* them? (Do not expect a simple, clear, or easy answer to this question! Perhaps it is something none of us can really understand.)

756. "Though he die, yet shall he live, and . . . never die" is a paradox, an apparent contradiction, since life and death exclude each other, like light and darkness. How can we both die rather than live and live rather than die? Is Jesus referring to two different kinds of death and two different kinds of life? If so, what are they?

She said to him, "Yes, Lord; I believe that you are the Christ, the Son of God, he who is coming into the world." (11:27)

757. How did Jesus do the same thing for Martha as he was about to do for Lazarus? (To answer this question, it may be helpful to

remember that Martha's previous faith, as expressed in verses 22 and 24, was not dead but halfway between death and life and that there can be different levels or degrees of life and death as well as different levels of faith.)

758. Why was what Jesus did for Martha harder than what he was about to do for Lazarus? (This question becomes easier if we put it the other way: Why was it easier for Jesus to raise Lazarus' body than for him to raise Martha's faith?) (Luther famously said that it was much easier for God to make the whole universe out of nothing than to make saints out of sinners. Why?)

When she had said this, she went and called her sister Mary, saying quietly, "The Teacher is here and is calling for you." And when she heard it, she rose quickly and went to him. (11:28–29)

759. Compared with Mary, Martha's personality seems at first to be sort of fast and fidgety rather than at peace (remember Lk 10:38–42) and somewhat shallow rather than deep. On the other hand, compared with Martha, Mary may seem at first to be sort of slow and stolid. Yet Martha showed a Marian depth in the previous exchange with Jesus and also now shows a Marian quiet and simplicity in her quiet, simple word to Mary. And now Mary shows Martha-like speed, immediacy, and action in response. (A) How did the greatest Mary also show both of these opposite virtues? (B) What do you think one of the saints meant when he said that we must do the works of Martha in the spirit of Mary?

760. (A) How do (I) the words Mary heard ("The Teacher is here and is calling for you") and (II) the response Mary gave ("when she heard it, she rose quickly and went to him") apply to everything in the Christian life? (B) If we followed this pattern, what more would we need? (C) If the answer is "nothing", why do we add something else and make our ultimate rules for living so manifold and so complicated? If the answer is something rather than "nothing", why do we also need this something else?

Now Jesus had not yet come to the village, but was still in the place where Martha had met him. When the Jews who were with her in the house, consoling her, saw Mary rise quickly and go out, they followed her, supposing that she was going to the tomb to weep there. Then Mary, when she came where Jesus was and saw him, fell at his feet, saying to him, "Lord, if you had been here, my brother would not have died." (11: 30–32)

761. Mary says the exact same words to Jesus as Martha had said. Do you think Mary said them in the same spirit or from the same state of soul as Mary, or do you think she meant something different "between the lines"? (This is probably a question a woman can answer better than a man. There is a hint in the text, in Mary's "body language".)

When Jesus saw her weeping, and the Jews who came with her also weeping, he was deeply moved in spirit and troubled. (11:33)

762. (A) Is being "deeply moved" and "troubled" a weakness or a strength? (B) Why? (C) When we are being "moved", we are not "movers and shakers", we are not in control. Why is that not a weakness?

763. (A) Is there any natural human emotion that Jesus never experienced? (Hint: See Heb 4:15.) (B) Why? (C) Look up the last paragraph of Chesterton's *Orthodoxy* for an apparent exception.

764. Old commonsensical Aristotle said that for every virtue there are two opposite vices, two opposite extremes. We can have too much or too little fear, anger, shame, sensitivity, etc. If we can also have either too much or too little sorrow and weeping, what makes for the right amount? Or is the rightness not a matter of amount? (See Rom 12:15.)

765. How different do you think men and women are in this?

And he said, "Where have you laid him?" They said to him, "Lord, come and see." (11:34)

766. This is the third time someone said "Come and see" in John's Gospel. Compare this with the other two.

Jesus wept. (11:35)

767. (A) This is the shortest verse in the Bible. But that is probably not the main reason you will remember it. What is? (B) Use your imagination and your empathy, and put yourself into this scene (as Saint Ignatius Loyola in his *Spiritual Exercises* advises to do for all the scenes in the Gospels). As you see this, what do you feel? Take some time to do this. Time is your servant, not your master.

H768. Unlike God the Son, God the Father did not become incarnate, so he does not have a human body or human learning processes (for instance, he does not learn new things through sense experience, as baby Jesus had to learn to speak Hebrew and Aramaic). And the Father does not have human passivities and passions and emotions, as Jesus has. The Father does not literally weep. Yet Jesus is the complete, final, and perfect manifestation of the Father: "in him all the fullness of God was pleased to dwell" (Col 1:19). So what does Christ's weeping show about God the Father? What divine perfection in the Father does this act in the Son show forth in human form?

769. (A) It's 3 A.M., and you are far from home, stuck in your car, which won't start. You call AAA, who will come in two hours with a new battery. But your friend comes immediately and sits with you in the cold car for two hours. Are you more grateful to your friend, who did not fix your car, or to AAA, which did? (B) Why? (C) Jesus did two things for Mary and Martha. First he wept with them, and then he resurrected Lazarus for them. His tears are God's tears. How are they like your friend who sits with you in the car? (D) Then, later, he also "fixes" things by raising Lazarus. Which is more important, and why?

So the Jews said, "See how he loved him!" But some of them said, "Could not he who opened the eyes of the blind man have kept this man from dying?" (11:36–37)

E770. (A) Do body language and seeing sometimes tell us more than spoken language and hearing? (B) Are bodily acts signs, just as words are? Are they sign-ificant? Do they mean things outside

themselves? Do they communicate? (C) If so, what did Jesus' tears
(v. 35) communicate?

771. In light of the last question, why did the Jews mentioned in
verse 37 not "hear" in Jesus' tears the same thing that the Jews
mentioned in verse 36 "heard"?

772. The previous question asked about the difference between the
two groups of Jews; this one asks about the difference between the
second group of Jews (v. 37) and the two sisters. The Jews' question
("Could not he who opened the eyes of the blind man have kept
this man from dying?") seems to make the same point as the sisters' complaint to Jesus, "If you had been here, our brother would
not have died." If these Jews and the two sisters both believed that
Jesus could miraculously prevent a sick man from dying, what do
you sense is the difference between what those words meant when
the Jews in verse 37 spoke them and what the same words meant
when the sisters spoke them?

*Then Jesus, deeply moved again, came to the tomb; it was a cave, and a
stone lay upon it. Jesus said, "Take away the stone." (11:38–39)*

773. (A) What emotional difference does it make to the reader that
the tomb "was a cave, and a stone lay upon it" rather than just
a grave under some earth? (B) How are these archetypal symbols?
(Look up "archetypes" if you don't know the word.)

774. (A) Again, use Saint Ignatius' method and imagine you are
there; what do you feel when Jesus commands, "Take away the
stone"? (B) Do you see any symbolic meaning here as well?

*Martha, the sister of the dead man, said to him, "Lord, by this time
there will be an odor, for he has been dead four days." Jesus said to her,
"Did I not tell you that if you would believe you would see the glory of
God?" So they took away the stone. (11:39–41)*

775. What does Martha's reply and Mary's silence tell you about
the difference between the two sisters?

776. What do you think was in the thoughts and feelings of those who heard Jesus say "Take away the stone"? What about the thoughts and feelings of those who actually took the stone away?

777. (A) Is verse 40 meant for us, too, not just for Mary and Martha? (B) If so, how? "The glory of God" that they saw was a very unusual miracle. What will we see if these words are meant for us, too?

778. What is the relation between faith, works, and sight in verses 40 and 41?

And Jesus lifted up his eyes and said, "Father, I thank you that you have heard me. I knew that you always hear me, but I have said this on account of the people standing by, that they may believe that you sent me." (11:41–42)

779. (A) Jesus began most of his prayers with praise and thanksgiving. Why? (B) What difference does that make to the rest of prayer? (C) What difference does it make to the rest of life?

780. Did Jesus perform this miracle (a) because he loved Lazarus, (b) because he loved Mary and Martha, or (c) because he loved the people who did not yet believe in him but would believe if they saw the miracle? (Hint: This is a trick question.)

781. Compare what Jesus did here for the people who saw it (question 780c) with what he did for "Doubting Thomas" (Jn 20:24–29, especially v. 29).

When he had said this, he cried with a loud voice, "Lazarus, come out." (11:43)

782. (A) What kind of word, voice, speech, or "*logos*" is this? Most of our words are labels for things that already exist—like the names Adam gave to the animals, new words for old things. But when Tolkien says "Let there be Hobbits", it is a new thing, part of a new world. So what kind of word did God use to make the world?

(B) What kind of word did Christ use to raise Lazarus? (C) What is the difference, then, between our words and God's?

783. One writer wrote that "Jesus also says to us what he said to Lazarus." What do you think he meant?

784. (A) Is it easier for Jesus to get the living or the dead to obey him? (B) In light of the answer to the previous question (A), what is one reason why it would be a terrible thing if we lived forever on earth and never died?

785. (A) Some apparently miraculous, apparently supernatural miracles of healing could possibly be explained by the power of "mind over matter" in man, e.g., the surprising sudden remission of a stage five cancer, since there is much that present-day science does not know about the power of the human mind over the body. But what about a sudden rising of a four-day-old decaying body? Did anyone who saw Jesus raise Lazarus think that advanced human science would some day explain that without anything miraculous or supernatural? (B) If one thousand atheists had seen this miracle, how many of them do you think would have been converted and believed? (C) Why? (D) Watch this scene in the movie *The Greatest Story Ever Told* and interpret the reactions on the faces of Jesus' different disciples.

The dead man came out, his hands and feet bound with bandages, and his face wrapped with a cloth. (11:44)

786. What is the radically life-changing consequence of the fact that the One who loves you enough to die for you has that kind of power? For the answer, read Romans 8:28–39. Read it aloud.

787. (A) Lazarus' resurrection is described very literally. Do you believe that yours will be that literal? (Hint: One of the twelve articles of the Apostles' Creed is "I believe in the resurrection of the body." The Greek word used for "resurrection" there, *anastasis*, means literally "standing up", and the Greek word used for "body", *nekron*, means "corpse". So how literal is your resurrection going to be?) (B) If it's that literal, how can all the atoms of your

body be gathered together again centuries after they decay and go elsewhere, e.g., into the ground, into the body of a worm that eats that dirt, into the body of a fish that eats that worm, and into the body of a man who eats that fish. Will those atoms be part of his body, your body, both, or neither? If that's a bad question, why is it? (Hint: Saint Paul in 1 Corinthians 15, is asked about the resurrection: "With what kind of body do they come?" [1 Cor 15:35], and he answers that we will be raised, not in a "physical" body, but in a "spiritual" body [1 Cor 15:44], which is very different. But that does not mean a non-material body; it means a body that is under the power of the Holy Spirit.)

788. (A) What is the difference between resurrection and resuscitation? (B) What kind of body did Lazarus have after Jesus resurrected it? (C) What kind of body did Jesus have after his resurrection? (D) What kind of body will we have after our resurrection?

789. In light of your answer to 788A, why do you think C. S. Lewis called Lazarus the first martyr?

Jesus said to them, "Unbind him, and let him go." (11:44)

790. Why do you think he had to say this? Why didn't they immediately unbind his grave clothes from him before Jesus told them to?

791. Compare this with Luke 8:55. How does Luke 8:56 tell you why Jesus had to say this? Compare it also with Luke 7:15b. How does Luke 7:16a explain why Jesus had to do this?

792. Do you see any symbolic truth as well as a literal one in Jesus words in 11:44?

793. Jesus was called "Savior" because he would save us from sin (Mt 1:21). He also saved Lazarus, the widow's son at Nain, and Jairus' daughter from death, and he will do the same for all of us (Jn 6:50, 54, 58; 11:24–25). What is the relation between sin and death? The answer is in Romans 6:23, but what does it mean?

*Many of the Jews therefore, who had come with Mary and had seen what
he did, believed in him; but some of them went to the Pharisees and told
them what Jesus had done. (11:45–46)*

H794. How could anyone see this miracle and not only not believe
in Jesus but be motivated by it to "squeal" on him to his enemies?

*So the chief priests and the Pharisees gathered the council, and said, "What
are we to do? For this man performs many signs. If we let him go on like
this, every one will believe in him, and the Romans will come and destroy
both our holy place and our nation." But one of them, Caiaphas, who
was high priest that year, said to them, "You know nothing at all; you
do not understand that it is expedient for you that one man should die for
the people, and that the whole nation should not perish." (11:47–50)*

E795. (A) The first commandment prohibits idolatry. Idolatry is
worshipping someone or something other than God as God. This
(idolatry, worshipping a false God) is quite compatible with religion, if religion is reduced to a means to this end (the false God). In
fact, the political aspect of their religion itself might be part of their
false God that they worship: thus they speak of their "holy place
and nation" as their primary concern. How does verse 48 show
that this is the kind of idolatry the chief priests and the Pharisees
were committing? (B) How common is this form of idolatry in our
culture today? (Hint: A Georgetown professor I know tells me that
whenever he asks his students whether they identify themselves as
Americans who happen to be Christians or Christians who happen
to be Americans, over 80 percent always choose the first option.)

796. Do you think Caiaphas is concerned with the people of the
nation in verse 50 or the nation itself?

H797. Suppose what Caiaphas said was literally true; that if Jesus
was not eliminated, such mass disorder would ensue that the Romans would come in with troops and restore order by a massacre.
Why would that not justify killing one innocent man in order to
save thousands? Why is it wrong for nine out of ten men in a
lifeboat to kill and eat one man so that nine of the ten will survive

rather than all ten die? Why doesn't a very good end justify an evil means if you believe there is no other possible means to attain that end? (The philosophy that teaches this principle, that the end of the greatest happiness for the greatest number justifies any means that is necessary to attain that end, is called Utilitarianism.)

He did not say this of his own accord, but being high priest that year he prophesied that Jesus should die for the nation, and not for the nation only, but to gather into one the children of God who are scattered abroad. (11:51–52)

798. What is the difference between the way Caiaphas meant his profound saying (v. 50) and the way God meant it (vv. 51–52)?

799. What does this verse say about God's sense of humor? (Hint: What is irony, and how is it a form of humor?)

800. What does it say about the relation between human purposes and divine purposes, between what we mean by our words and deeds and what God means by them?

801. Do you see any resemblance between Caiaphas' prophecy and that of Balaam's ass in Numbers 22? (This is a "stretch" question: if you don't see the connection, forget it. It's more funny than profound.)

So from that day on they took counsel about how to put him to death.
Jesus therefore no longer went about openly among the Jews, but went from there to the country near the wilderness, to a town called Ephraim; and there he stayed with the disciples. (11:53–54)

802. (A) One of Pope Saint John Paul II's favorite sayings was that Jesus reveals to us not only who God is but also who we are. He is perfect man, our model in all things. What is he teaching us here? (B) Why isn't Jesus a coward for hiding in the wilderness from the Jews in Jerusalem? (C) How did St. Thomas More do a similar thing in *A Man for All Seasons*? (A truly great movie.)

Now the Passover of the Jews was at hand, and many went up from the country to Jerusalem before the Passover, to purify themselves. They were looking for Jesus and saying to one another as they stood in the temple, "What do you think? That he will come to the feast?" Now the chief priests and the Pharisees had given orders that if any one knew where he was, he should let them know, so that they might arrest him. (11:55–57)

803. (A) Why does Jesus cause such dramatic controversy and such division? (B) If you are accused of being "divisive", is that necessarily bad? (C) Is that necessarily good? (D) Are Christians necessarily "divisive", as Christ was?

John 12

Six days before the Passover, Jesus came to Bethany, where Lazarus was,
whom Jesus had raised from the dead. There they made him a supper;
Martha served, and Lazarus was one of those at table with him. Mary
took a pound of costly ointment of pure nard and anointed the feet of
Jesus and wiped his feet with her hair; and the house was filled with
the fragrance of the ointment. But Judas Iscariot, one of his disciples (he
who was to betray him), said, "Why was this ointment not sold for three
hundred denarii and given to the poor?" This he said, not that he cared
for the poor but because he was a thief, and as he had the money box he
used to take what was put into it. Jesus said, "Let her alone, let her keep
it for the day of my burial. The poor you always have with you, but you
do not always have me." (12:1–8)

804. (A) Once again, try to use Saint Ignatius' method, and imagine
yourself present in this scene. How do you instinctively feel when
you see Mary do what she did? (B) If, like the other disciples at the
time, you didn't know that Judas was a thief and a liar, would you
tend to agree with Judas' reaction? Why or why not?

805. (A) Who else once did what Mary did here in Lazarus' house?
See Luke 7:36–50, in a Pharisee's house, and Mark 14:3–9, in the
house of Simon the leper. (B) What did this last incident (in Mark)
provoke Judas to do (Mk 14:10)? (C) Why do you think seeing
that act, which Mary also performed here, was Judas' turning point
(in Mk 14:10)?

806. Here is a little textual detective work for you. Could the incident in John 12 be the same as the incident in Mark 14? On the
one hand, both are in Bethany shortly before the Last Supper (Mk
14:17ff.) and Judas' betrayal (Mk 14:10ff.). Could this woman have
been copying Mary's act? There are often "copycat murders"; could
there be copycat love? On the other hand, the incident in Mark is
in the house of Simon the leper, while the incident in John is in

the house of Lazarus, Mary, and Martha. Could Lazarus have been living in Simon the leper's house?

807. (A) Verse 12 implies that our efforts to abolish poverty will never be wholly successful. Does this truth dampen our charity to the poor? (B) If not, why not? If so, can truth (if it is true that we will never abolish poverty) lead us away from charity? Can truth and charity contradict each other?

H808. Jesus says the poor are blessed (Mt 5:3). Our charity to the poor makes them less poor; why is it a good work if it lessens what is their blessing?

809. (A) How does the fact that Jesus is about to die (thus this expenditure is for his "burial") change the economics of the situation here? (B) Why isn't it wasteful to spend considerable money on funerals? (C) Do all cultures do this, or only Christian cultures? (D) Why? (E) The poorer the culture, the greater the proportion of its income they spend on weddings and funerals. Why?

When the great crowd of the Jews learned that he was there, they came, not only on account of Jesus but also to see Lazarus, whom he had raised from the dead. So the chief priests planned to put Lazarus also to death, because on account of him many of the Jews were going away and believing in Jesus. (12:9–11)

810. What different things do you think could have been in the minds and motives of those Jews who came to see Lazarus?

811. Do you think Lazarus was happy, unhappy, or both to have been resurrected? Why?

The next day a great crowd who had come to the feast heard that Jesus was coming to Jerusalem. So they took branches of palm trees and went out to meet him, crying, "Hosanna! Blessed is he who comes in the name of the Lord, even the King of Israel!" And Jesus found a young donkey and sat upon it; as it is written,
  "Fear not, daughter of Zion;
  behold, your king is coming,
  sitting on a donkey's colt!"

His disciples did not understand this at first; but when Jesus was glorified, then they remembered that this had been written of him and had had been done to him. The crowd that had been with him when he called Lazarus out of the tomb and raised him from the dead bore witness. The reason why the crowd went to meet him was that they heard he had done this sign. The Pharisees then said to one another, "You see that you can do nothing; look, the world has gone after him." (12:12–19)

812. (A) What is the connection between the raising of Lazarus and the events of "Palm Sunday" the very next day? (B) Do you think Jesus foresaw the events of Palm Sunday when he decided to raise Lazarus, or was he surprised by them? (C) Why? (D) If he foresaw them, do you think he encouraged them? (E) If not, why do you think he let the crowd cheer him on?

813. (A) Exactly what false expectations seem to have been in the minds and motives of those who cheered Jesus on so passionately on Palm Sunday? (B) Does this explain why this same crowd cried "Crucify him!" a few days later?

814. What do you think Judas thought and felt when he saw the Palm Sunday procession?

815. The Jews who praised Jesus' triumphal entry into Jerusalem knew the Messianic prophecy that John quotes, for they were far more biblically literate than most of us are. Did Jesus do this in order to fulfill the prophecy, or was the prophecy made in order to help the Jews identify their Messiah? Or is there something wrong with that question?

816. Why did he ride a donkey rather than a horse?

817. (A) It is sometimes said that Christians are Christ's vehicles in the world now, his hands and feet. It is also sometimes said that Christ still chooses to ride jackasses. Can both sayings be true? (B) Why isn't the first saying too flattering? (C) Why isn't the second one too insulting? (D) Why do we hear the first saying more frequently than the second?

818. (A) Saint Francis of Assisi called his own body "Brother Ass". Analyze that: How do we feel about a donkey? Is it obedient and

wise, or is it stubborn and stupid? On the other hand, does any sane person hate humble, useful donkeys? (B) Is it wise to laugh at our own bodies as we laugh at donkeys? (C) Do you think Saint Francis was laughing or serious when he said that? (D) Why do we so seldom think of saints as laughing and making jokes?

Now among those who went up to worship at the feast were some Greeks. So these came to Philip, who was from Bethsaida in Galilee, and said to him, "Sir, we wish to see Jesus." Philip went and told Andrew; Andrew went with Philip and they told Jesus. And Jesus answered them, "The hour has come for the Son of man to be glorified. Truly, truly, I say to you, unless a grain of wheat falls into the earth and dies, it remains alone; but if it dies, it bears much fruit. He who loves his life loses it, and he who hates his life in this world will keep it for eternal life." (12:20–25)

819. Why the intermediaries (Philip and Andrew) between the Greeks and Jesus?

820. Jesus' answer seems to have nothing to do with the Greeks' request. What is the connection between his answer and their question?

H821. (A) Do you find Jesus' reply connecting the lowest things (seeds) with the highest things (how we may attain eternal life) a surprising "stretch", or is it natural and obvious? (B) Is Jesus referring to his own unique saving death as the answer to the second thing (how we attain eternal life), or is he referring to a general principle for everyone, the principle of selfless charity as the way to happiness both in this world and in the next? (C) If it's both, why is it both? (D) If the connection in question A is natural, why do we not see it as natural anymore, as pre-modern societies did? Why are we surprised by it? (E) Why is there such a similarity between the biological principle of earthly, physical growth and the spiritual principle of heavenly sainthood? (Hint: Where did they both come from?)

H822. Why is Christ's principle about spiritual life and spiritual death (vv. 24–25) true? Why does it work? How does it come about that if we die to ourselves, if we say with our hearts, i.e., with our love, "Not my will, but yours, be done", then our own deepest will, the will to our deepest happiness, is also done; while if we say "not your will, but mine, be done", then our own deepest will is not done—how does that work? That sounds impossible and self-contradictory. Yet it works. Why?

823. How else do we know that it works, besides faith, i.e., faith that since God revealed it to us, it must be true?

824. Compare the way we come to know natural truths, i.e., truths in the natural sciences (e.g., that air has weight, that oxygen and hydrogen can combine, or that all objects fall at the same rate of speed) with the way we come to know supernatural truths (e.g., that we must die to ourselves in order to fulfill ourselves). How are these two things—the way we know supernatural truths and the way we know natural truths—different? (That's the easy question.) How are they similar? (That's the harder question.)

"If any one serves me, he must follow me; and where I am, there shall my servant be also; if any one serves me, the Father will honor him." (12:26)

H825. Put in your own words what you think Jesus means here by each of these four things: "serving" him, "following" him, being "where he is", and being "honored" by his Father.

826. Jesus is using an analogy or metaphor here. If we follow a man physically, we will go where he goes and therefore be where he is. What is the spiritual equivalent of this?

"Now is my soul troubled. And what shall I say? 'Father, save me from this hour'? No, for this purpose I have come to this hour. Father, glorify your name." Then a voice came from heaven, "I have glorified it, and I will glorify it again." The crowd standing by heard it and said that it had thundered. Others said, "An angel has spoken to him." Jesus answered, "This voice has come for your sake, not for mine." (12:27–30)

E827. We are sometimes told that we should never be (inwardly) troubled, that to experience distress in our souls is to lack the deepest level of faith. How does verse 27 conclusively prove that to be wrong? (See also Lk 22:44.)

828. (A) Is "trouble" or "distress" the same as "worry" or "anxiety"? Or is it different? (B) If it is different, then what do you think about this: If we cannot and should not try to avoid all trouble or distress, do you think we can and should overcome all worry or anxiety? (C) Why or why not? (Cf. Phil 4:6–7.)

829. Why doesn't verse 27 contradict Matthew 26:39?

830. In the course of his prayer, in moving from verse 27 to verse 28, Jesus changes the object of his attention and focus and concern. This elicits the Father's audible voice in a miraculous response. Jesus says that this voice is for our sakes. So what can we learn about how we ought to pray from this prayer, especially its change of focus?

"Now is the judgment of this world, now shall the ruler of this world be cast out; and I, when I am lifted up from the earth, will draw all men to myself." He said this to show by what death he was to die. The crowd answered him, "We have heard from the law that the Christ remains for ever. How can you say that the Son of man must be lifted up? Who is this Son of man?" (12:31–34)

H831. Jesus is praying about his forthcoming crucifixion and death, by which he would effect the salvation of the world. Why does he call it "the *judgment* of this world"?

832. Explain the last half of verse 31. Hint: When you watch Mel Gibson's *The Passion of the Christ* again, listen for a very strange sound that seems to come from below the ground at the moment Christ dies. If you know *The Lord of the Rings*, compare this "judgment" and "casting out" of Satan with what happens to Sauron when the Hobbits finally destroy the Ring.

H833. (A) How and when did Satan become "the ruler of this world"? (B) How and when is he "cast out"? (C) If he is now "cast out", why does he still seem to be doing so much damage? (D) To what event do you think Jesus is referring in Luke 10:18? Is it the same as John 12:31 or not? (E) Do you think Revelation 20 is about the same thing as either or both of these verses or about something different? (This is a very difficult question, and Bible scholars have disagreed about it for almost two thousand years.)

834. How does the fact that Christ acknowledges that Satan is indeed "the ruler of this world" (until the moment when he is cast out) explain Christ's second temptation in the wilderness (Lk 4:5–8)?

835. Many modern Christians regard the idea of the devil and demons as embarrassing, superstitious, and "unenlightened". They think it makes little difference whether the devil is literally real or merely a primitive symbol for human evil, a concrete image for something abstract. This question consists of a thought-experiment: suppose it true that Satan is not a reality but a symbol. Subtract Satan from the story of the Bible. What difference would it make? Better yet, suppose it was Jesus who did the thought-experiment. Suppose he became "enlightened" and realized that Satan did not exist. What difference would that make to him and his work?

836. (A) If you had been there at the time and heard Jesus say what he said in verse 32 for the first time, would you have interpreted it as John did in verse 33? (B) If not, how does verse 34 show that the unbelieving crowd of Jews were more biblically literate than you?

H837. This is a complicated question—in fact the question is more complicated than the answer!—but it tests whether you can participate in the typically Jewish enterprise of "midrash", poring over and probing into Scripture deeply. (This whole book tries to do that; that's why it's called *Probes*!) In verse 32, Jesus is repeating what he had said to Nicodemus in 3:15, interpreting Moses' "lifting up" the serpent in the wilderness (Num 21:4–9) as a symbol and prophecy of the Messiah's saving the whole world ("I will draw all men to myself") by his death by crucifixion (being "lifted up" on the Cross). Let's call that prophecy A. In verse 34, the Jews protest against this by pointing to the many prophecies in their Scriptures ("the law") that say that the Messiah, David's son, will reign "for ever". Let's call that prophecy B. (They also rightly assume that Jesus is claiming to be the Messiah to whom these prophecies refer because he claims for himself a Messianic term, "the son of man" [Dan 7:13].) Now suppose you were there and heard their very reasonable question; how would you explain to them, in a way they could understand, how both of these two prophecies, A and B, could be true and did not contradict each other?

838. How could the Jews who had just seen Jesus raise Lazarus from the dead possibly disbelieve in him? How should that event have changed their understanding of the prophecies referred to in the last question?

Jesus said to them, "The light is with you for a little longer. Walk while you have the light, lest the darkness overtake you; he who walks in the darkness does not know where he goes. While you have the light, believe in the light, that you may become sons of light." (12:35–36)

839. John's favorite terms for Christ are "light", "life", and "love". Explain this passage by explaining how it is love—the *"agape"* love of self-giving and self-sacrifice—that is the point of Christ's life on earth, and how that life, which manifests that love, is the world's last and only "light" in the "darkness". (What "light"? What "darkness"? Christians are not necessarily smarter or non-Christians more unintelligent. How is *wisdom* different from *intelligent*?)

H840. Jesus seems to be talking about his life ("the light"), which "is with you for a little longer", and his forthcoming death ("the darkness" that is the absence of that light). And then he says "walk while you have the light lest the darkness overtake you." But after his death, there was not darkness (except a sudden literal darkness for a short time when he died, which was probably a solar eclipse) but new light, namely, his Resurrection and the preaching of the Gospel to the world. What, then, is the "darkness" of which he speaks here? Is it each individual's death? But one does not "walk" in the darkness of death, for walking, whether physical or spiritual, is an activity of the living. Is he speaking of the general resurrection and the Last Judgment at the end of the world? How do you interpret this verse?

H841. Verse 36 is puzzling when you think about it. Jesus tells us to believe in the light. Do you have to *believe* the sun is shining? Why, then, do you have to choose to "believe in the light"? If "the light" is truth, isn't that to our minds what sunlight is to our eyes? If not, why not? Why do you have to choose to "believe" in this truth if you are to know it? About what kind of truth (or "light") is Jesus talking here? (Cf. Jn 8:12.)

H842. Why do you think Jesus said "children of light" rather than "disciples of light" or "followers of light" or "students of light"? (You should think about this one for awhile!)

When Jesus had said this, he departed and hid himself from them. Though he had done so many signs before them, yet they did not believe in him; it was that the word spoken by the prophet Isaiah might be fulfilled:
*   "Lord, who has believed our report,*
*   and to whom has the arm of the Lord been revealed?"*
*   Therefore they could not believe. For Isaiah again said,*
*   "He has blinded their eyes and hardened their heart,*
*   lest they should see with their eyes and perceive with their heart,*
*   and turn for me to heal them."*
Isaiah said this because he saw his glory and spoke of him. Nevertheless many even of the authorities believed in him, but for fear of the Pharisees they did not confess it, lest they should be put out of the synagogue: for they loved the praise of men more than the praise of God. (12:36–43)

843. The Jews, like us, have three options: (1) to believe in him because of his miracles, (2) to believe for better reasons, even if they did not see the miracles, or (3) not to believe. In light of what Jesus said to "Doubting Thomas" (Jn 20:29), how many of these three options does Jesus accept?

844. How does John explain the stubbornness and irrationality of those who saw Jesus' miracles and still refused to believe?

845. If, as Isaiah said, it is God who "has blinded their eyes and hardened their heart", does this mean that God is responsible for their unbelief? That they wanted to believe but God forcibly prevented them? Why couldn't it mean that?

846. (A) How does John evaluate those "authorities" who believed but feared to confess their faith (vv. 42–43)? (B) Is their fear a mere footnote to their faith, or is their faith a mere footnote to their fear? (C) What verb in verse 43 is the key to the answer to question B? (D) Whom do you think God would criticize more severely, such dishonest believers or honest unbelievers? (E) Why? (Hint: Is belief an act of the mind or an act of the heart [or will]? Is honesty a choice of the mind or of the heart [or will]?)

And Jesus cried out and said, "He who believes in me, believes not in me but in him who sent me. And he who sees me sees him who sent me. I have come as light into the world, that whoever believes in me may not remain in darkness." (12:44–46)

847. In light of verse 44, what do you think Jesus would say to someone who truly loves and trusts in him but thinks of himself as an atheist?

H848. We cannot see God, right (Jn 1:18)? So how can Jesus say here that we can (12:45)? How can he say "He who has seen me has seen the Father" (14:8–9) if he is visible and the Father is not? (Hint: Colossians 1:19 helps to explain this great mystery.)

849. How does the image of light that Jesus uses for himself explain this mystery (the previous question)? (Does light reveal itself, or does it reveal the things, colors, and shapes on which it shines? Does Jesus say he comes with his own mind and teaching or with the Father's? To do his own will or the Father's?)

"If any one hears my sayings and does not keep them, I do not judge him; for I did not come to judge the world but to save the world. He who rejects me and does not receive my sayings has a judge; the word that I have spoken will be his judge on the last day." (12:47–48)

E850. (A) Should Christians take the same attitude as Jesus about judgment? (B) If so, what does this mean?

E851. (A) If Christ does not judge you, does that mean there is no judgment? (B) When you get an F on your math exam (assuming it is a fair and just exam), is it your teacher who is judging you, or is it truth and justice that is judging you? If your exam was graded by a computer instead of a human teacher, would that change your answer?

"For I have not spoken on my own authority; the Father who sent me has himself given me commandment what to say and what to speak. And I know that his commandment is eternal life. What I say, therefore, I say as the Father has bidden me." (12:49–50)

852. If even Jesus himself subordinates his mind and will to the Father and carries out his Father's commandment; if even he is receptive of higher authority; then why do we think it is demeaning to be receptive and "conformist" and obedient? Why do we think it better to be "original" and "creative" and "self-fulfilled"? (That's not a rhetorical question but a real one. It demands an answer.)

853. Mary says and does very few things in the Bible. Yet Christians have traditionally exalted her as the greatest of saints. (This was true for many of the Protestant Reformers as well as for Catholics and Eastern Orthodox. It is true also for Muslims.) How does your answer to the previous question explain this?

H854. The Christian dogma of the Trinity says that (1) there is hierarchy and subordination and authority and obedience as well as equality even in God; and also that (2) there is equality among the divine Persons as well as hierarchy and subordination and authority and obedience. How does this dogma of the Trinity have radical social consequences (A) for the relation between citizens and rulers? (B) For the relation between husbands and wives? (C) For the relation between parents and children?

Now before the feast of the Passover, when Jesus knew that his hour had come to depart out of this world to the Father, having loved his own who were in the world, he loved them to the end. (13:1)

855. (A) Does loving us "to the end" mean only "to the end of his life" in time or "to the end of his power", doing everything that could possibly be done for us? (B) Apply this answer to what comes next, after this verse and illustrating this verse, namely, his choice to do three utterly unpredictable and apparently crazy things: (I) to wash his disciples' feet, (II) to give us his very body and blood sacramentally, in the Last Supper, and (III) to give this to us physically, on the Cross. (C) One drop of his divine blood, spilled at his circumcision, would have been sufficient to atone for all the sins of the world; why, then, did he give all twelve pints of his blood on the Cross?

And during supper, when the devil had already put it into the heart of Judas Iscariot, Simon's son, to betray him, Jesus, knowing that the Father had given all things into his hands, and that he had come from God and was going to God, rose from supper, laid aside his garments, and tied a towel around himself. Then he poured water into a basin, and began to wash the disciples' feet, and to wipe them with the towel that was tied around him. (13:2–5)

H856. Why does John mention Judas here before describing Jesus' washing his disciples' feet? What is the connection?

H857. Why does John next mention Jesus' relation to his Father? What is the connection with the foot washing?

H858. Why does John next mention Jesus' knowledge of his forthcoming death? What is its connection with the foot washing?

859. Imagine you are one of the disciples. How do you feel about this act?

860. Why does John describe this act in specific detail? What do those details add to the narrative's effectiveness? Suppose you read merely that "Jesus washed his disciples' feet" instead; what would be missing?

861. (A) When Jesus here implies, and later says, that we should wash each other's feet, do you think he means this literally? (B) Do you think he means that there should be no servants and masters with defined roles in a Christian society? (C) Why or why not?

He came to Simon Peter; and Peter said to him, "Lord, do you wash my feet?" Jesus answered him, "What I am doing you do not know now, but afterward you will understand." Peter said to him, "You shall never wash my feet." Jesus answered him, "If I do not wash you, you have no part in me." Simon Peter said to him, "Lord, not my feet only but also my hands and my head!" Jesus said to him, "He who has bathed does not need to wash, except for his feet, but he is clean all over; and you are clean, but not all of you." For he knew who was to betray him; that was why he said, "You are not all clean." (13:6–11)

862. (A) How does Peter's reaction in verse 8 show his personality? Why is that what you would expect from him? (B) Is that personality trait (your answer to question A) a strength, a weakness, both, or neither?

863. What do you think Jesus meant by verse 7? Did he mean by "afterward" after his death? After his Resurrection? After the coming of the Holy Spirit (cf. 16:12–13)? When Peter, too, was martyred? After Peter's death, in heaven?

864. (A) Since we are not saved by foot washing, what did Jesus mean by his reply to Peter in verse 8? What do we have to be washed of in order to "have part in" Christ? (B) And how do we do that?

865. What did Jesus mean by verse 10? He seems to be dividing people into four categories: (I) those who are not clean at all; (II) those who can become clean but only by bathing all over; (III) those

who are clean but still need to wash their feet but do not need to bathe all over; (IV) those who do not need to bathe at all. How would you identify each of these categories?

When he had washed their feet, and taken his garments, and resumed his place, he said to them, "Do you know what I have done to you? You call me Teacher and Lord; and you are right, for so I am. If I then, your Lord and Teacher, have washed your feet, you also ought to wash one another's feet. For I have given you an example, that you also should do as I have done to you. Truly, truly, I say to you, a servant is not greater than his master; nor is he who is sent greater than he who sent him. If you know these things, blessed are you if you do them." (13:12–17)

866. (A) In what sense is Jesus asking us today the same question he asked the Twelve in verse 12? (B) In what sense do we know what he has done for us, and in what sense do we not understand that? (To answer this question, imagine Jesus asking you exactly what he asked the Twelve; what would you reply?)

867. (A) Do verses 12–13 mean that he washes our feet *despite* the fact that he is Teacher and Lord or *because* he is? (B) If the latter, how does that radically change the Christian's definition of lordship? (C) Of teaching?

868. Jesus literally washed dirt off his disciples' feet (which was the job of the lowest servants in his culture). Is he saying we must imitate him literally? Or, if his washing physical dirt from his disciples is taken to symbolize his washing away their sins, how can we imitate him there, since only God, not we, can forgive all the sins of the world? Give a specific example of what you think he means by what all Christians are commanded by their Lord to do, namely, "washing one another's feet".

869. (A) Suppose we shrink back from washing each other's feet (whatever you take that to mean, whatever your answer to question 868 was). According to verse 16, what does that imply about what we are claiming to be in relation to Jesus? (B) So is this "foot washing" a maximum for saints, an ideal to aim at; or is it a minimum for beginners in the life of Christian discipleship?

E870. We learn here a radically new knowledge, a new ethic. Suppose we learn and know and understand this new ethic of Jesus; what is the role of that knowledge in making us blessed? There are two questions here: (I) Is it necessary? (II) Is it sufficient? (Read v. 17 for the answer. Compare Mt 7:24–27.)

871. (A) In light of the two passages above (Jn 13:17 and Mt 7:24–27), who do you think pleases God more, an ignorant unbeliever who practices a great degree of unselfish love without understanding it and without understanding why he does it, or a Christian who believes in it and understands it and its "why" but who practices it only to a very tiny degree? (B) If you are lost, what two things do you do with a road map, and which of the two is the more necessary?

872. (A) The two previous questions seemed to put knowledge in second place, as a preliminary thing, an instrument, a means to a further end, namely, action, living out your knowledge in obedience and right choices, choices to love. Yet in John 17, Jesus says "This is eternal life, that they know you the only true God." There he makes knowledge the ultimate and eternal end. Is there a contradiction here? (B) If not, how do you know there cannot be a contradiction here, even before you have figured it out and explained it? (C) Now let's try to figure it out. If there is no contradiction here, "knowledge" must be used to mean two different things in these two different passages. What are they?

H873. Theologians have debated whether our supreme joy in heaven would be an act of knowledge or of love; an act of the mind, intellect, or reason or an act of the heart or will. What do you think? (Hint: Your answer to question 872C might help you here.)

"I am not speaking of you all; I know whom I have chosen; it is that the Scripture may be fulfilled, 'He who ate my bread has lifted his heel against me.' I tell you this now, before it takes place, that when it does take place you may believe that I am he." (13:18–19)

874. How can you explain Jesus' first words in verse 18? Doesn't Jesus address his words and works to *all* of us, especially what he

just said about the foot washing? Did he not come to preach to Judas, too? When he said to the self-righteous Pharisees, "Those who are well have no need of a physician, but those who are sick. . . . I came not to call the righteous, but sinners" (Mt 9:12–13), is he saying that he did not come to save Pharisees? (Hint: Remember Jesus' very first words in John's Gospel, in 1:37.)

EH875. E(A) In light of 874, why are pride and self-righteousness the very worst and most dangerous of all sins, and why is humility and the repentance and confession that follow it the first and most necessary virtue? E(B) In light of that, evaluate pop psychology's first and greatest commandment, to "accept yourself as you are", to "feel good about yourself." H(C) How is that different from the proper self-love that God assumes when he commands you to "love your neighbor as yourself"? For if you don't love yourself, you can't love your neighbor as yourself, can you?

H876. (A) Is Jesus saying in verse 18 that the whole providential point and purpose and end of Judas' betrayal of Jesus was to fulfill the Old Testament prophecy? That the Scripture was not so much for the sake of the event as the event was for the sake of fulfilling the Scripture? (B) If not, why not? What refutes that interpretation? If so, why? What justifies that interpretation?

877. (A) How does verse 19 show that the purpose of prophecy is not to give us foresight to predict the future but hindsight to learn something else afterward from the events that have fulfilled the prophecy? (B) What is that "something else"? Is it something about the prophesied events or about the prophet?

"Truly, truly, I say to you, he who receives any one whom I send receives me; and he who receives me receives him who sent me." (13:20)

878. Who is the "you" to whom Jesus is speaking here? His apostles, of course. The literal meaning of "apostle" is "one who is chosen to be sent on a mission". So is Jesus saying this only to his twelve apostles or to all Christians? Or are all Christians apostles? On the one hand, it seems that it is all Christians, for all Christians are "sent" by Christ with the "mission" (*missio* means "to send") to "make disciples of all nations" (Mt 28:19). But, on the other

hand, Jesus picks out the Twelve and gives them a special authority as apostles, so that Paul asks the rhetorical question "Are all apostles?" (1 Cor 12:29), implying that not all are.

H879. Here are five hard questions in a row. They are all about the same great mystery, but they are five separate questions. You can have whoever answers it answer all parts of it, one by one. Or you can split it up. If the person who gets this question feels utterly at sea, it seems reasonable to put this question up for grabs, i.e., for volunteers.

(A) Why doesn't Jesus simply say that he will count our receiving those whom he sends *as if* we were receiving him? How could receiving his authorized representatives *really* be receiving him, not just "as if"? (This question confronts us whether we interpret these representatives to mean the twelve apostles and those whom they authorized to succeed them [the typically Catholic focus, the bishops whom the apostles authorized in "apostolic succession"] or whether we interpret them to mean all Christians who are authorized by Christ in his "great commission", his universal call to "missionary" work [the typically Protestant focus of "the priesthood of all believers"] or both.)

(B) In Matthew 25:40 he says something similar: "As you did it to one of the least of these my brethren, you did it to me" (Mt 25:40). Here, too, he does not say "as if". Does he really mean what he says? If so, what radical consequences follow?

(C) How does this explain what Jesus said to Paul on the Damascus road when Paul was persecuting Christians, "Saul, Saul, why do you persecute *me*?" (Acts 9:4)?

(D) Those whom Jesus sends with his authority as his authorized representatives speak "in his name". What does that "in the name of" mean? "What's in a name? A rose by any other name would smell as sweet", right?

(E) When Jesus says "he who receives me receives him who sent me [namely, the Father]", he is not denying that he and the Father are distinct Persons. They are. Yet we accept this saying without doubt. But when he says to his apostles "he who hears you hears me" (Lk 10:16), we find it difficult to accept this, because Jesus and his apostles are distinct persons. Why? Is this difficulty wrong for us to feel, or right?

When Jesus had thus spoken, he was troubled in spirit, and testified, "Truly, truly, I say to you, one of you will betray me." The disciples looked at one another, uncertain of whom he spoke. One of his disciples, whom Jesus loved, was lying close to the breast of Jesus; so Simon Peter beckoned to him and said, "Tell us who it is of whom he speaks." So lying thus, close to the breast of Jesus, he said to him, "Lord, who is it?" Jesus answered, "It is he to whom I shall give this morsel when I have dipped it." So when he had dipped the morsel, he gave it to Judas, the son of Simon Iscariot. Then after the morsel, Satan entered into him. Jesus said to him, "What you are going to do, do quickly." Now no one at the table knew why he said this to him. Some thought that, because Judas had the money box, Jesus was telling him, "Buy what we need for the feast"; or, that he should give something to the poor. So, after receiving the morsel, he immediately went out; and it was night. (13:21–30)

880. The medievals often interpreted the persons and events in the Gospels both literally and symbolically, and one of the symbolic meanings was what they called the moral meaning, each character in the Gospels being a part of our own personality and each event like an event in our lives. Suppose we do that as a thought-experiment. What difference would it make to this passage? What is the difference between (1) our standing outside this event two thousand years later and observing Jesus saying this to the Twelve and (2) our being one of those addressed by Jesus, hearing Jesus say this to us? You can interpret (2) either by putting yourself into the scene as one of the apostles or by interpreting Jesus' words as addressed to his whole Church today, of which we are a part. In either case, what difference does Jesus' direct gaze into the faces of your group make when he says "One of you will betray me"? Don't just think about this; take the time actually to do the thought-experiment, and then tell us what you discovered. Is there a Judas in you? A Peter? A John? A Mary?

881. If you did this thought-experiment, were you, too, like all the apostles, "uncertain of whom he spoke"? If so, why? If not, why not?

E882. What do we learn about John from (I) his not naming himself, (II) his calling himself the disciple "whom Jesus loved", (III) his leaning on Jesus' breast, and (IV) his being the one Peter asked to ask Jesus the question about which all the apostles were secretly wondering but did not dare to ask Jesus themselves?

H883. Why did Jesus answer the question with a morsel of bread rather than simply with a word?

884. Why was it *at that moment* (receiving the morsel) that Satan entered into Judas?

H885. (A) Did John mean that "entering" literally? ("Literally" does not always mean "physically"; of course nothing can enter into our spirit or soul physically, as bread enters our body. When we say "that idea never entered my mind", we mean it *literally* though not *physically*.) (B) If so, if Satan literally entered Judas, then how can God blame Judas if Satan took "possession" of him? (C) Can Satan possess you if you do not invite him to, if you do not choose to give yourself to him? (D) Can God "possess" you (in a very different way) if you do not invite him to, if you do not freely choose to give yourself to him? (E) How is the "freedom" in case (D) different from the "freedom" in case (C)?

886. Why does John add that the disciples did not understand Jesus' words to Judas? What does that contribute to the story?

E887. What is added by the last words, "and it was night"? What effect did those words have on you the reader?

888. (A) Are those last words literal, symbolic, or both? (B) If both, and if that is common in the Gospels, then why do we usually argue about whether a given passage is to be interpreted literally or symbolically?

When he had gone out, Jesus said, "Now is the Son of man glorified, and in him God is glorified; if God is glorified in him, God will also glorify him in himself, and glorify him at once." (13:31–32)

889. Why does Jesus say "glorified" here, since he has just lost an apostle (whom he loved) and is about to be crucified, which is the least glorious way to die?

890. What do "glory" and "glorify" mean, anyway?

H891. Can you make any sense, any order or map, of the Trinitarian relationships in this saying? Jesus is saying three things: (I) the Son is now glorified; (II) because of this (I), the Father is glorified; and (III) because of this (II), the Father will glorify the Son. (This is a very tough question; if you wish, you may skip it entirely rather than flounder and flop about like a dying fish.)

H892. Do you see any significance in the change of the tense of the verbs? (I) is present ("now"); (II) is also present, though it is an effect or result of (I), so that the cause and effect are simultaneous; and (III) is future, yet "at once", and thus in a sense also present. (The same parenthetical "fishy" remark applies to 892 as to 891.)

"Little children, yet a little while I am with you. You will seek me; and as I said to the Jews so now I say to you, 'Where I am going you cannot come.'" (13:33)

893. Why does Jesus call his apostles "little children" here? (Hint: John was the youngest apostle and the last to die. Probably the last thing he ever wrote was the last verse of his longest letter, 1 John: "Little children, keep yourselves from idols." How does the fact that he was soon to die explain his calling us "little children"?)

E894. What does Jesus mean by his last sentence? How do verses 36–37 explain it?

"A new commandment I give to you, that you love one another; even as I have loved you, that you also love one another. By this all men will know that you are my disciples, if you have love for one another." (13:34–35)

895. (A) How is this commandment new? (B) How is it old?

896. (A) What kind of love is this? (B) Why is it the only kind of love that can be commanded?

897. (A) "Love one another" is Jesus' most important commandment. Why did he not explain it by defining "love" for us, since there are many different kinds of love and much confusion about it, both in thought and in life? What did he do that was an even more

effective way to teach than by a clear definition? (Hint: The answer is in the 13th to 18th words in verse 34.) (B) How does this explain why we learn the most about love not from great theologians and philosophers but from great saints even when, like Mother Teresa, they speak mainly in one-syllable words?

898. Explain how James 2:18 explains John 13:35.

899. A popular interpretation of Jesus' great commandment (to love one another) is to see it as something everyone can do simply by being born into the human race and human life (*bios*) by nature rather than something supernatural that requires being "born anew" (Jn 3:3) from above (into *zoe*, supernatural life). How does verse 35 refute this?

H900. As background for this difficult question, we need to explain four Greek words. The New Testament's usual word for "love" is *agape* (ah-gah-pay), which is unselfish gift-love, not natural need-love or desire (*eros*) (air-ros), sexual or otherwise; or natural human friendship (*philia*) (fill-lee-ah); or natural liking or spontaneous affection (*storge*) (store-gay). *Agape* is supernatural; it comes from God. It is not the three natural loves together, even in their perfection. It goes far beyond feelings of compassion or liking or human friendship, and far beyond justice. Now here is the difficult question. Because of what Jesus said in verse 35, we sing: "They will know we are Christians by our [distinctive kind of] love [*agape*]." But is it really distinctive to Christianity alone? Can't Hindus or Muslims or Buddhists or even secular humanists also love in this unselfish way? Let's make this general question very specific: Didn't Gandhi, who was not a Christian, love in a distinctively Christian way? If so, how do you explain that? Let's think this through: one of the following three statements must be false; which one? (1) *Agape* is supernatural, not natural; you get it not by being born (into human nature), but by being "born anew" (by God's supernatural grace). (2) Gandhi was not "born anew". (3) Gandhi had *agape*. If 1 and 2 are true, 3 must be false; if 1 and 3 are true, 2 must be false; and if 2 and 3 are true, 1 must be false. (If you are cynical about Gandhi, pick another non-Christian holy person.)

901. John clearly teaches that Christ is in objective fact the only one who can give us supernatural, divine life (*zoe*, with its supernatural, divine love, *agape*). But Mark 9:38 seems to imply that some who

do not think of themselves as Christians also manifest this love and will be rewarded for it; and John himself seems to make room for this by saying, in 1:9, that Christ enlightens "every man" and that "he who loves [*agape*] is born of God and knows God" (1 Jn 4:7). Do you think that means that non-Christian saints (like Gandhi) are "anonymous Christians"? (This is a highly speculative question.)

902. (A) Is it true that we do not claim to know, and therefore to judge, who is or is not in fact in union with Christ and his supernatural *agape*? (B) If that is true, does it logically follow that we should evangelize in two ways rather than just one? The traditional way (which is clearly right, and clearly commanded) is to preach Christ, the whole Christ, to those who do not know him. Would a second way be to preach him to those "anonymous Christians" who seem to be practicing his *agape* love without consciously knowing where it comes from, not as someone they need but someone whose grace they already have but do not recognize? Would that be part of evangelism too? Or is that too optimistic?

H903. (A) If Christian love (*agape*) is broader than Christianity (if Gandhi, e.g., can practice it) but not broader than Christ (how could anything be broader than Christ?), is Christ then broader than Christianity? (B) If your answer to question (A) is Yes, then answer this question: Don't you have to believe in Christ and receive him into your soul and into your life in order to live in Christian love? Can you do it without him, on your own power? Of course not. The answer to that question is very clear, and Christians do not disagree about it. But can you do it without *knowing* him or *believing* in him? Can he be present anonymously? The answer to this question is not clear, and Christians do disagree about it. (C) If your answer to question (A) is No, then answer this question: If Christ and the distinctively Christian love (*agape*) is not broader than Christianity, then go back to question 900: How do you account for non-Christian saints like Gandhi?

Simon Peter said to him, "Lord, where are you going?" Jesus answered, "Where I am going you cannot follow me now; but you shall follow afterward." Peter said to him, "Lord, why can I not follow you now? I will lay down my life for you." Jesus answered, "Will you lay down your life for me? Truly, truly, I say to you, the cock will not crow, till you have denied me three times." (13:36–38)

904. Does Peter's "Where are you going?" mean (I) "Are you going away from this place, away from Jerusalem?" Or does it mean (II) "Are you really going farther *into* Jerusalem, to the place where they will kill you?" Or does it mean (III) "Where are you going when you die? What is heaven like?" Or does it mean (IV) "Don't you realize that if you go to Jerusalem, they will kill you?" Or does it just mean (V) "I don't know where you are going, but I want to be with you wherever you go"?

905. (A) Why does Peter think he is ready to die for Christ (v. 37)? (B) How does Jesus know he is not (v. 38)? Of course Jesus knows all things as God, but is there a human psychological dimension here, too, in his knowledge of Peter? (C) On the human level, explain how Jesus "knows" things *about* Peter (that Peter will not be as courageous as Peter thinks he will be) because Jesus "knows" *Peter*. How do those two kinds of knowledge influence each other?

906. (A) What do you think Peter *felt* when he heard Jesus say that he would deny him three times? (B) What do you think he *thought*? (C) Did his thoughts move his feelings, or did his feelings move his thoughts before Jesus said that, when he thought he was ready to die for Christ? (D) What about after he heard Jesus say that he would deny him? (E) Is it possible, then, for Jesus' thoughts and feelings (revealed in the Gospels) to move ours? (F) Can his thoughts move our feelings? (G) Can his feelings move our thoughts? (H) Can his thoughts move our thoughts? (I) Can his feelings move our feelings? (J) If so, is that why we are here in this Bible study?

"Let not your hearts be troubled; believe in God, believe also in me. In my Father's house are many rooms; if it were not so, would I have told you that I go to prepare a place for you? And when I go and prepare a place for you, I will come again and will take you to myself, that where I am you may be also." (14:1–3)

H907. Jesus says "Let not your hearts be troubled." How can we control our hearts? If the answer is the next word ("believe"), then how does that work? (Hint: Compare a believer's and an unbeliever's attitudes toward the greatest "trouble", death. How does faith make that great difference to our hearts in facing that "trouble"? How does it work?)

H908. (A) "Heart" can mean (a) any feelings, (b) higher, distinctively human feelings like gratitude or compassion, not animal feelings like tiredness or sexual desire, (c) will, or (d) the "I" who possesses "my" feelings and "my" will and "my" mind, the mysterious center of our souls. Which do you think it means here? (B) Why? (C) In which of these four senses can we exercise some control over our hearts?

909. (A) What does verse 2 imply about human individuality and uniqueness and God's attitude toward it? (B) How do Psalm 139:13, Isaiah 44:2, and Revelation 2:17 confirm this answer?

910. Jesus was a carpenter on earth. Does this passage also reveal him as (I) an architect, (II) a developer, (III) an engineer, (IV) an interior decorator, and (V) a travel agent in heaven?

911. (A) What is Jesus' end and purpose in all this work? What does he want to attain from it (v. 3)? (B) Can we thwart this desire of his? If so, how? (C) Can we help him fulfill it? If so, how?

912. (A) Is it true that Jesus is still human as well as divine, that the Ascension was not the undoing of the Incarnation? (B) If so,

does it follow that he still has human love for us as well as divine love? (C) If so, what does human love want the most? Explain how verse 3 is the answer to that question and how this proves that not philanthropy or impersonal charity but marriage is the greatest human love.

913. Why doesn't Jesus say "take you to heaven" rather than "take you to myself"? What is the relation between Jesus and heaven? If you had to choose, would you prefer Jesus without heaven or heaven without Jesus?

"And you know the way where I am going." Thomas said to him, "Lord, we do not know where you are going; how can we know the way?" Jesus said to him, "I am the way, and the truth, and the life; no man comes to the Father, but by me." (14:4–6)

E914. The disciples thought they did not know the way to where he was going (v. 5). Jesus said that they were wrong; that they did know the way (v. 4). What did he mean by that (v. 6)?

H915. Verse 6 is one of the most loved verses in the Bible for Christians and one of the most hated for non-Christians, who see this "only one way to heaven" idea as narrow and unjust and unloving on the part of God. How would you answer them?

H916. "What is the way?" seeks a general thing, like a road map, not a concrete individual. It also seeks an impersonal thing, like a highway, not a person. How can Jesus say that he not only shows or teaches the way but *is* the way?

H917. Even harder to understand, how can a concrete individual person be not only true but truth itself ("I am the truth")?

918. (A) Of what kind of "life" is Jesus speaking when he says he is "the life"? (See question 25.) (B) Is this merely a "life-style"? Or is it literally life itself? (C) How do we get this life?

919. (A) These three things that Jesus says he is correspond to many other triads of human needs or human goods or human desires. What is one of these triads? In other words, give three synonyms

for "way" and "truth" and "life". (B) Connect the three "theological virtues" (faith, hope, and charity) with these three things. (C) Connect them with the three powers of the soul, the mind, desires and will.

920. Hinduism says that the three knowable attributes of the one supreme God (Brahman) are *sat*, *chit*, and *ananda*, which translate as infinite being, infinite understanding, and infinite bliss—very close to John's three favorite words for God in his First Letter, "life", "light", and "love". (A) What is the connection between "bliss" and "love" in your experience? (B) By the way, Jesus' three words in this verse, "way", "truth", and "life", also begin with the same letter in Latin; they are *via*, *veritas*, and *vita*. By your Christian standards, do you think this real and not just verbal similarity between John 14:6 and Hinduism is (I) just a historical coincidence, (II) a wise psychology of universal human needs, (III) a vague but profound theological insight into the nature of God, or (IV) a deliberate divine revelation from God? (C) Why do you think that?

921. What does Christianity add to all three of these universal human needs and/or divine attributes that no other religion has?

922. Are there Trinitarian echoes here? Are the three Persons of the Trinity specially associated with these three human needs or powers (even though all three Persons always work together, never alone)?

923. Compare this with Jesus' other "I Am" statements in John's Gospel.

"If you had known me, you would have known my Father also; henceforth you know him and have seen him."

Philip said to him, "Lord, show us the Father, and we shall be satisfied." Jesus said to him, "Have I been with you so long, and yet you do not know me, Philip? He who has seen me has seen the Father; how can you say, 'Show us the Father'? Do you not believe that I am in the Father and the Father is in me? The words that I say to you I do not speak on my own authority; but the Father who dwells in me does his works. Believe me that I am in the Father and the Father is in me; or else believe me for the sake of the works themselves." (14:7-11)

H924. (A) What kind of "knowledge" is Jesus talking about in verse 7? See John 17:3. (B) Why does Jesus teach again and again in John's Gospel and here again in verse 7 these four things: (I) that all who know the Father know him, (II) that all who know him know the Father, (III) that all who do not know the Father do not know him, and (IV) that all who do not know him do not know the Father?

H925. Pat Robertson once said publicly (I think he took it back later) that "God does not hear the prayers of Jews." That is not only personally insulting and morally judgmental but theologically impossible, since Jesus and all his disciples were Jews as were all the Old Testament saints. But why doesn't Jesus' teaching here (v. 7) mean that no Muslims or Jews who are not Christians can know the true God or know God truly? Which of the following statements is false? (1) God the Father and Christ the Son are a "package deal". (2) Jews and Muslims do not know Christ. (3) Jews and Muslims know God.

H926. Why is it easier to see why disbelief in the Father (i.e., atheism) must mean disbelief in the Son than to see why disbelief in the Son must mean disbelief in the Father?

927. God the Father remains invisible. He does not become incarnate. So why does Jesus say in verse 7 not only that his disciples "know" the Father but also "have seen him"? (Jesus himself answers that question, but what does his answer mean?)

928. Philip's question in verse 8 implies that he is not satisfied with Jesus. How does Colossians 1:19 answer him and also explain Jesus' answer in verse 8?

929. What is Jesus implying about the relation between "know" and "believe" in his answer?

H930. What does Jesus mean by "in" when he says that he is "in" the Father and the Father is "in" him? (Do not expect a clear and full answer to this question. One theologian said that if we only understood the whole meaning of this word, we would understand all the mysteries of Christian theology.) Perhaps the following more specific question will make the general question about "in" a little clearer and easier to answer; if it makes it harder rather than easier for you, you may hand this question off to someone else. What is the difference between (I) the Father being "in" the Son and the Son being "in" the Father, and (II) Christ (in fact the whole Trinity) being "in" the Christian (and, indeed, in his whole Body the Church) and the Christian (and the Church) being "in" Christ? How are these two "ins" different?

931. How is Jesus distinguishing between the same two levels of faith in verse 11 as he does in John 20:29?

"Truly, truly, I say to you, he who believes in me will also do the works that I do; and greater works than these will he do, because I go to the Father. Whatever you ask in my name, I will do it, that the Father may be glorified in the Son; if you ask anything in my name, I will do it." (14:12–14)

932. What Jesus said in verse 12 certainly seems untrue. Do all Christians perform miracles? Do they raise the dead? So did Jesus mean this literally? Is it a lie? An exaggeration? Is there a hidden symbolic meaning there? (Hint: Perhaps the answer is simpler than it seems to be. Does "he" mean "all" and does "do" mean "always"? Hint no. 2: look at the lives of the saints, beginning with the Acts of the Apostles.)

933. (A) In what sense could the works believers do be "greater" in some sense than the works Jesus did? (B) In what sense could they not be "greater"?

934. Why does Christ say that it is "because I go to the Father" that "he who believes in me will also do the works that I do"? (Hint: Read John 16:7.)

H935. What Jesus says in verse 13 also certainly seems to be untrue, for many prayers seem unanswered, or answered with a No. Yet Jesus repeats his point in verse 14, for emphasis. What do you think he means? Evaluate the following three possible answers to this question: (I) "In my name" means "in perfect faith and union with me", which is very rare. Our prayers are not answered perfectly because our faith is not perfect. (II) "In my name" means "in union with my perfect will, which is always done". "Thy will be done" is the perfect prayer not only because it defines the deepest desire of a saint but also because it is always answered with a Yes. (III) Jesus himself did not have all his prayers answered, for he prayed in Gethsemane that the cup of suffering on the Cross be taken from him, and it was not; yet he added "not my will, but yours, be done" (Lk 22:42). So all Christian prayers, in conformity with his, implicitly add "if it be your will", and we can be absolutely assured that that prayer is always answered. Prayer exists, not to change God's will to conform to ours, but to change our will to conform to his. (IV) All prayers are indeed answered perfectly, but in the next life rather than in this one. Could all four answers be true?

936. How does this verse refute the common notion that love is essentially a certain *feeling*?

937. Does Jesus say here that love is nothing but keeping his commandments? If so, isn't that Phariseeism, legalism? If not, what else is it? (Hint: What *are* his commandments?)

H938. We usually contrast love (as something invisible and subjective and freely chosen rather than commanded) and obedience (as something visible and objective and not freely chosen but commanded). How is faith (in the sense of trust) the link between these two things? Give a human example of this principle, then apply it to our relationship with Christ.

"And I will ask the Father, and he will give you another Counselor, to be with you for ever, even the Spirit of truth, whom the world cannot receive, because it neither sees him nor knows him; you know him, for he dwells with you, and will be in you." (14:16–17)

939. (A) Can anyone receive any one of the three Persons of the Trinity without receiving the other two? (B) Why or why not? (See Jn 16:7 and Acts 19.)

940. When and how do we "receive" the Holy Spirit? When do we "know" him?

941. Why is he a "he" rather than an "it"?

"I will not leave you desolate; I will come to you. Yet a little while, and the world will see me no more, but you will see me; because I live, you will live also. In that day you will know that I am in my Father, and you in me, and I in you." (14:18–20)

942. Does Jesus' promise "I will come to you" in verse 18 refer to (I) his Resurrection, as verse 19 seems to imply, (II) his sending the Holy Spirit, (III) his coming into our lives more fully many times in our earthly lives, or (IV) our meeting with him in heaven?

H943. How can Jesus ever leave his disciples desolate (forsaken, abandoned)? But verse 18 implies that before he comes to us, he does leave us desolate for a little while. Is that desolation an event only in the lives of the apostles, or is it also in our lives? Is he speaking of what the saints call "the dark night of the soul"? (Look it up.) Also compare 16:16–22.

944. Explain "because I live, you will live also." What is the connection? Is it simply his power to resurrect in verse 20? (Hint: Remember the question about the word "in"!)

H945. In light of verse 20, explain the following: "It is only the mutual indwelling of us in Christ and Christ in us that enables us to believe the mutual indwelling of the Father in the Son and the Son in the Father." Is it *easy* to believe that this man of flesh and blood, this man who was born as a baby, this man who looks like all other men and is indeed just as completely human as all other men in every way except sin, is literally God? Does mere human nature, fallen human nature, suffice to believe and accept this and live it out and change the whole meaning and hope of your life, in time and in eternity, because of it? If not, how does God get us to believe it? Does he just "zap" us? Is it magic? Is it a kind of brain surgery?

"He who has my commandments and keeps them, he it is who loves me; and he who loves me will be loved by my Father, and I will love him and manifest myself to him." Judas (not Iscariot) said to him, "Lord, how is it that you will manifest yourself to us, and not to the world?" Jesus answered him, "If a man loves me, he will keep my word, and my Father

will love him, and we will come to him and make our home with him.
He who does not love me does not keep my words; and the word which
you hear is not mine but the Father's who sent me." (14:21–24)

H946. Elsewhere Jesus says "If you love me, you will keep my
commandments." Here he says "If you keep my commandments,
you love me." If these two things are connected as cause and effect,
how can A be the cause of B and at the same time B be the cause
of A? If they are not connected as cause and effect, how are they
connected?

H947. Here are twelve ingredients in the Christian life. In light of
all the things Jesus says in John's Gospel put together, can you map
at least some of the relations between them? (1) believing in Jesus,
(2) personally knowing Jesus, (3) being personally known by Jesus,
(4) loving Jesus, (5) being loved by Jesus, (6) obeying Jesus, (7) believing in the Father, (8) personally knowing the Father, (9) being
personally known by the Father, (10) loving the Father, (11) obeying the Father, (12) being loved by the Father. (Hint: You might try
making a map of these relationships by using arrows to express cause
and effect. Some of the arrows will be double-pointed, two-way arrows. Warning: Do not spend too much time worrying or arguing
about this very difficult question, just give it your best shot.)

948. What is behind Judas' question? (Hint: The Jews believed that
only when the Messiah came would the whole world know of the
God of the Jews, the true God.)

949. How is Jesus' reply relevant to Judas' question? (Hint: Suppose
you translated the second word of Jesus' reply as "any" instead of
"a".)

950. In light of your answers to the two previous questions, why
does Jesus repeat what he says in the last part of verse 24 here?
(Hint: Ask yourself two questions: [I] At this time in history, how
many people had met and heard Jesus? [II] How many people have
reason and conscience enough to know God, according to Paul in
Romans 1?)

"These things I have spoken to you, while I am still with you. But the Counselor, the Holy Spirit, whom the Father will send in my name, he will teach you all things, and bring to your remembrance all that I have said to you." (14:25–26)

951. (A) Why does Jesus call the Holy Spirit "the Counselor"? What is the essential job of a "counselor"? (B) He is also called our "Advocate". What does that mean? How is it related to "Counselor"?

H952. (A) How is the role of the Spirit in relation to the Son, as Jesus describes it, parallel or similar to the role of the Son in relation to the Father, as Jesus describes it? (See also 16:13–14 on this.) (B) How does this show that "God is love" and what that love essentially is?

953. The Roman Catholic Church and the Eastern Orthodox Churches differ on only one theological dogma: whether the Holy Spirit proceeds (eternally) from the Father and the Son (the Catholic claim) or from the Father only, "through" the Son. How can both sides appeal to this passage?

954. How does verse 26 explain the fact that the four Gospels, unlike all secular biographies, are so powerful and convincing and without errors?

"Peace I leave with you; my peace I give to you; not as the world gives do I give to you. Let not your hearts be troubled, neither let them be afraid." (14:27)

955. Peace is one of the "gifts of the (Holy) Spirit". But here Jesus calls it "my" peace and says it is he who gives peace. Why is that not a contradiction?

956. (A) What is the essential difference between the kind of peace that Christ gives and the kind of peace that the world gives? (B) What is the essential difference between the way the world gives its peace and the way Christ gives his peace?

957. (A) How can we "let" or "not let" our hearts be troubled and afraid? Is fear something we have the power to allow or disallow in our hearts, as we have the power to allow a visitor through our door and into our house? (B) If so, what in us has the power over the heart so as to be able to do this? (Hint: "Heart" can mean a range of things in Scripture. Here it refers to that in us which feels fear and trouble. What is that? Is that the deepest and most powerful thing in us? If not, what is?) (C) What is *faith's* role here?

"You heard me say to you, 'I go away, and I will come to you.' If you loved me, you would have rejoiced, because I go to the Father; for the Father is greater than I." (14:28)

958. Do you think when Jesus says "I will come to you" he means (1) the Resurrection, (2) Pentecost (sending the Spirit), (3) his Second Coming at the end of time, (4) his saving us and taking us to heaven after death, (5) the many repeated visitations of his grace to our souls, or (6) something else?

959. Why is Jesus' going away from his disciples to his Father in heaven a reason for his disciples to rejoice?

960. Why does Jesus not say "If you understood me, you would have rejoiced" instead of "If you loved me, you would have rejoiced"?

961. What is the connection between Jesus going to the Father (the Ascension) and sending the Spirit (Pentecost)?

H962. (A) In what way is the Father "greater" than the Son? (B) In what way(s) is he not? (C) Is the Son also "greater" than the Spirit in the same or a similar way? (D) How can we ignorant mortals possibly know the answer to those questions? (If you gave answers to those questions, on what did you base your answers?)

"And now I have told you before it takes place, so that when it does take place, you may believe. I will no longer talk much with you, for the ruler of this world is coming. He has no power over me; but I do as the Father

has commanded me, so that the world may know that I love the Father.
Rise, let us go from here." (14:29–31)

963. What is the "it" of which Jesus is speaking in verse 29? (1)
His going away by death? (2) His coming back by Resurrection?
(3) His going away by his Ascension? (4) His sending the Spirit?
(5) This whole series of events which Christians have called by the
singular noun "the Paschal (Passover) Mystery"?

964. Why does Jesus imply that the disciples cannot or at least will
not believe this "it" until it happens?

965. (A) Who is "the ruler of this world"? (B) Isn't Jesus giving
too much credit to him in calling him that?

966. Where is "the ruler of this world" coming and what is he
coming to do?

967. (A) Why does Jesus have to assure his disciples that "the ruler
of this world" has no power over him? (B) Didn't he have power
over him at 3 P.M. on Good Friday? (Hint: See Jn 10:18.)

968. Jesus says that one of the purposes of his forthcoming death
is "so that the world may know that I love the Father". How does
this explain why, although one drop of his divine blood (e.g., at
his circumcision) would have sufficed to pay for all human sins and
redeem the world, Jesus nevertheless let himself be crucified?

969. Jesus said that he gave up his life; no one took it from him
(Jn 10:18). Why doesn't this make him a suicide?

John 15

"I am the true vine, and my Father is the vinedresser. Every branch of mine that bears no fruit, he takes away, and every branch that does bear fruit he prunes, that it may bear more fruit." (15:1–2)

H970. Verse 1 is another "I AM" statement and another image or metaphor. Do all divine "I AM" statements have to be images or metaphors or analogies? (Jesus is not a literal vine or door.) If so, why? If not, which are literal?

971. Why does he choose the image of a vine? What do vines and Jesus have in common?

H972. There are false ideas and false (lying) persons but no "false vines", except in modern artificial flower shops. So why does Jesus call himself "the *true* vine"? (To answer this question, review 6:55 and question 461. Hint: Is Christ a little bit like a vine, or is a vine a little bit like Christ? Does *bios* resemble *zoe*, or does *zoe* resemble *bios*? Did God make man in his image, or did man make God in his image?)

973. If Christ is the vine and the Father is the vinedresser and the vinedresser is the one who prunes the vine, then it logically follows that the Father must prune Christ, right? If so, how? If not, what's wrong with that reasoning? (I) Is it illogical? (II) Is it taking a metaphor too literally? (III) Or is it forgetting the intended point of the image, the relationship between the vine and its *branches*? What is that relationship?

974. How is the answer to that question, and thus the point of Jesus' "vine and branches" analogy, made clear by Christ's answer to Paul's question on the Damascus road in Acts 9? Paul asked "Who are you, Lord?" and Christ answered, "I am Jesus, whom you are persecuting." But Paul was persecuting Jesus' disciples, not Jesus, right? Jesus had ascended into heaven.

E975. Think about the use of the concept of *life* in the image of the vine. (I) You and a dog have different kinds of life. (II) You and your friend have the same kind of life, but your lives are two different and independent lives; you do not die when he does, and you are not blamed for his sins or rewarded for his virtues. (III) But you and your fingers have not only the same kind of life but the same life, the life of the same organism. The same life-blood flows through you and your fingers. Your fingers depend on you, not vice versa. Which of these three is the kind of relationship that exists between you and Christ?

976. In light of your answer to the last two questions, does Jesus mean it literally when he says, in Matthew: "as you did it to one of the least of these my brethren, you did it to me"? Do we abort Jesus when we abort a baby? And if we are Christ's body, do we make Jesus commit adultery when we do? See 1 Corinthians 6:15 for the startling answer to this question.

H977. How can that (the answer to the last four questions) possibly be? (Notice how similar this question is to the question Nicodemus asked in John 3:9.)

978. How does the last thing Jesus says in this passage explain the problem of evil (why God lets bad things happen to good people)?

979. Does God do this "pruning" for the sake of the "fruit" or for the sake of the branch (individual) or for the sake of the whole vine (i.e., the other branches)? (Is this a trick question?)

"You are already made clean by the word which I have spoken to you. Abide in me, and I in you. As the branch cannot bear fruit by itself, unless it abides in the vine, neither can you, unless you abide in me. I am the vine, you are the branches. He who abides in me, and I in him, he it is that bears much fruit, for apart from me you can do nothing. If a man does not abide in me, he is cast forth as a branch and withers; and the branches are gathered, thrown into the fire and burned." (15:3–6)

980. Why does Jesus have to *assure* his disciples that they are "already made clean" if in fact they are already made clean?

981. Jesus does not say simply that they are clean but that they are "*made* clean". What difference does that additional word make?

982. What does he mean by "clean"? Surely we are not sinless or perfect.

H983. (A) How can a *word* make us clean? (Hint: Why did the centurion say to Jesus: "Only say the word, and my servant will be healed"?) (B) How does Genesis 1 show us the answer to that question? (What instrument did God use there to create the world?) (C) Are there any remote human analogies to this power of a word?

984. What more does "abide" mean than "remain"? (Hint: Read the hymn "Abide with Me." Why is it often sung at funerals?)

985. How do we "abide in" Jesus?

986. (A) What is the "fruit" here? (A) Why is "abiding" the key to "bearing fruit"? Explain the cause and effect principle here. (Hint: See question 975.) (C) Why are all other causes insufficient to produce this effect, namely, the "fruit" of which Jesus is speaking?

H987. (A) There is an African language in which the word for greeting (our "hello") means literally "I am here, you are there." What does Jesus do to this ordinary mode of thinking when he says "I am the vine, you are the branches"? Is the vine "here", and are the branches "there"? (B) Why isn't this pantheism (us being "parts" of God) or subjectivism (God being a "part" of us)? (Hint: If you think in terms of space, you will not see the point Jesus is making, but if you think in terms of life and distinguish *bios* and *zoe*, maybe you will. "Life" is a better way than "space" to think about more-than-physical things because there are non-physical kinds of life [the life of God, the life of angels, your own "inner life"], but there are no non-physical kinds of space.)

H988. Jesus does not say that apart from him we can do very little; rather, he says that apart from him we can do nothing. What does he mean by that? Can't we lift our hand into the air without him? Can't we even love in a human way (with *bios* and its *eros*, though not with *zoe* and its *agape*) without him? (Hint: Interpret this in context: remember his analogy of the vine and the branches.)

H989. (A) Put together John 15:5 ("without me you can do nothing") with Philippians 4:13 ("I can do all things in him [Christ] who strengthens me") and what do you get? (B) Put together verse 5 ("He who abides in me, and I in him, he it is that bears much fruit") with verse 6 ("If a man does not abide in me, he is cast forth as a [dead] branch and withers; and the branches are gathered, thrown into the fire and burned"), and what do you get? (Hint: It is the same truth that you find in Psalm 1.) (C) But there seem to be many degrees of goodness or godliness in us: "There's a little good in the worst of us and a little bad in the best of us, so it ill behooves the best of us to speak ill of the worst of us." How does that truth fit into and not contradict the truth of John 15:5–6 and Psalm 1? (Hint: Remember John 3:3. Use the analogy of pregnancy.)

990. (A) Is Jesus talking about hell in verse 6? If so, is he saying that if you don't have enough good works (bear enough fruit), you will go to hell? If so, where is the cutoff point? Do you go to heaven if you do one hundred good deeds but not ninety-nine? (Hint: Remember the parable of the sower in Matthew 13.) (B) Oh, just by the way, do you happen to know the answer to the most important question in the world? How *do* you get to heaven? If you died tonight and God asked you why he should let you into heaven, what would you answer?

"If you abide in me, and my words abide in you, ask whatever you will, and it shall be done for you." (15:7)

991. (A) This promise seems untrue, for many of our prayer petitions are not done for us. What does Jesus mean here? Here are four possible answers: evaluate them. (I) All petitions are granted in heaven. (II) The deepest desires of our hearts, what we most deeply and truly want, are always granted even though what we think we want is not. (III) There are two kinds of prayer: from below, where we are somewhat separated from God, and from above, where we are in him or with him. The latter kind of prayer is always granted. Only if we are "abiding in" him do we literally get everything we ask for, but this is a rare degree of sanctity, to be aimed for but rarely and only temporarily attained. (IV) If we "abide in" him, we will want only one thing, "thy will be done", and always get it,

since God's will is always done, at least in the end, and even, providentially, in the means to the final end. (Romans 8:28 does not say that all things are good but that all things work together for good.) (B) Can all four answers be true? Evaluate each one.

"By this my Father is glorified, that you bear much fruit, and so prove to be my disciples. As the Father has loved me, so have I loved you; abide in my love. If you keep my commandments, you will abide in my love, just as I have kept my Father's commandments and abide in his love. These things I have spoken to you, that my joy may be in you, and that your joy may be full." (15:8–11)

H992. (A) What is it to "glorify" God? (B) If he already has infinite glory, how can we increase it?

993. What does Jesus mean by "prove to be my disciples"? Is our bearing fruit (the works of love) the *cause* or the *effect* of our being or "abiding" in him? When a detective "proves" that Bubba was the murderer because his fingerprints are on the gun, is the reasoning moving from cause to effect or from effect to cause? So how does that help us to understand what Jesus means by "prove" here?

H994. (A) The Greek word for "as" in verse 9 is *hos*. It means not merely a similarity or an imitation but an identity. It is the word used in the Lord's Prayer when we pray "Forgive us our trespasses *as* we forgive those who trespass against us." In other words, it is the very same total forgiveness that God gives to us that we must give to others. And if we do not do this, we pray for our own damnation in praying this *hos*! ("God, if I don't forgive others totally, don't forgive me totally.") So how can we be loved by Jesus as (*hos*) totally as Jesus is loved by his Father if we are undeserving sinners and largely unlovable while Jesus is perfect and totally lovable? (B) Why does God love us so much? Is that question even answerable?

H995. (A) In Genesis 1, God knows (thinks, speaks) the world into existence. His knowing, unlike ours, does not *discover* what is but *creates* it. Thus Psalm 1 says that God "knows the way of the righteous [and they are therefore really righteous], but the way of the wicked will perish" (because he does not know them—in the Last Judgment he says to them, "I never knew you; depart from me"). How does this difference between divine knowing and human knowing parallel the difference between divine love (*agape*) and human love? Does God's love actually create value and worth in the ones he loves rather than respond to their already existing value and worthiness (since that would be only justice)? (B) Can we, too, do that to other people by loving them with *agape*? (C) If so, does that *agape* then come from us, or does it come from God through us as his instruments? (D) Can you give a real or fictional example of someone else's *agape* love creating new value in a person? For instance, Jean Valjean in Victor Hugo's *Les Miserables*; Alyosha in Dostoevski's *The Brothers Karamazov*; Gerasim in Tolstoy's *The Death of Ivan Ilyich*; or David Wilkerson's *The Cross and the Switchblade*.

996. (A) What is the relation among the following: (I) being "in" Christ, (II) "abiding" in Christ, (III) abiding in his love, (IV) keeping his commandments, and (V) having the fullness of his joy in us? Are these five things identical, or are they five different things or five stages of the same thing, one after the other, or five dimensions of the same thing, all at once? (B) If they are not the same thing, are they also in a causal sequence (I causes II, II causes III, etc.)?

997. (A) Does God love us only to the extent that we keep his commandments? (B) Does he most want actions of a particular kind or persons of a particular kind? (C) Which of these two (actions or persons) do human love and esteem most want (1) in families? (2) in business? (3) in science and technology? (4) in sports? (5) in politics?

998. (A) What is the connection between love and joy? (B) Is Jesus speaking about just any old kind of love and joy in verse 11? If not, what kind of love and what kind of joy? (C) If love multiplies joys, does it not also multiply miseries because both the joys and the miseries of the beloved become yours? (D) If not, why not? If so, what makes the enterprise of love worthwhile if it multiplies miseries as much as joys?

"This is my commandment, that you love one another as I have loved you. Greater love has no man than this, that a man lay down his life for his friends. You are my friends if you do what I command you. No longer

do I call you servants, for the servant does not know what his master is doing; but I have called you friends, for all that I have heard from my Father I have made known to you." (15:12–15)

999. What kinds of love cannot be commanded, and what kind can?

1000. (A) How can we love each other as (*hos*) Jesus has loved us? (B) Does this mean with the same kind of love, with the same degree or amount of love, both, or neither?

1001. Can we be both friends and servants to Jesus?

E1002. Of what kind of love is this the supreme manifestation?

1003. (A) Jesus says that we are his friends if we do what he commands us. Exactly what does he command us? (B) How far in the Bible from this verse do you have to go to get his answer to this question? (Hint: He begins the sentence by saying: "This is my commandment . . .")

1004. When Jesus says that we are his friends if we do what he commands us, does he mean that if we do not do what he commands us we are not his friends? Can't there be disobedient friends and obedient non-friends? (Hint: Greek, unlike English, distinguishes between two forms of a verb. One means a one-time or this-time or occasional action; the other means a habitual action. A single good act does not make a good habit or a good person, and a single evil act does not make an evil habit or an evil person. So how does this distinction answer the question? Which form of the verb "to sin" do you think John used in 1 John 3:4–10?)

1005. Why is the greatest love to lay down your life for your friends?

1006. (A) How does Jesus distinguish between "friends" and "servants"? (B) There are many differences between friends and servants; why does he focus on *that* particular difference? (C) What is the deeper source or cause of that difference?

H1007. Explain how verse 15 here and Jesus' answer to Philip's request to "Show us the Father" (in Jn 14:8–11) explain each other.

H1008. (A) Jesus tells us in verse 15 that the proof that he and we are friends is that he has revealed everything about the Father to us. Why do friends reveal everything to each other, even things that they keep secret from other people? That is, what prior relationship must there be in order to motivate this intimacy and full revealing? (Hint: Which of the three greatest virtues according to Paul in 1 Corinthians 13 motivates you to put your money into a bank? The word is often in the bank's name: "the First National Bank and _____ Company".) (B) Why is this word not surprising when it refers to something in us that is directed to Jesus, but is very surprising when it refers to something in him that is directed to us? (C) Why does he do that to us? (D) Did he do it to us when he created us with free will in the first place? Didn't he know how badly we would misuse that gift? (E) Since we made such a mess of it, and continue to do so, why does that thing, that attitude, that relationship on his part not prove that he is foolish and naïve? (F) Why isn't 1 Corinthians 13:7 a prescription for naïveté?

"You did not choose me, but I chose you and appointed you that you should go and bear fruit and that your fruit should abide; so that whatever you ask the Father in my name, he may give it to you. This I command you, to love one another." (15:16–17)

H1009. (A) What could Jesus possibly mean by his first five words in verse 16? They seem obviously untrue because we did choose him. If we did not really choose him, then either we are robots without free choice, or we chose against him. How do the next four words explain what he means by the first five? If we did choose him, is our choice of him the effect of his prior choice of us? If so, in that light, interpret his first five words again. (B) Does this reconcile free will and predestination?

1010. Here is that promise again, that you will get "whatever you ask the Father in my name", the promise that seems falsified by experience, since we often do not get the good things we ask for, such as health and healings and immediate sanctity and justice and peace. How does Jesus' image of growing fruit explain this promise? (Hint: How do you grow instant fruit?)

H1011. What is the relationship between (I) bearing more and more fruit (good works, the works of love, in obedience to Jesus' fundamental commandment in verse 17) and (II) more and more getting whatever we ask God in Jesus' name, as he promises in verse 16? Does (I) cause (II)? Does (II) cause (I)? Does it work both ways? Or does some even more fundamental thing cause both?

"If the world hates you, know that it has hated me before it hated you. If you were of the world, the world would love its own; but because you are not of the world, but I chose you out of the world, therefore the world hates you. Remember the word that I said to you, 'A servant is not greater than his master.' If they persecuted me, they will persecute you; if they kept my word, they will keep yours also." (15:18–20)

H1012. Christians, like Christ, love (the people in) the world. So why does the world hate Christians? Is it not true that "everybody loves a lover"? Christ answers that question in verse 18: they hate Christians because they hate Christ. But why does the world hate Christ? Why are Christians persecuted, tortured, and martyred so much, today around the world just as in the early Church?

1013. Someone asked, "If you were brought to trial on the charge of being a Christian, would there be enough evidence to convict you?" When was the last time you did or said something that made someone else hate you or fear you or be very uncomfortable around you and wish you were not there, just because you believed Christ wanted you to?

1014. In what way is it harder to be a Christian in a majority-Christian society? In what way is it easier?

1015. What does Jesus mean by the word "world"? What does he mean by saying "I chose you out of the world"? Aren't we still here? What does he mean when he says we are not "of the world" in verse 19? How can we be "in the world" (17:11) but "not of the world" (17:14)? How can the New Testament speak so negatively of "the world" if "God so loved the world that he gave his only-begotten Son" to die for it? Didn't God create the world and find it good in Genesis 1? (Hint: There are two Greek words for "world". One, *gaia*, is a spatial word. It means the planet earth. Scripture never uses this word negatively. The other, *aion*, is a temporal word. It means either "eon", "historical era", or "age"—the whole era between the Fall and the Second Coming—or the fallen, foolish, selfish, sinful cultures of that age or era. Scripture always uses that word negatively.)

1016. (A) In light of the above, in what sense are Christians expected always to be "counter-cultural" even in a so-called Christian culture? (B) In what sense are Christians expected always to be friends of their culture even in a so-called secular culture? (Hint no. 1: What did Jesus mean when he told us to "Render therefore to Caesar the things that are Caesar's" [Mt 22:21]? Hint no. 2: Jn 3:17.)

"But all this they will do to you on my account, because they do not know him who sent me. If I had not come and spoken to them, they would not have sin; but now they have no excuse for their sin. He who hates me hates my Father also. If I had not done among them the works which no one else did, they would not have sin; but now they have seen and hated both me and my Father. It is to fulfil the word that is written in their law, 'They hated me without a cause.'" (15:21–25)

E1017. What in verse 24 explains verse 22?

1018. (A) Is Jesus saying in verse 22 that we can know that non-Christians who persecute Christians do not really know God the Father even though they think they do? (B) Is this parallel to the suggestion in the question about Gandhi above that non-Christians who live by *agape* love do "know" God, at least "anonymously", even though they may not know that they know him, even perhaps if they are agnostics or even atheists? (C) If not, why not? If so, can we tell where is the dividing line between those who do and those who do not "know" God? (D) If we cannot judge this, then what course of action on our part logically follows from that ignorance?

1019. (A) Good moral theology and also common sense say that three things are necessary for a human act to be a serious sin (in the language of Catholic theology, a "mortal" sin, i.e., one that can kill your soul eternally if not repented of): (1) an objectively weighty matter, (2) clear knowledge that it is a sin, and (3) full consent of the will. Why does this seem right or not right to you? (B) How many of these three factors are mentioned or implied by what Jesus says in verse 23? (C) Compare Jesus' words from the Cross: "Father, forgive them; for they know not what they do" (Lk 23:34). (D) Which of these three factors is the clearest and easiest to judge, and which is the least clear and hardest to judge?

1020. (A) Why does it not logically follow from what Jesus says in verse 23 that we should call back all the missionaries because their work will send some unbelievers to hell by removing the "escape clause" or excuse of ignorance that they had before they heard the gospel truth? (Hint: Perhaps question 1018 helps to answer this question. If not, forget it.) (B) Is our primary reason for preaching the Gospel to maximize the population of heaven and minimize the population of hell, or is it something much simpler than that?

1021. How does verse 24 illustrate the maxim that "actions can speak louder than words"?

1022. (A) Is it possible for us freely to choose anything at all (especially love or hate) without any kind of cause or reason or explanation or motive whatever? (B) If not, of what kind of "cause" is Jesus speaking in verse 25 when he says they hated him "without a cause"?

1023. In verse 25, Jesus is speaking of something even worse than unbelief: hate. (A) Did you ever meet anyone who said "I hate Jesus"? (B) If not, is that because everyone is much more saintly today than the Jews were in Jesus' time? Could post-Christian modern pagans be that much more saintly and wise than God's chosen people? (C) If not, how do people hate Jesus today? Did you ever meet or read about anyone who said he hated Christians? Were these people whom they hated good Christians, who were preaching Jesus' words and doing Jesus' deeds? If so, why were they hated? Was it for the same reason Jesus was hated? (What answer to that question logically follows if we the Church are his very body, as the New Testament says? Why?)

"But when the Counselor comes, whom I shall send to you from the Father, even the Spirit of truth, who proceeds from the Father, he will bear witness to me; and you also are witnesses, because you have been with me from the beginning." (15:26–27)

1024. The Eastern Orthodox Church and the Western Roman Catholic Church split in 1054 over the Western Church's addition of the words "and the Son" (in Latin, *filioque*) to the article in the Nicene Creed that confesses that the Holy Spirit "proceeds from the Father". It is the major theological difference between these two churches. Is verse 26 evidence that the West is right, that the East is right, or that both are right?

H1025. What does it mean to "bear witness to" a person? How is this different from bearing witness to a fact or event?

1026. (This question is much longer than no. 1025 but probably easier.) (A) Can mere human beings ("you" refers to Jesus' twelve apostles, to whom he is speaking) do the same thing as God himself (in the Person of the Holy Spirit) can do, namely, "bear witness" to Jesus? (B) How do we do this differently from the way the Holy Spirit does it? In other words, distinguish between our role (or task or work) and the Spirit's role (or task or work) in this "witnessing". What does he do that we cannot do (see 1 Cor 12:3), and what do we do that he cannot do? (C) Jesus mentions the reason why the Twelve can do this "witnessing" to him in verse 27; how does this apply also to the Holy Spirit? (D) Can both the Holy Spirit and we do this same thing ("witnessing") at the same time? (Hint: Read Luke 1:26–38; when Mary said Yes to the Holy Spirit "coming upon" her [v. 35], was Jesus then conceived in her womb by Mary or by the Holy Spirit? Hint no. 2: Why is that a trick question? Hint no. 3: How do both the Apostles' Creed and the Nicene Creed answer that question when speaking of Jesus' conception and birth?)

1027. Jesus has said that his teaching is not his own but comes from the Father and that he came into the world not to do his own will but the will of the Father. Now he says that the Holy Spirit will bear witness, not to himself, but to Jesus (and therefore to the Father, since Jesus bears witness to the Father). So whom does the Father bear witness to, get his teaching from, or do the will of? (Hint: Why is that a trick question?)

1028. Here are three statements that seem to contradict one another, in such a way that if any two of the three are true, the third one must be false. Which one is false, then? (I) Jesus obeys the Father's will (II) Jesus is not inferior but equal in nature to the Father; (III) The one who commands is superior to the one who obeys (a soldier must obey his "superior" officer), and thus the one who obeys is inferior to the one who commands. (This is the third time this question was asked. It needs repeating because it changes all human relationships. How? That is the next question.)

1029. (A) What are the consequences of your answer to question 1028 for the relationships between parents and children, husbands and wives, and political rulers and citizens? (B) What does the New Testament say about these three relationships? (C) In world history, how radically new is this Christian social principle? Do you find it in paganism or classical Roman society? (D) So how "relevant" is this dogma of the Trinity for the future of human civilization?

"I have said all this to you to keep you from falling away. They will put you out of the synagogues; indeed, the hour is coming when whoever kills you will think he is offering service to God. And they will do this because they have not known the Father, nor me. But I have said these things to you, that when their hour comes you may remember that I told you of them." (16:1–4)

1030. Suppose Jesus had not ever said this to his disciples. What difference would that have made when his disciples encountered persecution?

1031. How does the mere fact that we can "remember" that Jesus predicted our persecution (v. 4) help to keep us from falling away (v. 1)?

1032. (A) Is it still true in our world that "whoever kills you will think he is offering service to God"? (B) If so, where? (C) What other forms of persecution besides killing do Christians encounter in our world? (D) How does Jesus explain the *motive* behind this persecution? (E) How does he explain the source of this motive? (F) Why is it ironic? (G) Where, especially, do you find this irony happening in the world today?

1033. Jesus' answer to the last question (1032E) was about knowing God. What does it mean to know God? (J. I. Packer wrote a classic book with that title: *Knowing God.*) This question can be answered very briefly or at great length and in depth. You might begin with John 17:3. What kind of "knowing" is this?

"I did not say these things to you from the beginning, because I was with you. But now I am going to him who sent me; yet none of you asks me, 'Where are you going?' But because I have said these things to you, sorrow has filled your hearts. Nevertheless I tell you the truth: it is to your advantage that I go away, for if I do not go away, the Counselor will not come to you; but if I go, I will send him to you." (16:4–7)

H1034. Why did Jesus leave us? Suppose he hadn't. Suppose he had remained incarnate in person in this world forever. Wouldn't that have improved everything in the world? Can you imagine a fantasy novel in which that's what Jesus did? If not, why not? If so, how might the plot line run?

1035. He left us in order to send us the Spirit, as he said. But why is it to our "advantage" that Jesus leaves us and sends the Spirit instead (v. 7)? Wouldn't it be more to our advantage to have Jesus here in the flesh? (Hint: God is love, and love seeks increased intimacy and interiority and union with the beloved. How are the revelation of the Father in the Old Testament, the revelation of the Son in the Gospels, and the revelation of the Spirit in the Church three stages of increased intimacy?)

1036. This is a "before and after" sketch. Compare the thoughts, attitudes, and behavior of the apostles (especially Peter, about whom more is written in the Gospels than any of the others) before and after the Spirit came upon them at Pentecost. (This is a long-range question that assumes you know both the Gospels and the Acts of the Apostles.) How does that data answer the two previous questions?

1037. Even though he left us physically in order to send the Spirit, as he said he had to do in this passage, Jesus also promised to be present with us himself "to the close of the age" (Mt 28:20). Name at least three different ways in which he is still present to us.

1038. So who is present in our souls now? Is it God the Father? Is it Jesus? Is it the Holy Spirit? Is it none of them? Or is it all of them? Defend your answer.

"And when he comes, he will convince the world of sin and of righteousness and of judgment: of sin, because they do not believe in me; of righteousness, because I go to the Father, and you will see me no more; of judgment, because the ruler of this world is judged." (16:8–11)

1039. How are these three things Jesus lists in verse 8—sin, righteousness, and judgment—related to each other? How are they a "package deal" in such a way that you can't have any one without the other two? (Think about it! It's not hard to figure out.)

1040. Many people in our society, if they read this saying of Jesus for the first time, would be shocked at how "judgmental" Jesus is. (A) Why are they shocked? (B) How do most people confuse two very different meanings of being "judgmental"? (C) Did our ancient ancestors tend to make the opposite mistake?

H1041. (A) What is the relation between sin and unbelief that is implied in verse 9? Is it merely that unbelief is one of many sins? (B) And what does the Spirit have to do with that?

H1042. What is the relation between the Spirit convincing the world of righteousness and Jesus' return to the Father that is implied in verse 10?

H1043. (A) Who is being judged in verse 11? (B) What does that mean? What is this judgment? How is he being judged now in a way he was not being judged before? (C) And what does the Spirit have to do with that?

"I have yet many things to say to you, but you cannot bear them now." (16:12)

1044. (A) The "deposit of faith" from Scripture, Christ, and his apostles is finished. (See Rev 22:18–19.) But our understanding and appreciation of them is not. Why do we tend to treat our understanding of divine things that God has revealed to us as a finished product that we *can* "bear" now? (B) What does Jesus mean by "bear"? "Believe"? "Understand"? "Not be turned off by"?

1045. (A) What does God have to do in us in heaven to allow us to "bear" the things Jesus refers to here that we cannot bear now? (B) What does God have to do to us on earth to enable us to "bear" these things on earth? (C) Are some of these things to which Jesus refers here things that he did not teach his apostles at the time but that he did later teach his Church through the Holy Spirit? (See verse 13.) Are there any such things? If so, give an example.

"When the Spirit of truth comes, he will guide you into all the truth; for he will not speak on his own authority, but whatever he hears he will speak, and he will declare to you the things that are to come. He will

glorify me, for he will take what is mine and declare it to you. All that the Father has is mine; therefore I said that he will take what is mine and declare it to you." (16:13–15)

1046. Jesus calls the Spirit (I) "the Advocate with the Father", (II) "the Comforter", and (III) "the Spirit of truth". (A) Why are all three necessary for us? (B) Which is the most absolutely necessary? (Hint: When, in the Bible [both in the Old Testament and in the New], people meet the true God, is their first reaction comfort? Does comfort come before, during, or after truth? Is it comfortable to confess the truth about your sins? And if you do not, do you seek an "advocate with the Father"?)

H1047. Since no human mind can know every single truth, what does Jesus mean when he says that the Spirit will guide us into "all" truth?

H1048. (A) Jesus says that the Spirit will guide us into all truth because he will not speak on his own authority but on Jesus' authority, as Jesus speaks not on his own authority but the Father's. Explain that connection, that "because". (B) The world's concept of authority is simply the power of some over others. How does Jesus give us a radically new concept of "authority" here? What is that new kind of authority? (Hint: Read Matthew 8:5–13. Where did the centurion get his power over his soldiers? Where did Jesus get his power over death itself?)

1049. Connect verse 15 with 1 Corinthians 3:22–23.

1050. (A) We tend to think that since Jesus said that "the Father is greater than I" (Jn 14:28), and because he submits his mind and will to the Father (Jn 7:16 and Jn 6:38), there must therefore be some things, some secrets, some powers, some qualities, in the Father that are not in the Son. How do verse 15 and Colossians 1:19 refute that error? (B) What are the consequences of that? What difference does it make to us and our lives as Christians? If you think this is just abstract, theoretical theology without practical human consequences, do a thought-experiment: try to imagine the opposite: that there is more in the Father than in the Son, less in the Son than in the Father. Now what are the consequences of that in your relationship with God, in your faith and in your prayer and in your life?

"A little while, and you will see me no more; again a little while, and you will see me." Some of his disciples said to one another, "What is this that he says to us, 'A little while, and you will not see me, and again a little while, and you will see me'; and, 'because I go to the Father'?" They said, "What does he mean by 'a little while'? We do not know what he means." Jesus knew that they wanted to ask him; so he said to them, "Is this what you are asking yourselves, what I meant by saying, 'A little while, and you will not see me, and again a little while, and you will see me'? Truly, truly, I say to you, you will weep and lament, but the world will rejoice; you will be sorrowful, but your sorrow will turn into joy. When a woman is in labor, she has pain, because her hour has come; but when she is delivered of the child, she no longer remembers the anguish, for joy that a child is born into the world. So you have sorrow now, but I will see you again and your hearts will rejoice, and no one will take your joy from you." (16:16–22)

1051. To what do you think Jesus is referring in verse 16? If it was simply his Resurrection, why did the apostles not "get it", since he clearly predicted it on numerous occasions (e.g., Lk 9:22, Mk 10:34, Mk 9:31–32, Mt 20:19)?

1052. (A) Jesus uses the analogy of a woman giving birth to a child not only to change his apostles' despair about the future into hope for the future but also to change their present sorrow; not to take our sufferings and sorrows away, but to inject joy into them, so that the bitter becomes neither simply bitter nor simply sweet but bittersweet. Does he do this with all our sufferings, too? (B) Can something that is thus "bittersweet" be more "sweet" than the simply sweet? How does that work? (C) Give an example from your own life and, if possible, also from the life or writings of someone holier than yourself. (D) Does God do this transformation for all suffering, no suffering, or some suffering? If all, what must we do to "get on board" his train and experience this transformation of all suffering? (See 2 Cor 1:3–7; 4:10.) If only some, which sufferings?

H1053. (A) Following Jesus' analogy or metaphor of childbirth here, what in our lives corresponds to the child that is born from the mother's painful pregnancy? Joy, of course, but what is it that gives us more joy in the end? (B) Do you think this principle applies on earth, in heaven, or both? If the sufferings are part of the joy, or increase the joy, might there be such sufferings in heaven, too?

1054. What joy, or what kind of joy, is it that "no one will take . . . from you" (v. 22)? Contrast it with joys that others can take from us. (Hint: Read Romans 8:28–39.)

"In that day you will ask nothing of me. Truly, truly, I say to you, if you ask anything of the Father, he will give it to you in my name. Until now you have asked nothing in my name; ask, and you will receive, that your joy may be full." (16:23–24)

1055. Does Jesus mean by "in that day" (I) after his Resurrection on earth, or (II) after the coming of the Spirit at Pentecost, or (III) in heaven? Does the rest of the passage give us clues?

H1056. Here again, as before, we have a promise that seems falsified by events, for we often ask God for things that he does not give us, such as miraculous healings. The "catch" seems to be "in his name". What does this mean?

"I have said this to you in figures; the hour is coming when I shall no longer speak to you in figures but tell you plainly of the Father. In that day you will ask in my name; and I do not say to you that I shall ask the Father for you; for the Father himself loves you, because you have loved me and have believed that I came from the Father. I came from the Father and have come into the world; again, I am leaving the world and going to the Father." (16:25–28)

1057. What is the "hour" (time) of which Jesus is speaking here? Is it (I) after the Resurrection, (II) after Pentecost, or (III) after death? Again, as with question 1055, which seems to be about the same time ("hour"), look carefully at the passage itself for clues.

H1058. Jesus says he will speak more "plainly" (more clearly) of the Father in that day than he did in the Gospels. Do we now know things about the Father that Jesus' disciples did not know then and that are now revealed to us, not "in figures", but "plainly"? If so, give an example.

1059. (A) Is Jesus speaking in verses 26–27 of a new, more direct access to God the Father that his disciples will have in the future? (B) If so, when will they have this? (C) And what is new in it? (D) Is Jesus saying in verse 23 and verse 26 that he will no longer be necessary as our mediator and our way to the Father, that "I am the way . . . no one comes to the Father, but by me" (Jn 14:6) will no longer be true?

H1060. Jesus speaks of a kind of "circular" journey in verse 28, from eternity to time and back again. (A) Do we, too, have a circular journey? If so, how is our journey different from his? (C) How is it in a way similar to his? (D) How is this "circular journey" a pattern for most epic or heroic stories in our literature? (Think of *The Odyssey, The Aeneid, The Lord of the Rings*, and—God's own story in the Bible!)

His disciples said, "Ah, now you are speaking plainly, not in any figure! Now we know that you know all things, and need none to question you; by this we believe that you came from God." Jesus answered them, "Do you now believe? The hour is coming, indeed it has come, when you will be scattered, every man to his home, and will leave me alone; yet I am not alone, for the Father is with me." (16:29–32)

1061. What do the disciples think they understand now that they did not before?

H1062. Notice that they did not reason this way: "Jesus came from God, therefore he knows all things", but this way: "Jesus knows all things, therefore he came from God." How did they know that he knew all things?

1063. Jesus is here predicting (v. 32) that his disciples will leave him alone and run away like sheep scattering from the wolf when their Master is arrested, not even returning when he is crucified (except for John and the women). But why does he call this a lack of *faith* (v. 31) rather than just a lack of courage?

1064. This is a long and psychologically demanding question, with many parts. Feel free to ask another person to be merciful and take it on his shoulders if you feel you cannot even try to answer it.

(A) Which do you think was more important to Jesus: (I) his disciples not forsaking him and leaving him alone or (II) his Father not forsaking him and leaving him alone? (B) How terrifying is absolute aloneness? Could that be an even more terrifying image of hell than the usual image of fire? (C) Is that what Jesus suffered most from on the Cross (Mt 27:46)? (D) Was that hell? (E) Was Jesus really forsaken by his Father on the Cross, in objective fact, or was it in his subjective feelings alone? (Hint: If he believed he was really forsaken by God, why did he pray this prayer *to God*?) (F) If you had to choose between (I) being forsaken by God in objective fact but not in your subjective feelings or (II) being forsaken by God in your subjective feelings but not in objective fact, which would you choose and why? (G) Imagine yourself dying and being forsaken by all your children. Then imagine dying and feeling forsaken by your (human) father. Compare the two feelings. Now compare that imagined experience in yourself to the thing Jesus really experienced on the Cross: being forsaken by his spiritual children and by his Father. Which do you think was harder for him? (H) The more you love someone, the more that person can pain you by forsaking you. So how much pain did Jesus suffer on the Cross?

"I have said this to you, that in me you may have peace. In the world you have tribulation; but be of good cheer, I have overcome the world." (16:33)

E1065. (A) Does Jesus mean that his disciples will have peace because of what he has told them, because of what he will do for them, or both? (Hint: Imagine that he had done either one of those two things without the other.) (B) So is "the Gospel" words (truths), facts (deeds), or both?

H1066. Explain that little preposition "in": What does it mean to have peace "in" Christ, not just "because of" Christ?

1067. (A) Is Jesus implying here that we can have peace and tribulation at the same time? (B) If so, how? (C) Have you ever experienced this?

1068. Two other famous people in history said "I have overcome the world." Alexander the Great said it after he conquered the whole

known world with his army. Buddha said it after his mystical experience of Nirvana convinced him that the world was an illusion.
Compare the way Jesus overcame the world with the way these two
did it. Jesus did not do either of those two things, but how *did* he
"overcome the world"?

John 17

When Jesus had spoken these words, he lifted up his eyes to heaven and said, "Father, the hour has come; glorify your Son that the Son may glorify you, since you have given him power over all flesh, to give eternal life to all whom you have given him." (17:1–2)

1069. I heard a very profound preacher once say that John 17 is the most intimate chapter in the Bible, a glimpse into Jesus' own interior prayer life and a glimpse into the eternal life of the Trinity. (A deep "probe" if ever there was one!) If that is true, how should that change our attitude toward this chapter when we read it and try to understand it? How should it change what method we use to try to answer these "probes" (questions) about it?

1070. Jesus is about to be horribly tortured and die, just to save *us* from eternal death. He is about to experience hell (being forsaken of God) to save *us* from that hell. Why does he turn to his Father, in prayer, rather than to his disciples at this time if it was primarily for love of them that he was about to die? Or did he also turn to his disciples? (Cf. Mt 26:40.) And was it primarily for the love of them or for the love of his Father that he did this? (Hint: Jesus certainly practiced what he preached. Did he preach that the very first and greatest commandment was to love our neighbors?)

1071. (A) Does Jesus' love for his Father diminish, increase, or leave unchanged his love of us? (B) Why? (C) Does our obedience to what Jesus calls the first and greatest commandment (to love God) diminish, increase, or leave unchanged our obedience to what he calls the second commandment (to love our neighbors)? (D) Why? (E) Jesus tells us to love our neighbor "as [we love] ourselves". How does our love of ourselves affect our love of our neighbor? (F) How does our love of ourselves affect our love of God? (G) How does our love of God affect our love of ourselves? (H) How does our love of God affect our love of our neighbor?

1072. (A) The first few words of verse 1 show that Jesus' words were *spoken*, that he prayed this prayer aloud in the presence of his disciples right after having spoken to them. Why do you think he did not keep it private? (B) Why do you think he kept most of his prayer in the Garden of Gethsemane private (Mt 26:36)? (C) What part of that prayer (in Gethsemane) did he not keep private but revealed to us? (D) How do we know that? (E) Why did he not keep that part private?

H1073. (A) Why does Jesus speak of his Passion and death as "glory"? (B) Does this passage tell us what he means, of what "glory" he is speaking? Is it the glory he had eternally in heaven? (C) Why do you suppose "glory" is a word that we hardly ever use anymore today? (D) If the answer to (C) is not very flattering, what can we do about it?

"And this is eternal life: that they know you the only true God, and Jesus Christ whom you have sent." (17:3)

E1074. (A) Is this the best definition of "eternal life" ever given? (B) Why (or why not)?

E1075. Of what kind of "knowing" is Jesus speaking here?

1076. (A) Does "eternal life" then begin in time? (B) Why (or why not)?

H1077. (A) Can we be in time and eternity at the same time? (B) If so, how? (C) Was Jesus in time and in eternity at the same time?

1078. Why does Jesus say "know" instead of "love"? (Hint: Perhaps this is a "trick question". Is love a kind of "knowing"? Is there an eye in the heart?)

"I glorified you on earth, having accomplished the work which you gave me to do; and now, Father, glorify me in your own presence with the glory which I had with you before the world was made." (17:4-5)

1079. (A) Our work is of course not the same as Christ's (unless we are either carpenters or martyrs), so how does our work, like

Christ's, "glorify" God? (B) What does it mean to "glorify" God? Can we add to God's glory if God is already infinitely glorious? If not, what can we add to? (Hint: Think of the second petition of the Lord's Prayer.)

1080. How can Jesus pray for something he knows he is going to get (v. 5)? How can we do the same?

H1081. (A) Will Christ share the eternal, divine glory of which he speaks in verse 5 with us, too? (B) Is that possible? (C) If he could add human glory to his divine glory, can he therefore also add divine glory to our human glory? (D) Which do you think is easier for him to do? (E) Why?

H1082. Since Einstein proved that time is not absolute, as Newton thought, but relative to matter, motion, and space, God must have co-created time with matter in the "Big Bang". So there is no such thing as any time "before" the world (i.e., the material universe) began. So why does Christ use the language of time to speak to us of eternity ("before the world was made")? (This question seems terribly difficult, theoretical, and abstract, but it really has a very simple answer.)

"I have manifested your name to the men whom you gave me out of the world; they were yours, and you gave them to me, and they have kept your word." (17:6)

1083. What difference does it make to your concept of yourself to realize that you are one of those "whom you [God] gave me [Christ] out of the world"—that you are one of the gifts the Father gave to his Son?

1084. What is it to manifest God's "name"? (Think of the phrase "in the name of. . .") (Hint: It's not just a sound or a set of letters!)

1085. Why does Jesus say that his disciples have "kept" his "word"? How do you "keep" a "word"? Is it like Scrabble? What does he mean by his "word", and what does he mean by "keeping" it?

"Now they know that everything that you have given me is from you; for I have given them the words which you gave me, and they have received them and know in truth that I came from you; and they have believed that you sent me." (17:7–8)

1086. (A) In saying "I have given them the words which you gave me", is Jesus saying that he literally tells us the word-for-word words that God the Father spoke to him? (B) If so, what language does God speak? If not, why does Jesus use such concrete language ("the words which you gave me") rather than something more safe and distant and abstract and general like "message" or "truth"? (Even the singular "word" is more general than the plural "words", for it can mean simply "will" or "law".)

1087. Why does Jesus say that it is his words, rather than his miracles, that caused his disciples to know that he was divine and came from the Father in heaven?

H1088. What's in a word, anyway? How can it be true that "in the beginning was the Word"? What more is a word than a label for something that already exists?

H1089. The divinity of Christ is the distinctive and central Christian belief. Why does Jesus always refer to it in terms of where he came from and who sent him rather than simply saying, as a theologian would say, that he has a divine nature?

"I am praying for them; I am not praying for the world but for those whom you have given me, for they are yours; all mine are yours, and yours are mine, and I am glorified in them." (17:9–10)

H1090. (A) What does Jesus mean by "the world"? Is it a place? A time? A people? Hint: You might want to google or briefly look up Saint Augustine's answer to that question in his classic *The City of God*. Hint no. 2: One way to clarify a thing is to contrast it to its opposite. This is what Augustine did in that classic about two "cities" (communities), the "City of God" and the "City of the World" (*civitas dei* and *civitas mundi*). (B) Why does Jesus not pray for "the world"? Didn't he come to save the world? (C) Does that mean just that he's not praying for the world now or that he doesn't do that at all? (D) Should we pray for the world? (E) If so, why? If not, why not? (F) Should we pray for the salvation of very evil men? Should we pray that Hitler converted just after he pulled the trigger to kill himself? (G) Should we pray for the salvation of demons? Why or why not?

1091. (A) To whom is Jesus referring when he says he is praying to the Father "for those whom you have given me"? (B) Does the Father give us to Jesus, or does Jesus give us to the Father? (Hint: Why is that a trick question?) (C) What difference does it make that Jesus himself is praying for us? What is the effect of his prayers?

H1092. (A) Is it easier to see how we are glorified "in" Christ or how he is glorified "in" us, as he says he is in verse 10? (B) How *are* we glorified in Christ? (C) How is he glorified in us?

"And now I am no more in the world, but they are in the world, and I am coming to you. Holy Father, keep them in your name, which you have given me, that they may be one, even as we are one." (17:11)

1093. What does it mean that Christians are "in the world but not of the world"? How does John 3:6 answer that question?

H1094. (A) What does Jesus mean by "kept"? (B) What does he mean by "in your name"? (Remember how much more that phrase means than labels or words in a book.) (C) How can we be "kept" by God himself in his own name?

H1095. (A) Jesus says "*which* you have given me" instead of "*whom* you have given me" because the phrase refers to God's name rather than Jesus' disciples. What does Jesus mean by saying that God's name is something his Father has given him? (B) Is this gift given on earth in time or in heaven in eternity? (C) Is the fact that your earthly father gave you his family name a reflection of that Trinitarian gift? (D) If so, how is it differently given?

1096. (A) When Jesus prayed to his Father that his children "may be one", the Church was not yet divided. Or was she? (B) Is Jesus praying for the healing of future divisions? (C) Of past divisions also? (D) When did divisions first arise? (E) When will they cease? (F) Which ones can cease before that time?

H1097. (A) Why are divisions bad? (This is not as simple a question as it looks.) (B) Are all divisions bad? Are some good, some neutral, some minimally bad, and some maximally bad? If so, give examples *of all four*.

1098. (A) What do you think Jesus would say about our present divisions? (B) How did you find your answer to that question? (C) What did the apostle (*Jesus'* apostle!) Paul think about divisions in the first chapter of 1 Corinthians?

1099. (A) What do you think we should do about this problem of divisions? Obviously, we begin by doing what Jesus did: sincere, passionate prayer. What next? (B) I could not decide whether to label this question H or E! If you find it hard, is it hard to *know* the answer or hard to *do* it? If both are hard, which is harder?

1100. Jesus does not merely say "that they may be one" but "that they may be one *even as we are one*." Isn't that an impossible ideal? How can we be one as Jesus and his Father are one? What kind of unity is that?

"While I was with them, I kept them in your name, which you have given me; I have guarded them, and none of them is lost but the son of perdition, that the Scripture might be fulfilled." (17:12)

1101. (A) Why does Jesus repeat so much in his prayer? What is the purpose of repetition? (B) Why do we find it more in song than in speech and more in poetry than in prose?

H1102. (A) Do Jesus' words about Judas mean that his being lost was a means to the end that the Scripture (the prophecies about this) might be fulfilled? If not, why not? (B) If divine prophecies are infallible, they are necessarily true and necessarily fulfilled. Does that mean that the human beings referred to in those prophecies lose their free will whenever such an infallible prophecy is made about them? If not, why not?

1103. Here are some very easy "leading questions" about a very hard issue. (A) In calling Judas "the son of perdition", is Jesus implying that perdition (damnation) is his "destiny", as being born to a certain biological parent is the "destiny" of a child? (B) "Fate" usually means the opposite of free will. Is destiny the same as fate? (C) Can it be your destiny to make certain free choices? If so, can destiny and free choice thus coincide? (D) Can you choose your destiny? Well, let's figure it out. Does your destiny, both in time and in eternity, depend on your character? (Judas, for example.) Does your character depend on your free choices? Does your destiny thus depend on your free choices? (E) Where do these two forces (destiny and free choice) come from? Well, let's figure that out, too. In a story, does the destiny come from the power of the author (since a story requires a storyteller) and the free choices come from the power of the characters (since the author is not telling a story about robots but about people)? If so, are those choices both free and destined at the same time? (F) In fact, can you think of a single story worth telling or hearing that does not have both a sense of destiny in its plot and free will in its characters? (G) Is your life a real story? If so, who is the storyteller? (H) If even a human storyteller can insert himself into his story and meet his characters (as both Alfred Hitchcock and M. Night Shyamalan did in their movies), can God do that, too? (I) Is that the plot of the story of the Bible?

"But now I am coming to you; and these things I speak in the world, that they may have my joy fulfilled in themselves." (17:13)

1104. Throughout his prayer, Jesus speaks *to* his Father and calls him "you". When he teaches, he speaks *about* his Father, and calls him "he". Both are necessary, but which is the source of the greater wisdom and makes the greater difference? (Hint: The reason God approved Job's wild words and not Job's three friends' correct and pious words [in Job 42:7] was probably that they never talked to God, as Job did, but only about him.)

1105. (A) Do Jesus' last nine words here mean that the ultimate end of all that Jesus said to us and did for us was our joy? (B) What is the difference between joy, happiness, and pleasure? How is happiness deeper than pleasure, and joy deeper than happiness?

1106. Jesus does not say merely that his desire is that we may have joy in ourselves but that we may have *his* joy in ourselves. How can we have Jesus' joy in ourselves? Jesus' joy is perfect and divine and eternal; we are imperfect and human and temporal. (Hint: When you see someone you deeply love moving from misery to joy, whose joy is in your soul?)

1107. The martyrs often died with hymns of joy on their lips even as they were being eaten by lions. How is that possible? Where could that joy *not* possibly have come from? Where *did* it come from?

"I have given them your word; and the world has hated them because they are not of the world, even as I am not of the world. I do not pray that you should take them out of the world, but that you should keep them from the evil one. They are not of the world, even as I am not of the world." (17:14–16)

1108. (A) When we do what Jesus did and give the world his word, in its fullness, what reaction can we expect from the world? (B) Why? (C) Here is a question whose answer you can logically deduce from your answer to the previous two questions: If no one in the world hates you or fears you, what does that prove about yourself?

1109. (A) In light of your answer to the previous question, why doesn't this mean that we should make pests of ourselves by confrontational polemics? Is there a better method than that for "witnessing" or preaching the gospel without compromise? Are there only two options for a Christian, namely, either to preach the whole gospel in a way that will offend others and make them our enemies, or to tone it down and compromise it for the sake of friendship? (B) If so, which of the two is better? If not, what would a third option be? (Hint: What is the single most effective way to preach the gospel? What made Mother Teresa so effective? How did Jesus himself do it? What was the single most powerful sermon he ever preached? [Hint: It was not the Sermon on the Mount, but it was preached from a high place, "lifted up" from the ground.]) (C) Saint Francis supposedly said, "Preach the gospel at all times, use words when necessary." When we "preach" the gospel in that nonverbal way; what difference will that make to the world's attitude to the verbal way, what difference will our actions make to our words? (D) Give a concrete example of this in a controversial situation, e.g., how to "witness" to those who are living a "gay" life-style or having an adulterous "affair".

1110. Why does Jesus not want us to be taken out of the world (v. 15)?

1111. What does Jesus mean by being "not of the world"? Is it merely that Christians do not live in the same way and by the same moral principles as most of the rest of the world? (Hint: "Of" means "caused by or having your being from". How does this relate to Jesus' speech to Nicodemus in chapter 3?)

"Sanctify them in the truth; your word is truth." (17:17)

H1112. We usually think of truth as something objective, impersonal, and hard-headed, and we think of sanctity, or sanctification, as something subjective, personal, and soft-hearted. We certainly do not want to be either soft-headed or hard-hearted. But Jesus combines and almost identifies these two things when he prays that we be "sanctified . . . in the truth". How does this change and expand our assumptions both about truth and about sanctity?

H1113. Why does he say not merely "your word is true" but "your word is truth"?

H1114. (A) What does Jesus mean by "your word"? The New Testament had not yet been written. Does he mean the Old Testament? Is truth found first of all in a book? (B) If not, where? Where did this book (the Bible) get its truth from?

"As you sent me into the world, so I have sent them into the world. And for their sake I consecrate myself, that they also may be consecrated in truth." (17:18–19)

1115. (A) In what sense are Christians the continuation or extension of the Incarnation (v. 18)? (B) In what sense are we not?

1116. (A) What does it mean to "consecrate"? (Look it up.) (B) Is it possible to consecrate yourself to yourself? (C) Is it possible to consecrate yourself to another for the sake of yourself rather than to consecrate yourself for the sake of the other? (D) Can you consecrate yourself to a cause or only to a person? (E) Can you consecrate yourself wholly to God and also to your neighbor?

1117. Why does Jesus first consecrate himself so that then and only then we may be consecrated?

1118. Why does Jesus add "in truth"? What does truth have to do with consecration? Can there be false consecrations, too?

1119. Were you consecrated? If so, when and how?

"I do not pray for these only, but also for those who believe in me through their word, that they may all be one; even as you, Father, are in me, and I in you, that they also may be in us, so that the world may believe that you have sent me." (17:20–21)

1120. For how many people is Jesus praying here?

1121. Can he know and love each one individually by name? If so, how can he do that?

H1122. (A) Someone once said that if you were the only person God ever created, God would have done no less for you alone than he did for the whole human race (including sending his Son to die for you). Do you believe that's true? Why or why not? (B) Someone else added that in fact, that's what he did: he died for you, not for "humanity". Do you believe that's true, too? Why or why not? (See Is 49:16.) (C) There is a Jewish proverb, made famous by the movie *Schindler's List*, that says "he who saves one soul saves the whole world." What could that possibly mean? (D) Do you see any connection between that saying (in the [C] part of this question) and the saying in the (A) part of this question?

H1123. (A) Jesus prays not just that we may be one but that we may be one *as Jesus and the Father are one*. What kind of unity is that? Perhaps it would be easier to say what kind(s) of unity that is not. For instance, it is not a confusion of persons, an abolition of individuality, like melting down two metal toy soldiers into one lump. But it is also not merely a relationship of friendship between two persons who remain only externally related to each other, as in a social club or a common workplace. So what is it like? What human relationship images it most clearly or approaches it most closely? (B) Jesus' answer to that question ("what kind of unity is that?") is that he is "in" us and we are "in" him as he is "in" his Father and his Father is "in" him. Here is an apparently very simple question that is inexhaustibly profound: What does "in" mean here? (C) But how can A be in B and also B in A? How can we be "in" Christ and Christ also be "in" us? How can Christ be "in" the Father and the Father "in" him? If a sardine is in a can, the can cannot be in the sardine.

E1124. (A) What does verse 21 imply will happen to the world if and when Christians attain the kind of unity for which Jesus prays? (B) What should we do about that?

1125. Christians of the "left" today, who emphasize ecumenism, usually shy away from evangelism, which they fear is too fiery and divisive and which they call "proselytizing". Christians of the "right" today, who emphasize evangelism and missionary work, usually shy away from ecumenism, which they see as too watery and which they fear is indifferentism, relativism, and compromise. How does this saying of Jesus address this division between Christians of the left and right?

1126. What, exactly, is the obstacle to the world accepting our witness and coming to believe that Jesus has divine authority ("that the Father has sent me")? Is it merely that we lack visible and organizational unity? That we lack total unity in our belief systems? The Nazis had all that, but the world did not lovingly embrace them! What kind of unity do we lack that Jesus is praying for, implying that if we had it, the world would recognize the truth about him? (B) Do you think he is implying that the whole world would recognize him? Isn't that impossibly large? Does he mean, then, merely a few more people? Isn't that trivially small? (Hint: When Mother Teresa first did her work in Calcutta, many non-Christians were suspicious of her and opposed her. But she eventually won over nearly everyone except for a very few supremely cynical antireligious people like Christopher Hitchens.) (C) Do you feel that Jesus is being naïve and overly optimistic here and ignoring the sinful and rebellious part of human nature? If not, what else does he see in human nature that is stronger? (Hint: Who designed human nature?)

"The glory which you have given me I have given to them, that they may be one even as we are one, I in them and you in me, that they may become perfectly one, so that the world may know that you have sent me and have loved them even as you have loved me." (17:22–23)

H1127. (A) Jesus is divine and eternal and perfect; we are not. So how can Jesus give us the same glory he has received from the Father? What is that "glory"? (B) And why does that "glory" make us "one" as the Father and the Son in the Trinity are one? (C) What is that "oneness"? Jesus speaks of it as perfect when he prays "that they may become perfectly one". What is the most perfect oneness? Let's think this through: (C1) How are the Father and the Son one? (C2) How is that their "glory"? (C3) How can Christ give us that glory; how can we get it from him? (D) Finally, how does that make the world know who Jesus is and where he comes from? (Hint: If you answer the last question first, you can figure out the answers to the other three, too. And you implicitly did answer that last question already, in answering question 1126.)

H1128. If Jesus' perfect glory is something he has "received" from the Father, so that he receives and reflects the Father's mind and conforms to and obeys the Father's will, and yet he is equal to the Father and not inferior to him, how does that radically transform human relationships of "receiving" (e.g., a woman "receiving" a marriage proposal from a man and "receiving" seed and pregnancy from a man) and obeying (e.g., citizens obeying their rulers and children obeying their parents)? (See Eph 5:21–33 on this.)

1129. (A) The Greek word for "as" in verse 23, *hos*, means not "an imitation or copy of", like a picture, but "in the very same way, with the very same reality and power", like fire kindling fire. Does that mean the answer to the question of how much Jesus loves you is the same as the answer to the question of how much he is loved by the Father? (B) If so, how can that be? We are not as lovable as Jesus is; there is not as much in us for him to love as there is in him for the Father to love. (Hint: What kind of love is dependent on how lovable its object is, and what kind of love goes beyond that?)

"Father, I desire that they also, whom you have given me, may be with me where I am, to behold my glory which you have given me in your love for me before the foundation of the world." (17:24)

1130. What does Jesus mean by "with me where I am" here?

H1131. Jesus says that he "desires" that we be there where he is and prays to the Father for it. How effective is that desire and prayer? If it is 100 percent effective, and if the answer to question 1130 is "heaven", and if Jesus loves everybody, how can anyone not get to heaven? (Hint: Notice words 7–11 in v. 24, and also v. 9.)

1132. (A) Is Jesus saying that in heaven we will behold something that goes back to before the act of creation, before what scientists call the "Big Bang"? (B) Since no matter goes back farther than that event, which was the beginning of all matter, and since bodies are made of matter, and since eyes are parts of bodies, then what eyes will we use to "behold" this glory?

"O righteous Father, the world has not known you, but I have known you; and these know that you have sent me. I made known to them your name, and I will make it known, that the love with which you have loved me may be in them, and I in them." (17:25–26)

H1133. Let's try to figure out why Jesus adds the word "righteous" here? (A) What does it mean? Is it essentially "rightness" or justice? (B) What is the connection between this "righteousness" of God and the fact that "the world has not known" God? (C) In Romans 1, Paul calls the gospel ("good news") that he preaches "the righteousness of God". But (C1) the fact that God is righteous does not seem to be good news but bad news, because it means that we must be judged by the standard of his perfect justice and holiness, which is a test we cannot pass. (C2) And the Gospel centers on the most unrighteous, unjust, unholy deed ever done, the murder of God Incarnate. What kind of strange "justice" is this? Yet when Paul writes Romans, which centers on Christ's atoning death, he calls the gospel "the righteousness (justice) of God". (Rom 1:17) How can this be?

H1134. (A) What is the relationship between knowing God the Father and knowing Jesus? (Cf. Jn 8:19; 1:18.) (B) What is the difference between knowing a person ("I know him") and knowing a fact ("I know that . . .")? (C) What is the relation in verse 25 between (I) knowing God ("the world has not known you, but I have known you") and (II) knowing that God has sent Jesus ("that you have sent me")?

1135. What is the *relation* between past and future in Jesus saying "I made known to them your [God's] name" and saying "I will make it known"? (Cf. Heb 11:8.)

1136. What is the relation between Jesus' love being in us and Jesus himself being in us (at the end of v. 26)?

John 18

When Jesus had spoken these words, he went forth with his disciples across the Kidron valley, where there was a garden, which he and his disciples entered. Now Judas, who betrayed him, also knew the place; for Jesus often met there with his disciples. So Judas, procuring a band of soldiers and some officers from the chief priests and the Pharisees, went there with lanterns and torches and weapons. (18:1–3)

1137. (A) Why do you think Jesus and his disciples "often" went to this garden? (B) What does a garden naturally symbolize? (C) Why does Genesis call Eden a "garden"? (D) What does this little event of Jesus going to the garden have to do with us and our lives, if Jesus is our perfect model in all things?

1138. (A) Why did Judas come? To betray Jesus, of course, but what do you think his motive was for betraying Jesus? (B) Why did the religious officers come? What was their motive? (C) Why did the soldiers come? (D) Why did they think they would need weapons?

Then Jesus, knowing all that was to befall him, came forward and said to them, "Whom do you seek?" (18:4)

1139. Compare this question of Jesus with the very first thing Jesus said in John's Gospel. Don't just compare the words; compare the meanings.

1140. (A) Why did Jesus ask the question "Whom do you seek" if he already knew that it was himself they were seeking? (B) Usually we ask questions to get new information. But what are some other reasons for asking questions besides getting information? For instance: (B1) Why did Jesus ask the sick man, "Do you want to be healed?" in John 5:6? (B2) Why do teachers ask questions of their students? (B3) Why do exorcists ask the demon to speak his name?

1141. If Jesus knew "all that was to befall him" (crucifixion and death) and yet "came forward" rather than hiding, why wasn't this "coming forward" an act of suicide?

H1142. Do you see any deeper or symbolic significance in the fact that Jesus "came forward"?

They answered him, "Jesus of Nazareth." Jesus said to them, "I am he." Judas, who betrayed him, was standing with them. When he said to them, "I am he," they drew back and fell to the ground. (18:5–6)

1143. (A) Jesus asked his first disciples "What do you seek?" (Jn 1:38). He asks us the same question. Here, he asks his enemies, "Whom do you seek?" (v. 4). Does he mean the same thing here, in this context, as he did in 1:38, or is it something different, in a different context? (B) "They answered him, 'Jesus of Nazareth'" (v. 5). Do we give him the same answer? If so, does it mean something different from what they meant?

H1144. Explain verse 6. Why would three simple little words ("I am he") make tough soldiers retreat and fall down? Is there a connection here to John 8:58 and Exodus 3:14?

Again he asked them, "Whom do you seek?" And they said, "Jesus of Nazareth." Jesus answered, "I told you that I am he; so, if you seek me, let these men go." This was to fulfil the word which he had spoken, "Of those whom you gave me I lost not one." (18:7–9)

1145. Why the repetition of Jesus' question and of their answer and of his response?

1146. Do you see any symbolic or allegorical significance in Jesus' words "If you seek me, let these men go"? How could these words be taken to summarize the whole "good news" of the gospel?

H1147. In verse 9, John says that Jesus saying "let these men go" fulfilled the prophetic word Jesus had spoken earlier in his "high priestly prayer" to his Father, "I lost not one" (Jn 17:12). Compare the meaning of "let these men go" as the soldiers understood these words with "I lost not one" as Jesus understood these words.

Then Simon Peter, having a sword, drew it and struck the high priest's slave and cut off his right ear. The slave's name was Malchus. Jesus said to Peter, "Put your sword into its sheath; shall I not drink the chalice which the Father has given me?" (18:10–11)

1148. What was Peter doing with a sword in the first place?

1149. Why was it Peter alone who drew his sword?

1150. What does the fact that John mentions Malchus' name and which ear was cut off tell you?

1151. What is the evidence in this text that Peter was left-handed?

H1152. In Matthew 26:52 Jesus also tells Peter to put his sword back into its sheath, but then adds, "for all who take the sword will perish by the sword." In John's account he adds, "Shall I not drink the chalice which the Father has given me?" Compare those two reasons Jesus gives for sheathing the sword.

1153. (A) Do you think that either of those two reasons proves the rightness of pacifism? (B) Why or why not?

1154. Why does Jesus call his death a "chalice"?

H1155. (A) Why does he speak of it as a *gift* given to him by the Father? (B) Are our sufferings gifts from God? (C) If so, how could that be? Don't gifts reflect love? Is suffering a gift? Would a God of love deliberately give it to someone he loves? If so, for what purpose? Could it be to release more love? For whose sake?

So the band of soldiers and their captain and the officers of the Jews seized Jesus and bound him. First they led him to Annas; for he was the father-in-law of Caiaphas, who was high priest that year. It was Caiaphas who had given counsel to the Jews that it was expedient that one man should die for the people. (18:12–14)

1156. Notice the composition of the crowd that came to arrest Jesus. (A) What is the significance of the fact that those who were

responsible for Jesus' death included both individuals (Judas, Annas, Caiaphas, Herod, Pilate) and groups? (B) What is the significance of the fact that it included both sides of all the opposing
groups (the Jews and the Gentiles [Romans], the secular and sacred
authorities, Zionist rebels and Herodian collaborators, soldiers and
priests, Pharisees and Sadducees [the "religious right" and the "religious left" of the time])? (C) How is this related to the fact that
the sign Pilate had put on the Cross was written in Latin, Greek,
and Hebrew (Jn 19:20)?

1157. Is the answer to the question "who crucified Jesus?" the same
as the answer to the question "for whom did Jesus die?" To answer
this question, ask why Mel Gibson put himself into his own movie
(*The Passion of the Christ*) as the voice that said to the Roman soldier
who had trouble nailing Christ to the Cross, "Here, let me show
you how to do that" and as the hand that held the hammer for the
soldier.

1158. (A) What does verse 14 show about how God's plans and
man's plans are related? (See Jn 11:45–51.) (B) Since this is an example of irony and since irony is a form of humor, is there any
kind of humor here? Cf. the joke: "If you want to give God a good
laugh, tell him your plans."

*Simon Peter followed Jesus, and so did another disciple. As this disciple
was known to the high priest, he entered the court of the high priest along
with Jesus, while Peter stood outside at the door. So the other disciple,
who was known to the high priest, went out and spoke to the maid who
kept the door, and brought Peter in. The maid who kept the door said to
Peter, "Are not you also one of this man's disciples?" He said, "I am
not." Now the servants and officers had made a charcoal fire, because it
was cold, and they were standing and warming themselves; Peter also was
with them, standing and warming himself. (18:15–18)*

E1159. Who is this "other disciple" in verse 15? Why doesn't John
name him?

1160. (A) Of the twelve Jesus chose as his apostles, one (Judas)
betrayed him and nine ran away. Only Peter raised his sword to defend Jesus (foolishly but bravely), and only Peter "followed Jesus"
together with John into the judgment hall, but then quickly denied

Jesus (v. 17). Only John stayed with Jesus to the end and was there
beneath the Cross with the women (19:25–27). Why do you think
Jesus chose this unreliable, motley crew, these twelve? (B) Why
did he include Judas? (C) Why did he single out Peter instead of
John for leadership? (It is clear from the Gospels that he did, even
if Protestants and Catholics differ on whether Peter was the first
pope.) Why did he call Peter "Rocky" (Jn 1:42 and Mt 16:18–19)
if he was so sandy? (D) When did Peter finally live up to his new
name and why?

1161. (A) There are many pagan myths about gods who came down
from heaven and performed miracles. Some myths even have them
dying and being resurrected. "Liberal" or "Modernist" theologians
claim that the Gospels are also myths, not eyewitness descriptions of
historical events, but imaginative inventions of the Church or "the
early Christian community", which divinized their human hero,
somewhat as the Greeks did to Achilles or some later Buddhists
(the "Pure Land Sect") did to Buddha—or perhaps even invented
him as a fiction, like Superman. What do little details like John
knowing the maid at the door or the servants, officers, and Peter
warming their hands by a charcoal fire do to that literary theory?
(B) If you compare the Gospels with all the pagan myths, what
striking difference in style do you find? (C) Is it reasonable that
a few Jewish fishermen invented modern realistic fantasy nineteen
centuries before Tolkien? Or is *that* the fantasy?

1162. Suggest some ways in which we today do the same thing
Peter did when he told the maid, "I am not [one of this man's dis-
ciples]."

1163. (A) When Peter disowned Jesus, did Jesus disown Peter? (B)
What was his reply to Peter's denial? (Cf. Lk 22:54–62.)

1164. When the Jews who clamored for Jesus to be crucified said,
"His blood be on us and on our children" (Mt 27:25), did God
accept that self-curse? Compare this with the previous question.

The high priest then questioned Jesus about his disciples and his teaching.
Jesus answered him, "I have spoken openly to the world; I have always
taught in synagogues and in the temple, where all Jews come together;
I have said nothing secretly. Why do you ask me? Ask those who have

*heard me, what I said to them; they know what I said." When he had
said this, one of the officers standing by struck Jesus with his hand, saying,
"Is that how you answer the high priest?" Jesus answered him, "If I have
spoken wrongly, bear witness to the wrong; but if I have spoken rightly,
why do you strike me?" Annas then sent him bound to Caiaphas the
high priest. (18:19–24)*

1165. (A) Annas the priest begins collecting evidence by questioning the accused, just as we would do today in court. Was the killing
of Jesus an act of raw power by a totalitarian dictatorship, or was
it a carefully planned use of the legal rules of evidence that were in
place? (B) Which of these two is the greater danger today in our
culture?

1166. Most religions in the ancient world were esoteric, that is,
their core teachings could be fully understood only by the few,
the elite, the "insiders", or the mystics. This was true also of at
least one Jewish sect of the time, the Essenes. However, mainline
Judaism has always been exoteric, i.e., public and egalitarian, with
the same truths (Scriptures) and rules (laws) for everyone. How
does the dialogue between Annas and Jesus show which kind of
religion Christianity is?

1167. Why isn't Jesus "copping out" or "passing the buck" in telling
Annas to ask his followers what he taught rather than asking *him*?

1168. Why did the officer who struck Jesus interpret his reply as a
personal insult to the high priest?

1169. (A) Take the time to do the kind of imaginative thought-
experiment that Ignatius of Loyola suggests in his *Exercises*: imagine yourself present in this event as an eyewitness. How do you
spontaneously feel when you see God incarnate being slapped in
the face by a soldier? (B) Why does it still shock and surprise you
if it is so well known and familiar?

1170. (A) What is surprising about Jesus' answer to the slap? (B)
Compare Paul's response to a similar slap in Acts 23:1–5.

H1171. Jesus rarely uses a cerebral, impersonal logical argument.
Here he does: a classic Socratic "choose either A or non-A" dialec-
tical argument. Why do you think he does that?

1172. (A) Is Jesus' very logical reply the kind that we typically hear from men or from women? (B) Why is that so, do you suppose? (Do not let this tempting question gobble up too much of your thought-time or inflame your thoughtless prejudices! It is a confusing and even dangerous question in our culture. The president of Harvard [Larry Summers] was fired for suggesting that it was an open and therefore discussable question whether one reason why more men than women went into the hard [mathematical] sciences was some innate difference between the "masculine mind" and the "feminine mind".)

Now Simon Peter was standing and warming himself. They said to him, "Are not you also one of his disciples?" He denied it and said, "I am not." One of the servants of the high priest, a kinsman of the man whose ear Peter had cut off, asked, "Did I not see you in the garden with him?" Peter again denied it; and at once the cock crowed. (18:25–27)

1173. Why do you suppose John twice tells us that Peter was standing around the fire warming himself? (Hint: What do we seek when we are warming ourselves? What should Peter have been seeking and thinking of in that situation?)

1174. Why is it important that Peter denied Jesus not once but three times?

1175. What back-story relationships might there be behind the fact that John knew the high priest (vv. 15–16) and the fact that the third person who fingered Peter was a relative of Malchus, the high priest's slave, whose ear Peter had cut off?

1176. What do you think John was doing or feeling or saying while Peter was denying Jesus three times?

H1177. If John knew the high priest, the high priest knew John. Why do you suppose he didn't expose John? Three people, including the high priest's servant, had just exposed Peter.

1178. Why do you suppose God arranged a cock to crow after Peter's third denial?

1179. (A) Are there ways in which we do the same thing Peter did? (B) Do you think our motive is the same as his?

Then they led Jesus from the house of Caiaphas to the praetorium. It was early. They themselves did not enter the praetorium, so that they might not be defiled, but might eat the Passover. (18:28)

H1180. Explain the irony in this verse. (Background: Jews were defiled ["dirtied"] if they entered Gentile houses, especially those of their pagan Roman oppressors; and no defiled person could partake of the greatest Jewish feast, the Passover, without ritual cleansing first.)

1181. (A) How did Jesus' death and Resurrection fulfill and show the real meaning of the Jewish Passover? (B) Why was it called the "Pass-over"?

1182. Celebration of the Passover was essentially an act of eating and drinking. When Christianity came into the world and claimed to be the fulfillment and real meaning of the Jewish Passover, did these Christians celebrate their fulfilled Passover also by an act of eating and drinking?

So Pilate went out to them and said, "What accusation do you bring against this man?" They answered him, "If this man were not an evil-doer, we would not have handed him over." Pilate said to them, "Take him yourselves and judge him by your own law." The Jews said to him, "It is not lawful for us to put any man to death." This was to fulfil the word which Jesus had spoken to show by what death he was to die. (18:29–32)

1183. Evaluate the two things Pilate says to the Jews here by the standards of legal justice.

1184. Evaluate the two replies the Jews make to Pilate here by the same standard.

H1185. How are both the Jews and Pilate doing the same thing in their dialogue with each other as Adam and Eve did in their dialogue with God after they ate the forbidden fruit?

E1186. Since the occupying Romans refused to grant to the Jews the right of capital punishment even when Jewish law mandated it, the Jews had to find a Roman-acceptable political excuse for having Jesus killed, since their motive was religious, not political: they accused him of blasphemy. How does that explain why their reply to Pilate's first question is so lame and vague?

1187. (A) Jewish execution for blasphemy was by stoning. Crucifixion was a Roman invention. How does that historical fact explain verse 32? (B) Why did Jesus suffer a Roman punishment for a Jewish crime?

E1188. Would you rather be stoned to death or crucified? Why?

Pilate entered the praetorium again and called Jesus, and said to him, "Are you the King of the Jews?" Jesus answered, "Do you say this of your own accord, or did others say it to you about me?" Pilate answered, "Am I a Jew? Your own nation and the chief priests have handed you over to me; what have you done?" (18:33–35)

1189. Count the number of times in this chapter Pilate re-enters the praetorium (Roman judgment hall or law court). Do you see any significance to that?

1190. Why does Pilate ask Jesus that question (v. 33)? What answer is he hoping to get?

1191. (A) Why doesn't Jesus answer Pilate's question with a simple Yes or No? (B) Jesus was a rabbi (teacher). Why does a rabbi always answer a question with another question? (C) Why is the best answer to that question "Why shouldn't a rabbi answer a question with another question?"?

1192. (A) Socrates and modern psychoanalysts have the same habit of teaching by questions rather than by answers. Why do they do that? (Pick either one.) (B) Does Jesus fit this pattern throughout his life or only now, at the end? (Hint: What is the very first thing Jesus says in John's Gospel?)

1193. Is there a way in which God does that same Socratic, rabbinic thing to us throughout our lives, every single day? (Hint: Viktor Frankl, in *Man's Search for Meaning*, noticed that in the Auschwitz death camp all his fellow prisoners asked the same question of life [or of God if they believed there was a God behind their lives]:

What is your meaning, life? What is the meaning of my suffering here? Why was I brought here? For what purpose? What good can possibly come of this horror? No one got a clear, direct answer to that question, but some of them made a 180-degree turn when they realized that it was life [or God] asking them that question, not vice versa, and they had to answer it, not in words but in deeds.)

1194. Why does Jesus ask Pilate this particular question ("Do you say this of your own accord, or did others say it to you about me?")? (Hint: Job 42:5 shows the difference between these two alternatives that Jesus distinguishes. It is the difference between theology [the objective, impersonal, universal truth about God that we learn from others, from teachers] and religion [the personal, subjective, individual, experienced relationship with God]. Hint no. 2: The Hebrew word for "truth", *emeth*, means "personal faithfulness, fidelity".)

H1195. (A) What does Pilate's answer ("Am I a Jew?") to Jesus' question ("Do you say this of your own accord, or did others say it to you about me?") reveal about what he is trying to do in this trial? (B) How does that hidden motivation compare with his duty as a judge or magistrate?

1196. This is a legal question. If anyone in this Bible study group is a lawyer, he should take this question. (A) Let's distinguish three aspects of people's lives: (1) what they do, (2) what they say, and (3) what they believe. Pilate asks Jesus question 1, "What have you done?" Is that the right question for a judge to ask? Why? (B) Are the Jews trying to get Jesus killed for what he has done (healing on the Sabbath?), or is it for what he said (calling them hypocrites?), or for what he believed (that he was God)? (C) Did the ancient Romans and/or Jews share our modern American notion of "freedom of speech"? (D) Do we ever legally punish public speech? If so, when? (E) Can the law judge and punish beliefs? (F) If not, is there any justification for the Spanish Inquisition?

Jesus answered, "My kingship is not of this world; if my kingship were of this world, my servants would fight, that I might not be handed over to the Jews; but my kingship is not from the world." (18:36)

1197. (A) When Jesus says his kingship is not "of" this world, he clearly means that it is not *from* this world. (That's what he says when he repeats this saying at the end of verse 36.) No one in this world crowned him king. He's not even a candidate for president! But is he also saying that his kingship is not *over* this world or about this world? (B) In order to answer that question, we need to know what he meant by "this world". As we saw in an earlier question, there are two Greek words translated "world". One is *gaia*, which means this place, this planet, the earth, or part of it; the other is *aion*, which means this time, this era or age or eon. Which of these two do you think it is here? (C) Why? (D) Could both meanings be implied?

1198. This-worldly kings (and their followers), even good ones, need to fight and wage war and have armies. Why doesn't Jesus (and his followers) fight in that way (with physical weapons like Peter's sword) to protect him?

1199. Is Jesus here saying that his followers also do not, or should not, fight in that way, i.e., (with physical weapons) to defend other things or people besides Jesus? Is Jesus teaching pacifism here? Why or why not?

1200. (A) Didn't Jesus come to earth to fight and conquer sin, death, hell, and Satan? Isn't that "spiritual warfare", i.e., fighting? Doesn't Saint Paul say we do fight, or wrestle, though not with flesh and blood enemies (Eph 6:12)? If so, how do you reconcile that with Jesus saying that his disciples do not fight? (B) To answer that question, why can't we simply contrast these two (Jesus and Paul) and buy into the popular view that Jesus was a nice, sweet, meek hippie pacifist and that Saint Paul spoiled his religion by being an angry, nasty, polemical, heretic-burning inquisitor? What is the textual evidence against that in the Bible?

Pilate said to him, "So you are a king?" Jesus answered, "You say that I am a king. For this I was born, and for this I have come into the world, to bear witness to the truth. Every one who is of the truth hears my voice." (18:37)

H1201. Why does Jesus answer Pilate's next question, "So you are a king?" with "You say that I am a king" (v. 36) when Pilate never did say that Jesus was a king, but only asked?

1202. Jesus says here that he "came into the world to bear witness to the truth". How did he do that? Was it primarily by his words? Many of his words (e.g., much of the Sermon on the Mount) can be found in the teachings of previous rabbis. Since most of Jesus' ethical and theological teachings were already in Judaism, what is "the truth" that Jesus alone could give us? (Hint: John 14:6 is the answer to that question.)

1203. (A) If John 14:6 is the answer to the above question, where and when did Jesus give us the truth that is himself? (B) All other sages and philosophers and mystics gave us their mind and said, "This is my mind." Jesus gave us his body and said, "This is my body." How is that "the truth"?

Pilate said to him, "What is truth?" (16:38)

1204. What is the almost-comic irony in this question to Jesus? (Remember Jn 14:6.)

1205. What do you think Pilate's tone of voice was when he asked this question?

1206. Be a creative actor. Pronounce these words "What is truth?" in three different ways, three different spirits, first Pilate's and then two others. See whether the others, who hear you, can detect what you are implying "between the lines".

1207. How does Pilate's question "What is truth?" (v. 38) relate to Hint no. 2 in question 1194?

1208. (A) What do these words of Pilate's reveal about his relationship to truth itself, truth as such, or truth in general? (B) What do his words reveal about his relationship to Christ? (C) How are those two relationships related?

After he had said this, he went out to the Jews again, and told them, "I find no crime in him. But you have a custom that I should release one man for you at the Passover; will you have me release for you the King of the Jews?" They cried out again, "Not this man, but Barabbas!" Now Barabbas was a robber. (18:38–40)

1209. (A) What game is Pilate trying to play? What irreconcilable forces is he trying to balance and satisfy and mollify? (B) Why does he not simply say "I find no crime in him" and let it go at that, ending the trial? (C) What is he hoping for in giving the Jews the choice between Jesus the King and Barabbas the robber? (D) What is the irony in their choosing their robber (who had robbed many of them) over their Savior?

1210. Go back to question 1208A: Do we sometimes play similar Pilate-like games (in lesser ways and for lesser stakes, of course)?

Then Pilate took Jesus and scourged him. And the soldiers plaited a crown of thorns, and put it on his head, and clothed him in a purple robe; they came up to him, saying, "Hail, King of the Jews!" and struck him with their hands. (19:1–3)

1211. (A) Who bears more responsibility for Jesus' scourging (whipping) and crucifixion, the soldiers who actually did these deeds or Pilate who told them to do it? (B) Why?

1212. Billions of Christians have recited, at least every Sunday, the Apostles' Creed and/or the Nicene Creed, both of which include the line "suffered under Pontius Pilate". If Pilate hears these billions of voices from hell (or purgatory, if you will), what do you think he feels?

1213. (A) Having felt safe and superior to Pilate in answering the last question, since you didn't hurt Jesus as Pilate did, how do you feel when you remember Jesus' saying "As you did it to one of the least of these my brethren, you did it to me" (Mt 25:40)? (B) What do you do about that? Look up the last line in the play "Judgment at Nuremberg."

1214. (A) If Jesus was destined to die anyway, why did (I) the Roman soldiers and (II) the Jews both enjoy adding to his torments by scourging and crowning him with thorns and sneering at him? (B) What state of soul must you be in, what attitude must you have, in order to *enjoy* watching someone else suffer? (C) What attitude does God have to our suffering? For the answer to that question, see the shortest verse in the Bible, John 11:35.

1215. What is the great irony in the *crown* of thorns and the purple (royal) robe?

E1216. Sometimes the concrete sensory imagination can teach us more than the abstract spiritual intellect. What do you feel when you imagine this scene, complete with sneering and spitting and slapping? What did you feel when you saw it in the movie *The Passion of the Christ*?

Pilate went out again, and said to them, "Behold, I am bringing him out to you, that you may know that I find no crime in him." So Jesus came out, wearing the crown of thorns and the purple robe. Pilate said to them, "Here is the man!" (19:4–5)

1217. "Pilate went out again."—How many times has Pilate done this? How many times has he tried some new ploy in this trial? Why does he keep trying?

1218. (A) What do Pilate's words "here is the man!" (or "behold the man") imply? (B) What is he hoping for? (C) Why didn't that happen?

When the chief priests and the officers saw him, they cried out, "Crucify him, crucify him!" Pilate said to them, "Take him yourselves and crucify him, for I find no crime in him." (19:6)

1219. (A) How many times has Pilate said "I find no crime in him"? (B) Why does he need to repeat it? (C) Why didn't that settle everything?

1220. (A) What is the implied relationship between the crowd and the chief priests and officers? (B) What does Matthew 27:40 add to this scene? (C) Is this a phenomenon that is typically pre-modern rather than modern? (D) Is it either more likely or less likely to be found in a democracy?

1221. Crucifixion was invented by the Romans, not the Jews. The Jews saw it (rightly) as a pagan and barbaric torture, especially when imposed on a Jew. Yet here their leaders passionately ask the pagan Roman Pilate, not just to take Jesus the Jew away or kill him, but to crucify him. Why do they hate Jesus so passionately? Were they just spectacularly wicked, or was there something about Jesus that explains why he divided mankind more radically than anyone else, into those who passionately loved him and those who passionately hated him?

The Jews answered him, "We have a law, and by that law he ought to die, because he has made himself the Son of God." (19:7)

1222. (A) How does this verse explain their passion? What kind of passion did the Jews have for their law? (B) Why is it hard for a modern person to understand that passion? (C) Could it even be said that in their minds this was a struggle between Jesus and the Mosaic law as two absolutes, almost two gods, or two saviors, two ways to the one God? (D) If so, why doesn't that (the fact that their passion was religious) excuse them? Weren't the Jews right, and even pious, to insist on applying the divinely revealed Mosaic law to Jesus? The law mandated capital punishment for blasphemy, and if Jesus was not God, as he claimed to be, then his was the worst and clearest case of blasphemy in history. So how can the Jews be faulted?

1223. How do these words disprove the popular idea (e.g., in *The Da Vinci Code*) that the dogma of Jesus' divinity was invented by the early Church, that Jesus never claimed to be divine and was killed for political reasons rather than religious reasons?

When Pilate heard these words, he was even more afraid; he entered the praetorium again and said to Jesus, "Where are you from?" But Jesus gave no answer. (19:8–9)

1224. (A) Why would these words of the Jews make Pilate "more afraid"? Of what is he now afraid? (B) So what does he do about it? (C) The first thing he does about it is to enter the praetorium again. He keeps going into and out of the praetorium like a yo-yo. Why is this not accidental but a perfect, visible symbol of what is happening in his soul?

1225. What does Pilate mean by his question "Where are you from?"

1226. (A) Why did Jesus give no answer? (B) Suppose he had?

Pilate therefore said to him, "You will not speak to me? Do you not know that I have power to release you, and power to crucify you?" Jesus answered him, "You would have no power over me unless it had been given you from above; therefore he who delivered me to you has the greater sin." (19:10–11)

1227. (A) What do you think Jesus' silence makes Pilate feel? (B) How does Pilate now deal with this problem of Jesus' frustrating silence? (C) Does it work? Does Pilate get what he wants?

H1228. (A) Why does Jesus' answer make Pilate try harder to release him? (B) Which part of Jesus' answer does that, the first part or the second part? (C) Why would the first part of Jesus' answer increase Pilate's fear? (D) Why would the second part lessen it? (E) (This part of the question is hard, and if you want to skip it or give it to someone else, feel free to do so.) Jesus connects the second part of his answer to the first part by a "therefore". But the first part increases Pilate's fear, and the second part decreases it. How can that be? "A therefore B" means that A is the reason for B; how can the reason for Pilate's increased fear also be the reason for his decreased fear? (Hint: The principle of a hierarchy of authority and the delegation of authority from above is presupposed in the answer to this question.) (F) Why is Judas' sin greater than Pilate's?

Upon this Pilate sought to release him, but the Jews cried out, "If you release this man, you are not Caesar's friend; every one who makes himself a king sets himself against Caesar." (19:12)

1229. (A) Why is Pilate now trying harder to release Jesus than before? (B) Why did he want to release him before, and why does he want to release him now? (C) Why is the second motive stronger than the first?

1230. (A) How is what the Jews say now the most effective thing they could possibly say to get Pilate to crucify Jesus? (B) Compare it with the reason they gave before (v. 7).

H1231. (A) Isn't what the Jews say here true? Didn't Jesus claim to be a king; in fact, isn't he literally the King of all kings? Why does that not set him against Caesar? (B) Or does it? Under what circumstances does it? (C) How do you reconcile Acts 5:29 ("We must obey God rather than men") with Romans 13:1 ("Let every person be subject to the governing authorities. For there is no authority except from God, and those that exist have been instituted by God")?

When Pilate heard these words, he brought Jesus out and sat down on the judgment seat at a place called The Pavement, and in Hebrew, Gabbatha. Now it was the day of Preparation of the Passover; it was about the sixth hour. He said to the Jews, "Here is your King!" They cried out, "Away with him, away with him, crucify him!" Pilate said to them, "Shall I crucify your King?" The chief priests answered, "We have no king but Caesar." (19:13–15)

1232. Why do these words make the indecisive and vacillating Pilate (the "yo-yo") suddenly more decisive now even though he is still trying to avoid crucifying Jesus?

1233. Why does John mention the exact place ("The Pavement", "Gabbatha") and time (the day and the hour) here?

1234. (A) With what tone of voice do you imagine Pilate said "Here is your King!" and "Shall I crucify your King?" (B) Why do you think he calls Jesus "King"? (Hint: Look at verse 12 again, and then verse 15.) (C) Why does he call him "*your* King"?

1235. What is the irony in verse 15? (Hint: Exactly who is saying this? Suppose you heard Jewish leaders in Nazi Germany crying out: "We have no Führer but Hitler!" What would you think?)

1236. Are there ways we, too, sometimes say "We have no king but Caesar"?

Then he handed him over to them to be crucified.
   So they took Jesus, and he went out, bearing his own cross, to the place called the place of a skull, which is called in Hebrew Golgotha. There they crucified him, and with him two others, one on either side, and Jesus between them. (19:16–18)

1237. (A) "He handed him over to them." Explore what that means. Didn't God the Father also "hand over" his Son to be crucified by putting him into our hands? How was that a different kind of "handing over" from Pilate's? (B) How was Judas' "handing over" Jesus a different kind of "handing over" from that of either God or Pilate? (C) "Handing over" is done by the hand. The hand is a bodily symbol of a more-than-bodily power, namely, authority (authority is not just power but the power of right and the right to use power), as the head is a symbol of intelligence and the heart a symbol of love. If all authority comes ultimately from God, did God hand over some of his authority to Caesar, who handed over some of his authority to Pilate, who handed over some of his authority to the Jewish priests in one way and the Roman soldiers in another way? Did God also hand over some of his authority to the priests of the Mosaic law that he instituted in Leviticus? If so, where did this chain of authority break down and become corrupt? (D) So who is responsible for the crucifixion of Jesus: Caesar, Pilate, the chief priests, the soldiers, or Judas?

1238. (A) Suppose Pilate or the chief priests or Judas had had to kill Jesus themselves instead of handing him over to the soldiers to do it. What difference would that have made? (B) What does that tell you about authority and its use and misuse? (C) Would you rather be the warden who pulls the switch on the electric chair or the judge who orders the execution? Would you rather be an infantryman or a general?

1239. Why did Jesus have to carry his own Cross?

1240. Why was the place of crucifixion called "the place of a skull"? (B) Why was it outside the holy city?

1241. This question has no one obvious right answer, for it requires you to try to guess some of the hidden designs of God's providence and to intuit what is most appropriate or fitting in a symbolic way, a kind of "poetic justice". (A) Why do you think God in his providence arranged for Jesus to be crucified between two thieves? (B) Why not alone? (C) Why not with one thief? (D) Why not with ten? (E) Why was he in the middle? (F) Why (as we learn in the other Gospels) did one of the two thieves repent, not both and not none?

Pilate also wrote a title and put it on the cross; it read, "Jesus of Nazareth, the King of the Jews." Many of the Jews read this title, for the place where Jesus was crucified was near the city; and it was written in Hebrew, in Latin, and in Greek. The chief priests of the Jews then said to Pilate,

"Do not write, 'The King of the Jews,' but, 'This man said, I am King of the Jews.' " Pilate answered, "What I have written I have written." (19:19-22)

1242. The sign on the Cross is mentioned in all four Gospels, and the wording is a little different in each version. Does that difference show that the Gospels are unreliable or reliable as historical documents?

1243. What is the irony in the sign?

1244. Hebrew, Latin, and Greek are the three languages, and the three cultures, that would last and that are the foundation for Western civilization. What does that show about (A) who is responsible for Christ's crucifixion and (B) those for whom Christ was crucified?

H1245. (A) What does it tell you about God and his providence that he arranged that sign? (B) We creatures can signify meanings with signs, i.e., with words and languages, which we make, but not with the things and events in the universe, which God makes. But God, in his divine providence, can signify and communicate and reveal to us truths by means of real things and events as well as by means of words. What are the consequences of this doctrine of divine providence concerning whether it is legitimate to interpret the things and events narrated in Scripture both literally and symbolically?

1246. (A) What is the difference between Pilate's version of the sign and the version the Jews demanded instead? (B) How is this also ironic?

1247. Why does Pilate now suddenly become stubborn instead of wishy-washy? What does it tell you about Pilate that he insisted on his version of the sign, even at the risk of offending the Jews, after being so afraid of offending them that he condemned to death a man he knew to be innocent?

When the soldiers had crucified Jesus they took his garments and made four parts, one for each soldier; also his tunic. But the tunic was without seam, woven from top to bottom; so they said to one another, "Let us not

*tear it, but cast lots for it to see whose it shall be." This was to fulfil the
Scripture,*

> *"They parted my garments among them,
> and for my clothing they cast lots." (19:23–24)*

1248. (A) John's account of Jesus' crucifixion contains many more specific details like this one than the accounts of any of the other three evangelists. Why? (B) How is the answer implied in 19:35? (C) How does 19:35 also tell you the importance of this question?

1249. (A) Matthew was one of Jesus' disciples, too; where was he when Jesus was crucified? (B) Mark probably got his information from Peter; where was Peter? (C) Luke, who was a Greek, not a Jew, and who probably became a Christian after these events, probably got much of his information from Mary (whom he mentions more often than the other three evangelists do); where was she?

1250. What is the symbolic value or point of the seamlessness of Jesus' tunic? What spiritual reality or truth might this seamlessness be taken to symbolize? (There is no single answer to this question; after giving one answer yourself, throw this question out for suggested answers by other people in the group.)

1251. What is the symbolic value or point of the fact that the soldiers gambled for the tunic?

1252. What is the point or importance of the fact that the life of Christ fulfilled many Old Testament prophecies like the one John quotes in verse 24?

E1253. Besides Jesus, what other person in history fulfilled as many specific prophecies that had been written centuries before him?

So the soldiers did this. But standing by the cross of Jesus were his mother, and his mother's sister, Mary the wife of Clopas, and Mary Magdalene. When Jesus saw his mother, and the disciple whom he loved standing near, he said to his mother, "Woman, behold, your son!" Then he said to the disciple, "Behold, your mother!" And from that hour the disciple took her to his own home. (19:25–27)

1254. (A) Men are supposed to be more courageous and to protect women. So why did the women who stayed with Jesus to the end outnumber the men three to one? (B) Where was Adam while Eve was being seduced by the serpent?

1255. Is there any possible significance to the fact that all three of these women bore the name Mary?

1256. Why do you suppose John calls himself "the disciple Jesus loved" rather than "John" throughout his Gospel?

1257. (A) What do Jesus' words here show about Jesus? (B) What do Jesus' words show about John? Why did Jesus select him for this task? (C) How important do you think that task was to Jesus? Why?

E1258. Is there any other man in history who got to choose his own mother when he came into the world?

1259. (A) Catholic and Orthodox Christians interpret these words of Jesus as giving his mother Mary not just to John but to all Christians as our spiritual mother and our ideal model of sanctity for the rest of time, to be taken into the home of our hearts just as John did. Is there any clear purely scriptural proof or disproof of this interpretation? (B) If so, where is it? If not, why, then, do Catholics and Orthodox believe it but Protestants do not (at least not today —Luther did)?

1260. (A) When Jesus said to Mary, "Behold, your son", what do you think Mary's reaction was? (B) When Jesus said to John, "Behold, your mother", what do you think John's reaction was?

1261. Mary is the only woman mentioned by name in the Qur'an. Muslims admire her perfect "surrender" to God at the Annunciation. Although Protestants reject what they regard as Catholic and Orthodox excesses when it comes to Mary, they also generally acknowledge her total surrender to God at the Annunciation. How do different ideas about Jesus' identity affect how one should think about Mary?

After this Jesus, knowing that all was now finished, said (to fulfil the Scripture), "I thirst." (19:28)

1262. What, exactly, is the "all" that was "finished"?

1263. Again John uses the formula "to fulfil the Scripture". Does that refer to Jesus' motive? Did Jesus say "I thirst", not because he was thirsty, but because he wanted to fulfill this prophecy? Compare Caiaphas' words in 11:49–51.

1264. (A) For what did Jesus thirst the most? Was it vinegar? (B) Can you do anything to help quench Jesus' thirst? (C) Google Mother Teresa of Calcutta's prayer by that title ("I thirst"). Read it aloud.

A bowl full of vinegar stood there; so they put a sponge full of the vinegar on hyssop and held it to his mouth. When Jesus had received the vinegar, he said, "It is finished"; and he bowed his head and gave up his spirit. (19:29–30)

1265. If the whole point of crucifixion was to instill fear through maximum pain, torture, and terror, why would they try to lessen that pain a little with vinegar (a mild painkiller and diversion)?

1266. Why would a Christian give a different answer from a non-Christian to the question in the title of the Southern spiritual, "Were You There When They Crucified My Lord?"

1267. Why does John use the active verb "gave up his spirit" rather than the passive "died"? What did Jesus mean when he said "I lay down my life. . . . No one takes it from me" (10:17–18)?

1268. (A) What, exactly, does it mean that Jesus "gave up his spirit"? Matthew uses the verb "yielded up his spirit" (Mt 27:50). Luke records that "Jesus, crying with a loud voice, said, 'Father, into your hands I commit my spirit.'" (Lk 23:46) Do all four expressions mean the same thing, or is there any slight difference? (B) Death seems to be the loneliest thing in life, for we lose all our friends in death, and even if we live together, we must die alone. How do Jesus' last words show that this is an illusion, that death is not an aloneness but an intimate interpersonal relationship?

1269. (A) Is this last moment of Jesus a unique way to die that is proper to Jesus alone (see the quotation in no. 1267), or do we have it in our power and choice to die in this way, also? (B) If so, what is the alternative way to die? (C) And if so, does that alternative way to die parallel and fulfill the alternative way to live? (D) What makes one of these alternatives better than the other? (This question is not as easy as it sounds; think of how an atheist would an-

swer it, or someone who dies in despair or unrepentant rebellion.)
(E) Think of the two thieves; what are the three ways to die that
are exemplified by the three crosses?

1270. Why does Jesus bow his head? Was that a deliberate act or
just an involuntary muscle movement? Suppose, instead, he had jut-
ted out his jaw?

1271. (A) The word "islam" means "surrender". The related word
"muslim" means "one who surrenders". Islam regards Jesus as a perfect "muslim" or one who submits to God. Christianity, of course,
affirms the same thing, but Christians, unlike Muslims, who deny
that Jesus really died, believe Jesus surrendered to the Father's will
that he suffer and die on the cross. How is Jesus shown to be the
perfect "surrenderer" here? (B) How was he the same in life as in
death? In other words, how did he live in the same "surrendering"
way he died? (C) Psalm 1 also defines the two opposite ways to
live: righteousness and wickedness, good and evil. What is the relationship between those two "ways" (good vs. evil) and the two
"ways" in question B (trusting surrender vs. untrusting rebellion)?

*Since it was the day of Preparation, in order to prevent the bodies from
remaining on the cross on the sabbath (for that sabbath was a high day),
the Jews asked Pilate that their legs might be broken, and that they might
be taken away. So the soldiers came and broke the legs of the first, and of
the other who had been crucified with him; but when they came to Jesus
and saw that he was already dead, they did not break his legs. But one of
the soldiers pierced his side with a spear, and at once there came out blood
and water. He who saw it has borne witness—his testimony is true, and
he knows that he tells the truth—that you also may believe. For these
things took place that the Scripture might be fulfilled, "Not a bone of him
shall be broken." And again another Scripture says, "They shall look
on him whom they have pierced." (19:31-37)*

1272. Why did breaking the legs of the crucified hasten their death?
(Ask your physician.)

1273. (A) Why did the Jews regard it as sacrilege to have bodies on
the cross during the Sabbath? (B) Why do nearly all cultures see the

burial of human corpses as a sacred obligation? (Use your intuition here rather than your practical, scientific, calculating mind.)

1274. Another specific fulfillment of a specific scriptural prophecy! Do you see any symbolic significance to this one?

1275. How did the fact that not just blood but also "water" (peritoneal fluid) came out of Jesus' chest cavity when pierced by the lance prove that Jesus was dead? (Again, ask your physician.)

1276. Do you see any symbolic significance to the blood and water?

1277. How carefully do we inspect the victims of capital punishment to be sure they are dead? How careful were the Romans about not botching a crucifixion, especially in religiously sensitive and riot-prone Judea?

1278. John uses a legal formula in verse 35, certifying this as eyewitness testimony. Why is that important? Why does he say that he says this so "that you also may believe"? What might the reader believe instead if this formula was missing? (Hint: If Jesus didn't really rise from death, what are the consequences for the Christian faith, according to Paul in 1 Corinthians 15:14–19? [Read it again!] And if Jesus did not really die, could he have risen?)

1279. Pursue this thought-experiment for a moment: imagine Jesus did not really die on the Cross and that the soldiers and John were mistaken. What happens next if they bury (in grave clothes that surround him like "swaddling" surrounding a baby) a living man instead of a corpse, and this man then recovers, escapes from his grave clothes, carefully folds them, pushes away the great stone at the door of the tomb all by himself, overcomes armed Roman guards, and appears to his disciples forty-eight hours later as the glorious God-man "risen from the dead" rather than a staggering, half-dead victim of a botched crucifixion badly in need of medical attention? Is that easier or harder to believe than the miracle of a resurrection? In light of the historical data, does it take more faith to believe in the Resurrection or to disbelieve?

After this Joseph of Arimathea, who was a disciple of Jesus, but secretly, for fear of the Jews, asked Pilate that he might take away the body of

Jesus, and Pilate gave him leave. So he came and took away his body.
(19:38)

1280. (A) Why do you think Joseph of Arimathea now, after Jesus'
death, comes forward and publicly reveals the fact that he was a
disciple of Jesus, which he had previously hidden from the Jews?
(B) Do you see any similarity between this sudden change into
forthrightness and Pilate's stubborn refusal to change the inscrip-
tion on Christ's Cross ("What I have written I have written")?
Or are the two cases quite different? What do you guess are the
psychological forces that are operating here?

1281. (A) Do you think it would have been morally better for
Joseph from the beginning not to have concealed the fact that he
was a disciple of Jesus and to have endured the consequences of
excommunication from the Jews? (B) Whom do you admire more,
a secret disciple of Jesus or an open opponent of Jesus? Why? (C)
We do not know whether Joseph of Arimathea had a family, but if
he did, his excommunication would have ruined their reputation as
well as his and probably much of their income; do you think that
would have changed the morality of the situation?

Nicodemus also, who had at first come to him by night, came bringing a
mixture of myrrh and aloes, about a hundred pounds' weight. They took
the body of Jesus and bound it in linen cloths with the spices, as is the
burial custom of the Jews. (19:39–40)

1282. Now a second secret disciple comes out into the open,
Nicodemus, who earlier came to Jesus "by night" for fear of the
Jews (Jn 3:1–2). Why does Jesus' death bring out the best in such
people?

1283. (A) These burial spices were also massive (one hundred
pounds!) and fairly expensive, but not unusual. Why did the Jews
spend so much money on their dead? (Hint: There are two answers
to this question. One is a very simple and physical explanation, but
there is also a religious one.) (B) Compare the Jews' attitude toward their dead with what you know of the attitude of the ancient
Egyptians.

1284. Where is this linen burial cloth today? (Someone might do a little fascinating research on its history.)

1285. If Joseph and Nicodemus (or others) had not buried Jesus, what would the Romans have done with his dead body?

1286. Where is Jesus' body now?

Now in the place where he was crucified there was a garden, and in the garden a new tomb where no one had ever been laid. So because of the Jewish day of Preparation, as the tomb was close at hand, they laid Jesus there. (19:41–42)

1287. What is fitting or symbolic about the fact that Jesus' tomb was in a garden?

1288. What is fitting or symbolic about the fact that Jesus' tomb was new? Why do you think John added this detail?

1289. Why did they have to hurry to bury Jesus' body some place close by? What was their deadline?

H1290. The story certainly seems to be over now. Suppose it was. How would the future of mankind have been radically changed if John's Gospel had ended with these words? Let your imagination roam on this one.

1291. On a number of occasions, Jesus clearly told his disciples that he would be handed over to the chief priests and be killed and that he would rise again on the third day. Why were his disciples not expecting that? Why were they cowering behind locked doors in the upper room? He had told them that he would rise, but the Gospel says (Mk 9:32), not that they understood what he said and did not believe it, but that they "did not understand" what he said. Why?

John 20

Now on the first day of the week, Mary Magdalene came to the tomb early, while it was still dark, and saw that the stone had been taken away from the tomb. So she ran, and went to Simon Peter and the other disciple, the one whom Jesus loved, and said to them, "They have taken the Lord out of the tomb, and we do not know where they have laid him." (20:1–2)

1292. Why is it Mary Magdalene who comes to the tomb first?

1293. In Jewish courts of law at the time, women's testimony was inadmissible evidence. If Jesus' disciples invented a lie or a myth about his Resurrection, why would they have made up a story to which women were the first witnesses?

1294. Is there a fitting or symbolic value to the fact that Mary comes in the dark?

1295. What do you think she felt when she saw the stone removed?

1296. Frank Morison was an atheist and a scientific historian who attempted to refute the central Christian claim of a literal resurrection of Jesus by purely rational scientific, textual, historical, and forensic arguments. After years of research, he came to the conclusion that the only possible explanation for all the data we have is that Jesus really did rise; and he became a Christian. His book about this investigation, *Who Moved the Stone?*, has been in print for almost a century now. (A) Why do you think he used that title? Why is the taken-away stone so important? (B) What are the possible answers to the question in that title? (There are four obvious possibilities.) (C) How likely is each one?

1297. Another similar question to which it is hard to give a convincing answer is "What happened to Jesus' body if he didn't really rise from the dead?" What are the possible alternative answers to that question?

1298. (A) Why did Mary Magdalene run? (B) Why did she go to Peter and John?

1299. Whom do you think she meant by the "they" who she thought took Jesus' body in verse 2?

1300. What does Mary's use of "we" instead of "I" in verse 2 imply?

Peter then came out with the other disciple, and they went toward the tomb. They both ran, but the other disciple outran Peter and reached the tomb first; and stooping to look in, he saw the linen cloths lying there, but he did not go in. Then Simon Peter came, following him, and went into the tomb; he saw the linen cloths lying, and the napkin, which had been on his head, not lying with the linen cloths but rolled up in a place by itself. Then the other disciple, who reached the tomb first, also went in, and he saw and believed. (20:3–8)

1301. Why are Peter and John running? What do you think they felt at that moment?

1302. Why did John outrun Peter? (Hint: John was the last apostle to die; most scholars think that he probably wrote the Book of Revelation in the final decade of the first century.)

1303. If John arrived at the tomb first, why did he stop and wait for Peter before he went in?

1304. Some medieval theologians interpret this passage allegorically (not to deny that it also happened literally), with Peter symbolizing faith and John symbolizing reason. Can you explain that allegory?

1305. Why is John so careful and detailed about the two separate piles of burial cloths?

1306. It is John who tells the story of "Doubting Thomas", who would not believe until he saw, in this chapter. Is John in verse 8 saying that he too, like Thomas, was so weak in faith that he did not believe until he saw?

For as yet they did not know the Scripture, that he must rise from the dead. (20:9)

1307. Once again, as with question 1291, we have this strange statement that none of the disciples expected that the Resurrection was going to happen. Here the explanation was that they did not "know" the Scriptures. This meant, not they were ignorant of the texts— all the Jews knew their Scriptures far better than most modern Christians do—but that they did not understand it. (A) Compare the prophecies of the Resurrection in the Jewish Scriptures (which Christians call the Old Testament) with the words of Jesus predicting his Resurrection. Compare the *clarity* of these two things. (B) Why do you think God was so deliberately unclear in the Scriptures about that? Would the Jews have "gotten" the point if God had been as clear in the Scriptures as Jesus was to his disciples? Did his disciples get it? Cf. Jesus' words in the parable about the rich man and Lazarus (Lk 16:19–31, especially verse 31).

H1308. To see God's strategy in being deliberately ambiguous, look at the two words "enemies" and "kingdom" in the Old Testament. The prophets had said that the Messiah, who would establish "the kingdom of God", would save Israel from its "enemies". Most Jews of Jesus' time interpreted their "enemies" as the Romans and the "kingdom" as a political one, like the kingdom under David and Solomon. Why? Because their answer to Jesus' first question, "What do you seek?" (Jn 1:38), was essentially worldly success and power. That is why they did not recognize the apolitical Jesus as their Savior. (That was quite possibly why Judas betrayed him.) They did not understand because it was not just their minds but their hearts that were darkened. But those who were wise enough to know that their enemies were their own sins and that the Messiah's kingdom would rule hearts rather than politics did recognize Jesus as the Messiah. Review questions 139–48 on how Jesus tests hearts with his questions and how what the mind sees depends on what the heart loves. Now summarize this whole complex and deep point in a few simple words, and apply it to the puzzle of why Jesus' disciples did not understand the Resurrection (v. 9).

Then the disciples went back to their homes.
  But Mary stood weeping outside the tomb. (20:10–11)

1309. How is the contrast between Mary and the disciples significant here?

1310. This is a rather long question, with many parts, but they all hang together, so it is best for a single person to try to answer all of them. (A) Compare 20:10 with 21:3. (B) What would you have done if you were one of the apostles at this point? (C) Compare also the question the apostles asked Jesus in Acts 1:6, especially in light of Acts 1:3–5. Why must this rank among the most stupid questions ever asked? (D) Is John's portrait of himself and the other apostles, here and in many other places in his Gospel, self-serving and flattering? If he had been writing a myth, would he have made all his male heroes such dummies? (E) Why did Jesus select such people to be his apostles? (Did he have any alternatives?)

And as she wept she stooped to look into the tomb; and she saw two angels in white, sitting where the body of Jesus had lain, one at the head and one at the feet. (20:11–12)

1311. (A) In Matthew's Gospel, only one angel is mentioned, but two women (Mt 28:1–8). In Mark, there are three women, and the angel is described as "a young man" (Mk 16:1–5). In Luke, the humans are simply "they", and the angels are "two young men . . . in dazzling apparel" (Lk 24:1–4). Do such differences make the story more or less credible, by the standards of human credibility on the part of witnesses in court? (B) Imagine yourself at this scene; what do you think you might say you saw? (Remember that the usual reaction to seeing a real angel is one that the angel addresses by the words "Fear not.")

1312. (A) Why do you suppose angels are always described as being in white? (B) Why "dazzling"? (Compare ghosts, which also often appear white but not "dazzling". What does this physical detail *signify*?)

1313. (A) If angels are pure spirits without bodies, why do you suppose they usually appear to humans in human form? (B) What practical consequence follows from this fact? (See Heb 13:2.)

1314. (A) How often do angels appear in the Bible? (B) At what kinds of occasions?

1315. Do you see any significance or symbolism in the fact that one angel is where Jesus' head had been and the other where his feet had been?

They said to her, "Woman, why are you weeping?" She said to them, "Because they have taken away my Lord, and I do not know where they have laid him." (20:13)

1316. (A) Why was Mary weeping because Jesus' body had apparently been removed? Why was Jesus' dead body now so important to her? (B) Wouldn't you expect that her answer to the angels' question would have been "Because they *crucified* my Lord"?

Saying this, she turned round and saw Jesus standing, but she did not know that it was Jesus. (20:14)

H1317. (A) Why, in nearly every one of Jesus' post-Resurrection appearances to those who knew and loved him best, did they not recognize him at first? If there was nothing different about him after the Resurrection, would this have happened? (B) But in each case they then did recognize him when he spoke or acted. If there was nothing the same about him after the Resurrection, would this have happened? (C) In each case (Lk 24:13–32; 36–43; Jn 20:11–16), how and when did they recognize him? What is the common cause in each case of their recognition? (D) How does that (your answer to question C) help us to recognize his presence in our lives today?

1318. In comparing the four accounts of Jesus' post-Resurrection appearances, why does the fact that Luke was (a) a Greek, (b) a physician, and (c) the only one of the four who claims that his account is "orderly" and "followed all things closely" (Lk 1:3) explain why he often observes more details than the others do?

1319. (A) What were the two ways Jesus' disciples recognized him in Luke's account of the disciples on the road to Emmaus? (Lk 24:30–32)? (B) How does that apply to Christians in all times?

Jesus said to her, "Woman, why are you weeping? Whom do you seek?" (20:15)

1320. Jesus certainly knew why Mary was weeping, so why did he ask?

1321. Compare his question here with the first words he spoke in John's Gospel (1:38). How does Jesus' question have the same meaning here as it did there, and how does it have a somewhat different meaning?

Supposing him to be the gardener, she said to him, "Sir, if you have carried him away, tell me where you have laid him, and I will take him away." (20:15)

1322. (A) Our "supposings" or expectations color what we see. How much? Make it a multiple-choice question, choose your answer, and defend it: (a) totally, (b) a lot more than we suppose it does, (c) a little more than we suppose it does, (d) as much as we suppose it does, (e) a little less than we suppose it does, (f) a lot less than we suppose it does, (g) not at all. (B) Give one other example, from fact or fiction, of a case of mistaken identity like this to illustrate your answer.

H1323. Why do we always refer to the newly dead body of a loved one as "him" or "her" even when we know that it is only his or her body and that he or she is now gone from this world?

1324. If this had been the gardener, if he had taken Jesus' body away, if he had told Mary where he had laid it, and if he had given the body to Mary, what would Mary have done?

1325. (A) Following up on question 1324, would Mary's deep and heartfelt remembrance and love for Jesus have been enough to get Christianity moving through the history of the world? If Jesus had not really risen from the dead, would a mere human loving memory of the greatest man who ever lived have sufficed to motivate martyrs and missionaries? (B) Why or why not?

H1326. This is a longer and more detailed version of question 1325B. If the answer to question 1325B is in 1 Corinthians 15:12–19, you might want to go through and explain each of these seven consequences of a non-resurrection that Paul lists there (two in v. 14 one in v. 15, two in v. 16, one in v. 17, and one in v. 18).

1327. In light of the answer to the two previous questions, what could the "liberal" or "modernist" theologian Rudolf Bultmann, the founder of "demythologizing", and his followers (who still abound today, e.g., in the so-called "Jesus Seminar") possibly mean by saying that "If the bones of the dead Jesus were to be found in some Palestinian tomb tomorrow, all the essentials of Christianity would remain unchanged"?

Jesus said to her, "Mary." She turned and said to him in Hebrew, "Rabboni!" (which means Teacher). (20:16)

1328. Why is this single word the most profound and powerful one Jesus could have spoken now?

1329. (A) Why does Mary call him "Rabboni" here? (B) What did she call him when she told the disciples he was risen (Jn 20:18)? (C) What did John call him when he saw him (Jn 21:7)? (D) What did John call him when he wrote about him (Jn 20:31)? (E) What did "Doubting Thomas" call him (Jn 20:28)? (F) What do you call him?

Jesus said to her, "Do not hold me, for I have not yet ascended to the Father." (20:17)

H1330. What did Jesus mean by "do not hold me"? How does the context tell you?

1331. Are there ways in which we too can try to "hold" him? (Cf. Jn 16:6-7; Acts 1:10-11.)

1332. How do you know he didn't mean simply "Do not touch me"? (See Mt 28:9; Lk 24:39; Jn 20:27.)

"But go to my brethren and say to them, I am ascending to my Father and your Father, to my God and your God." (20:17)

E1333. He says we should not "hold" him; we should not stop the unrolling film, which must go on to his Ascension. If all of human history is only the prelude to Jesus' birth, and Jesus' birth is only the prelude to Jesus' life, and Jesus' life is only the prelude to Jesus' crucifixion and death, and Jesus' death is only the prelude to Jesus' Resurrection, and Jesus' Resurrection is only the prelude to Jesus' Ascension, and Jesus' Ascension is only the prelude to the descent of the Holy Spirit on the Church, and the descent of the Holy Spirit on the Church, and all her history, is only the prelude to Jesus' Second Coming, then to what is the Second Coming the prelude? When do we get to hear the symphony?

1334. (A) What is the connection between Christ saying we are his brethren and saying that his Father is our Father? (B) Is this a mere metaphor, or is it literally true? (C) Can it be literally true if it is not biological? (D) Which kind of fatherhood defines the other one: divine fatherhood or biological fatherhood?

1335. (A) Why does Jesus call the Father both "my Father and your Father"? (B) When did God become Christ's Father? (C) When did God become your Father? (D) In the early Church, catechumens were told they had the right to pray the Our Father only after they were baptized. Why?

H1336. (A) If Christ is God, how can he call the Father "my God"? (B) How can Christ say in John 14:28 that "the Father is greater than I" if he is equal to the Father? Greater in what way? (C) How does the context of both passages, here and in John 14:28, explain this? Does his forthcoming Ascension help to answer the question?

H1337. (A) The Bible often uses vertical-vs.-horizontal imagery. For instance, Eve is horizontal, not vertical, to Adam; she was not taken from Adam's head, to be his lord, or his feet, to be his servant, but from his side, to be his equal. But the New Jerusalem comes "down" from heaven in Revelation 21, and the Tower of Babel (Gen 11), which tried to lift itself "up" to heaven, falls down. We "look up to our superiors". So what is suggested by the vertical imagery of Jesus ascending "up" to the Father, not down or sideways? (B) Suppose he had departed downward into the ground; how would the whole Christian religion be radically changed? (C) Suppose he had sailed away over the sea?

Mary Magdalene went and said to the disciples, "I have seen the Lord";
and she told them that he had said these things to her. (20:18)

1338. (A) Can we say what Mary said here? (B) If so, how? (C)
Why are both of the following answers insufficient? Answer no. 1:
No, because we never saw Jesus and Jesus never spoke to us. We
were born two thousand years later. Answer no. 2: We "saw" him
in the same way as we "saw" Lincoln: by reading about him in
history books; and he "spoke" to us in the same way as Lincoln's
words speak to us today: because we feel different after we read his
inspiring words, like the Sermon on the Mount or the Gettysburg
Address.

On the evening of that day, the first day of the week, the doors being shut
where the disciples were, for fear of the Jews, Jesus came and stood among
them and said to them, "Peace be with you." (20:19)

1339. (A) The first day of the week was not the Jewish Sabbath.
Why did it become the Christian Sabbath? (B) On whose authority
was one of the Ten Commandments (Ex 20:10) changed?

1340. (A) Can we also interpret these locked doors symbolically?
How do we also often sit behind doors that are shut? (B) What
does God do about this? (Rev 3:7)

1341. (A) What were they afraid of? (B) How strong is that fear?
(C) What is stronger? (Cf. 1 Jn 4:18.)

1342. (A) Why did Jesus speak the word "peace" rather than some
other word on this occasion? (B) How was this more than a mere
wish, like "Have a nice day"? What power was in his word? (Compare Jn 20:21–22.) (C) What is the connection between peace and
the Holy Spirit? (See Gal 5:22.)

When he had said this, he showed them his hands and his side. Then
the disciples were glad when they saw the Lord. (20:20)

1343. (A) Why did he show them his hands and his side rather than
just his face? (B) Why did this make them glad? Did they doubt

it was he? (C) Why will the sight of his hands and side make you glad in heaven?

1344. Someone (I do not remember who, but it sounds like Mother Teresa) said that Jesus continues to show us his hands and his side in every single human being we ever meet. What do you think she meant? Was it an exaggeration? Sentimentalism?

Jesus said to them again, "Peace be with you. As the Father has sent me, even so I send you." (20:21)

1345. Why does he have to repeat "Peace be with you"?

H1346. How are the two "sendings" the same? The Father "sends" Jesus out from himself eternally within the Trinity, as his *Logos*, Word, or Mind; but Jesus sends us out temporally in the world; so how can that be the same? And Jesus was sent to us from heaven, "downward", so to speak; but he sends us out "horizontally", from earth and time, so how can that be the same?

1347. (A) Are all Christians thus "sent" as missionaries, or only the apostles? (B) How do you know?

And when he had said this, he breathed on them, and said to them, "Receive the Holy Spirit. If you forgive the sins of any, they are forgiven; if you retain the sins of any, they are retained." (20:22–23)

1348. Here is a verse about which the different churches (Protestant vs. Catholic and Orthodox) differ. (A) What do you think it means? Do you think it might possibly mean exactly what it says it means? (B) There are two questions here: First, did Jesus mean it literally? Second, did he intend this power to be passed on by the apostles to the successors they ordained ("bishops" or "presbyters")? What different theological beliefs follow from different answers to these two questions? (C) How do you think we should try to find the answer to the question of what Jesus meant here? What method should we use? What should we look at to find the answer? Where is our data? (D) How do you think we should try to find the answer to the question of whether Jesus intended this power to be passed on? What method should we use, and at what data should we look to answer that question?

H1349. If they received the Holy Spirit on this occasion, what did Pentecost add?

H1350. (A) How does "breath" mean more than merely the moving of molecules of air? (B) Why do you think the very same word (*ruah'* in Hebrew, *pneuma* in Greek) means "air", "breath", "life", and "spirit"? (C) We moderns wonder how the same word can mean both something physical and something spiritual. People in pre-modern societies, like ancient Israel, did not. Why do you suppose that is so?

Now Thomas, one of the Twelve, called the Twin, was not with them when Jesus came. So the other disciples told him, "We have seen the Lord." But he said to them, "Unless I see in his hands the print of the nails, and place my finger in the mark of the nails, and place my hand in his side, I will not believe." (20:24–25)

1351. Use your imagination for this one. If Thomas was called the Twin, what do you think happened to his twin brother? Could you imagine the plot of a novel about him?

1352. Why do you think Thomas was not with the other apostles when Jesus first came?

1353. Most of us have both good and bad points, virtues and vices, strengths and weaknesses, wisdoms and follies. Do you see both in what Thomas says here? (Thomas has always been known as "Doubting Thomas", but Thomas was an apostle, a believer, and a saint, so he must have had some pretty strong good points, too.)

H1354. Many people say, "Seeing is believing." But of course it isn't; faith always goes out to something more than what is seen, for what is seen immediately impresses itself on our mind as indubitable. (A) So what do you think is the relation between faith and sight, or faith and data? Is faith simply a leap in the dark, or is it a leap in partial light? (B) If the latter, how much light, how much sight, how much data, do you have to have in order to believe? For instance, imagine Romeo proposing marriage and elopement to Juliet. On the one hand, he is not a total stranger, but, on the other hand, he does not prove, with dozens of lawyers, psychologists, and philosophers, that Juliet must accept his offer. Just where between these two extremes does faith lie? Or is that the wrong question? (C) All religions require faith, but how would a Christian give a different answer from what a Muslim, a Hindu, or a Buddhist would give to the question of how much data, and especially what kind of data, motivates the believer to believe? (D) How is this difference dependent on the fact that the object of the Christian's faith is different from the object of faith for these others? (What *is* the object of a Christian's faith? [If you get the answer to that question wrong, you should hang your head in shame.])

Eight days later, his disciples were again in the house, and Thomas was with them. The doors were shut, but Jesus came and stood among them, and said, "Peace be with you." (20:26)

1355. Why do you think Thomas was with them this time?

1356. Why were the doors still shut?

1357. What doors can keep Jesus out?

Then he said to Thomas, "Put your finger here, and see my hands; and put out your hand, and place it in my side; do not be faithless, but believing." (20:27)

1358. Why are we surprised at how compassionately and almost compromisingly Jesus comes down to Thomas' level and meets his demands? What does that say about our understanding of Jesus?

1359. Is Jesus now saying that for Thomas, at least, "seeing *is* believing"? How could Thomas *not* believe what his eyes have seen and his hands have touched?

1360. Read the first three verses of John's First Letter (1 Jn 1:1–3). Why might John have had this exact scene in mind when he wrote that letter?

1361. How much of a free choice do we have to be either "faithless" or "believing"?

1362. (A) What makes the difference in this choice? What makes someone decide to believe? (B) How many different kinds of answers are there to that question for different people?

1363. Is it possible for us to sort out and distinguish the role of divine grace and of human motives and reasons in this choice to be "not faithless but believing"?

Thomas answered him, "My Lord and my God!" (20:28)

1364. This is the most explicit act of faith in the Bible. It came from "Doubting Thomas". Do you see any connection between these two facts?

1365. Why did Thomas say "My Lord and my God"? Wouldn't "Lord God" have been enough?

1366. On what occasion(s) is this prayer a fitting one for us to pray?

1367. (A) Compare this five-word formula with the three-word formula that was probably the first Christian creed, "Jesus is Lord" (1 Cor 12:3). (B) How is this the central and most distinctive belief that separates all Christians from all non-Christians? Why does believing this make you a Christian and not believing it make you not to be one?

1368. "Jesus is Lord" contains the same word Thomas uses here in addressing Jesus, the word "Lord" (*Kyrios*). (A) What does the word "lord" mean? (B) Why couldn't this creed (1 Cor 12:3) or Thomas' confession be interpreted simply as referring to an earthly lord, like Caesar? (C) How is Jesus' lordship different from all earthly lordship? Of course no other lord is divine, and that is the difference *in him*, but what difference does that make to his relation to us, his lordship over us? (See Jn 13:12–16.) (D) Connect 20:28 with 19:15.

H1369. (A) How does Thomas' confession implicitly contain not only the dogma of Jesus' divinity but also every dogma taught by Scripture and the Church, insofar as the Church speaks with his authority, which he gave to his apostles (Lk 10:16)? (B) Look up the word "dogma" in a theological dictionary. How does the meaning given there differ from the popular use of the word?

Jesus said to him, "You have believed because you have seen me. Blessed are those who have not seen and yet believe." (20:29)

1370. (A) Jesus implies in this verse that believing because you see is second best to believing even though you have not seen. Does Jesus accept a second best from us? (B) Is he pleased with it? (C) Is he satisfied with it? (D) Compare Jesus with a "hard" earthly father and with a "soft" earthly father. Which is hard to please and hard to satisfy? Which is easy to please and easy to satisfy? Which is easy to please and hard to satisfy?

E1371. How many Christians, after Jesus' Ascension, are in the category of those who have not seen and yet believe?

1372. (A) Do you think you would be more "blessed" if God gave you a mystical experience in which you actually saw Jesus with your eyes? (B) If you think Yes, does Jesus contradict that thought here? (C) If so, why do we so naturally think that thought? (D) Here is a similar question: Why do we think that it would be better for us if Jesus had not left this world visibly by his Ascension and given us the invisible Holy Spirit instead? (See Jn 16:7.) H(E) Why isn't that thought true? Why is it better for us to have the Holy Spirit invisibly than to have Jesus visibly in the flesh? Why does Jesus speak the truth in John 16:7?

1373. Is there any other way for us to "see" Jesus? (See Heb 2: 8–9.)

1374. How is faith an "eye"?

1375. How do you get that "eye"?

Now Jesus did many other signs in the presence of the disciples, which are not written in this book. (20:30)

1376. Why has no author, however pious and however brilliant and however imaginative, ever written a successful novel imagining these other things that Jesus said and did? Why do all attempts at imaginative historical fiction about Jesus fall flat on their face? (This may sound like a very hard and mysterious question, but the answer is really a very simple and obvious one.)

1377. (A) The last verse of chapter 21 (v. 25) says just about the same thing as the next-to-last verse of chapter 20 (v. 30). Does that make it more or less likely that chapter 21 (or at least its last few verses), was added by an author other than John? (B) See also 21:24: does its distinction between "we" and "he" speak to this question?

1378. (A) Might some of the stories about Jesus in the apocryphal gospels that the Church rejected as not canonical and not infallible divine revelation nevertheless be true? (B) Aren't myths often mixtures of fact and fiction? (C) Is there any way of telling which are true and which are not?

But these are written that you may believe that Jesus is the Christ, the Son of God, and that believing you may have life in his name. (20:31)

1379. In what sense is this the most important verse in the book?

E1380. Many scholars have written many books and articles on why John wrote his Gospel. Why are they all superfluous?

1381. John admits that he wrote this book, not out of a strictly impersonal, scientific curiosity, but for a very personal reason: to persuade readers to believe in Christ. Some modern writers say that this makes the book "propaganda" and "subjective" rather than "objective" and, therefore, not to be trusted. How would you answer this objection?

E1382. (A) There are two Greek words for "life", as we saw in Jesus' talk with Nicodemus in chapter 3. (Review them if you have forgotten them.) Which one do you think is used here? (B) Why?

1383. (A) What is the connection between belief (the cause) and heaven or eternal life (the effect)? Why should belief determine whether you go to heaven or hell? Isn't that like a father saying to his son, "If you believe some very strange things about me—that I am from another planet and seven thousand years old—then I will give you the thing you want the most, a very expensive red Jaguar convertible"? The connection between the cause and the effect in John's formula might seem as arbitrary as the one in the Jaguar parable. Can you explain it? (B) Hint: What does "faith" mean in the Gospels? Is it merely a mental opinion? (C) Hint no. 2: Why do lovers require "faith" of each other? (D) Why does God wait for our consent to his spiritual marriage proposal?

1384. (A) What two things does John say here that we must believe about Jesus? (B) What does "Christ" mean? (C) How does "Son of God" mean divinity? (Hint: What do all fathers give to all their children even before they give education, love, time, attention, etc., and even if they do not give those things?) (D) But aren't we all sons and daughters of God, whether we believe or not?

1385. What does "in his name" mean? Is it a verbal formula, like a password on a computer? (Hint no. 1: When a poor man with a billionaire father tries to cash a million dollar check in his own name, what happens? When he cashes it in his father's name, what happens? Hint no. 2: Why do exorcisms work only "in Jesus' name"?)

After this Jesus revealed himself again to the disciples by the Sea of Tiberias; and he revealed himself in this way. Simon Peter, Thomas called the Twin, Nathanael of Cana in Galilee, the sons of Zebedee, and two others of his disciples were together. Simon Peter said to them, "I am going fishing." They said to him, "We will go with you." They went out and got into the boat; but that night they caught nothing. (21:1–3)

1386. (A) Does Jesus keep revealing himself today, or is revelation finished? (B) If he does, name at least two ways in which his revelation is different today from what it was when he was physically on earth. If he does not, then how can we meet him today, as distinct from just reading about him in a book as we read about dead people?

1387. (A) Why was the Sea of Galilee renamed the Sea of Tiberias? (B) Why is that important enough for a question in a Bible study? (C) Why are names important? (Remember "in the name of . . .")

1388. Why is Peter always mentioned first whenever a list of the apostles is given in the Gospels?

1389. (A) Who were "the sons of Zebedee"? (B) Why doesn't John name them?

1390. (A) Do you see anything lame and lacking in Peter's "I'm going fishing"? (B) If you had been one of the apostles, what would you have said and done at this time? (C) Why didn't they go out and tell the world the amazing "good news" that Jesus the Messiah had risen from the dead?

1391. Do you see anything symbolic in the fact that they caught nothing that night?

Just as day was breaking, Jesus stood on the beach; yet the disciples did not know that it was Jesus. (21:4)

1392. Why do you think Jesus waited until the day was breaking?

1393. Do you see anything symbolic in Jesus standing on the beach while the apostles are out at sea?

1394. Why do you think the apostles did not recognize Jesus? Was it because of something in him, something in them, or both?

1395. (A) Jesus had said of his sheep, "I know my own and my own know me." How do we "know" him today? (B) Where do we fail to "know" him the most often? (Hint: Mt 25:45.)

Jesus said to them, "Children, have you any fish?" They answered him, "No." He said to them, "Cast the net on the right side of the boat, and you will find some." So they cast it, and now they were not able to haul it in, for the quantity of fish. (21:5–6)

1396. Why does Jesus call them "children"?

1397. (A) Is Jesus asking for fish? Does he need fish? (B) Is Jesus asking us for our fish, our "stuff"? (C) If so, why, if he does not need it? If not, what is he asking for, then?

1398. (A) Our fish is part of our "stuff", our physical possessions. Jesus obviously does not need our "stuff". Does Jesus care if we get "fish" (stuff) or not? (B) Why or why not? (C) Does he tell us how to "fish" for "stuff"? (D) Does he tell us how to fish for anything else? (Cf. Mk 1:17.)

1399. (A) When he gives us "fish", as he did to his apostles, how generous is he; how much does he give? (B) When he gives us something more than fish, how generous is he? (C) Can we believe this is happening also when we are apparently failing and poor and weak and suffering? (D) If so, why can we believe this? If not, why not?

That disciple whom Jesus loved said to Peter, "It is the Lord!" When Simon Peter heard that it was the Lord, he put on his clothes, for he was stripped for work, and sprang into the sea. But the other disciples came in the boat, dragging the net full of fish, for they were not far from the land, but about a hundred yards off. (21:7–8)

1400. What details in this story show that it is an eyewitness description rather than invented fiction? (See also vv. 9–11.)

1401. Why was John the first one to recognize Jesus?

1402. How is Peter's reaction typical of Peter?

1403. Should the other disciples have jumped into the sea with Peter instead of taking care of the boat and the fish?

When they got out on land, they saw a charcoal fire there, with fish lying on it, and bread. Jesus said to them, "Bring some of the fish that you have just caught." So Simon Peter went aboard and hauled the net ashore, full of large fish, a hundred and fifty-three of them; and although there were so many, the net was not torn. (21:9–11)

1404. (A) Do you see any significance in the fact that Jesus had already prepared breakfast on the beach for his apostles? (B) Will he serve us like that in heaven? (C) Does he do so on earth? (D) Why did Jesus both have his own fish on the grill and ask the apostles for their fish when he did not need their fish and either pile of fish without the other (his pile or theirs) would have sufficed to feed them? (E) How do wise parents do the same kind of thing to their children as Jesus did here?

1405. Why do you think John includes the exact number of fish?

1406. (A) Was this catch of fish literally miraculous? (B) Can we always be sure when a given physical event is miraculous and supernatural and when it is not? (C) If so, how can we know this? If not, give another example of such a borderline case.

Jesus said to them, "Come and have breakfast." Now none of the disciples dared ask him, "Who are you?" They knew it was the Lord. Jesus came and took the bread and gave it to them, and so with the fish. This was now the third time that Jesus was revealed to the disciples after he was raised from the dead. (21:12–14)

1407. Jesus says to his disciples both "come" ("Come and have breakfast") and "go" ("Go into all the world and preach the gospel" —Mk 16:15). What is the relationship between these two commands?

1408. Do you see any significance (perhaps symbolic?) in the fact that it was breakfast rather than lunch or supper that Jesus served?

1409. (A) Why did the disciples not "dare" to ask Jesus "Who are you?" What did they fear? (B) If it was fear that paralyzed their tongues, what does that say about how well they really "knew it was the Lord"? (C) What is the difference between knowing "who he is" and knowing *him*? (Do the demons know who he is? Do they know him?)

1410. Do you see any significance in the fact that this meal consisted of two parts, bread and fish? Would its meaning change in any way if it had been nuts, berries, and milk?

1411. Why does Jesus reveal himself as resurrected at least three times rather than just once?

When they had finished breakfast, Jesus said to Simon Peter, "Simon, son of John, do you love me more than these?" He said to him, "Yes, Lord; you know that I love you." He said to him, "Feed my lambs." A second time he said to him, "Simon, son of John, do you love me?" He said to him, "Yes, Lord; you know that I love you." He said to him, "Tend my sheep." He said to him the third time, "Simon, son of John, do you love me?" Peter was grieved because he said to him the third time, "Do you love me?" And he said to him, "Lord, you know everything; you know that I love you." Jesus said to him, "Feed my sheep." (21: 15–17)

1412. Why does Jesus address Peter by his former and formal name here?

1413. (A) Why does Jesus ask Peter if he loves him "more than these"? (See Mt 26:33.) (B) Why three times? (See Jn 18:15–27.)

1414. Greek has four words for "love": (1) *storge* (spontaneous natural affection), (2) *eros* (desire), (3) *philia* (friendship), and (4) *agape* (charity, self-giving). Which word does Jesus use? What kind of love does he demand from us?

1415. (A) Which word for "love" does Peter use in reply? (B) This reply shows both a positive virtue and the lack of a positive virtue. What positive virtue (other than the love itself that he confesses) is shown by the fact that Peter does not use the same word Jesus uses? (C) What is lacking? What else does Jesus demand?

1416. (A) Why does Jesus demand more? Why does he say we must become perfect (Mt 5:48)? (B) Suppose he didn't. Would that be better for us? (C) Why or why not?

1417. (A) What does this "second chance" for Peter say about Jesus' relation to us? (B) To which of the other apostles did Jesus give a gracious "second chance"? (Hint: Think of the last apostle you would think of. Then read Matthew 26:50.) (C) How does he do the same to us? (D) What difference does that make? If your teacher gives you a chance to retake a test that you flunked the first time, what is the difference between your preparation for that test the first time and your preparation for it the second time? (E) How many times does Jesus do this to us? (F) How many times should we do it to each other? (Hint: How about "seven times"?) (G) How does that help to answer the question of what Jesus means by being "perfect" in Matthew 5:48? (Read the context before that verse.)

1418. (A) What does Jesus mean by "feed my lambs"? (B) Why does he also say "feed my sheep"?

1419. (A) Why does he say that to Peter as soon as Peter confesses that he does love Jesus? (The question is about the timing of what Jesus says, not its meaning. Its meaning was answered already in question 1418.) (B) Why does Jesus say that even though honest Peter has been able to confess only the highest human love, or natural love (*philia,* friendship), for Jesus so far, and not supernatural charity (*agape*)?

H1420. (A) Was Peter "grieved" because he made Jesus repeat his question three times or because his answer made Jesus change his question? To answer this question, you have to look at the Greek word for love Jesus used the third time. What, exactly, is making Peter "grieved" here? (B) What does Jesus' use of that word for love now, in his third question, indicate about what is going on in Jesus' mind and heart at this moment?

1421. (A) Why does Peter reply, not simply "I do love you", but "You know that I love you"? And the third time, "You know all things; you know that I love you"? (B) In light of the context of the personal relationship between Peter and Jesus, and remembering Peter's past, what is Peter feeling now?

"Truly, truly, I say to you, when you were young, you fastened your own belt and walked where you would; but when you are old, you will stretch out your hands, and another will fasten your belt for you and carry you where you do not wish to go." (This he said to show by what death he was to glorify God.) And after this he said to him, "Follow me." (21:18–19)

1422. Why does Jesus preface this prophecy with the formula "truly, truly, I say to you"? What does that add?

1423. Why does John have to interpret and explain to the reader Jesus' words here (v. 19)? He hardly ever does that in his Gospel.

1424. How did Peter in fact die?

1425. How much of what Jesus says here do you think Peter understood? Don't just give the safe, obvious answer: "Not much", or "Only a little". Try to be more specific by using your imagination: put yourself into Peter's position here.

H1426. What is the relation between Jesus' last command here ("follow me") and his three previous ones ("feed my lambs", "tend my sheep", and "feed my sheep")? Why doesn't he just say "feed my sheep" again?

1427. What does it mean to "follow" him? (It would be useful and educational for many people in the study group to answer this question, for there are many good answers to it.)

Peter turned and saw following them the disciple whom Jesus loved, who had lain close to his breast at the supper and had said, "Lord, who is it that is going to betray you?" When Peter saw him, he said to Jesus, "Lord, what about this man?" Jesus said to him, "If it is my will that he remain until I come, what is that to you? Follow me!" (21:20–22)

1428. Why is Peter turning around looking for a diversion here and trying to turn Jesus' attention away from himself and onto John?

1429. How does Jesus respond to this diversion?

1430. (A) How do we, too, do what Peter did when we ask "Will Buddhists be saved? Will atheists be saved? Will more than half of all mankind be saved?" (B) How does Jesus do to us the very same thing he did to Peter here? (How did he answer the disciples' question, "Lord, will those who are saved be few?" [Lk 13:23]?) (C) How is this the same thing he did when the Pharisee asked him "Who is my neighbor?" (Lk 10:29)?

1431. Do you see any irony in John's use of the word "following" in verse 20, in light of the previous situation? (Who followed Jesus to Calvary, John or Peter?)

H1432. Throughout his Gospel, John has used many extra words of circumlocution (look it up!) to describe himself without using his name, and in verse 20 he does it again. Why do you think he does this clumsy thing even here at the end rather than signing his book, so to speak, by revealing that the author and this unnamed disciple are the same person?

1433. What does Jesus mean by his answer to Peter's silly question (v. 22)? Interpret it in the context of the previous conversation, the psychological tension between Jesus and Peter, and Jesus' insistence on teaching Peter something Peter wants to avoid learning.

The saying spread abroad among the brethren that this disciple was not to die; yet Jesus did not say to him that he was not to die, but, "If it is my will that he remain until I come, what is that to you?" (21:23)

1434. How do the other disciples now (in verse 23) make exactly the same mistake Peter has made?

1435. (A) "What is that to you?"—how does that mean something very different from "who cares?" (Surely Peter should care about the fate of his friend John, right?) (B) Compare these words with the words Jesus said to Mary at Cana in John 2:4.

E1436. Do you think this was a really stupid misunderstanding on the part of the other disciples? Do you think that if you had been there your understanding of Jesus' words would have been more accurate? Do you think that now that you have answered 1435 questions about the words of Jesus, or the words of John describing Jesus, you are wiser than the apostles and free from misunderstanding? So you don't need to undertake another Bible study course and ask 1500 more questions, right?

E1437. John does not say when this misunderstanding started. But we have three clues about why it may have persisted. First, John was the youngest of the apostles. Second, John was the only one not martyred—he was only exiled on the island of Patmos. Third, John lived to a ripe old age, writing the last book of the Bible ("Revelation", or the Apocalypse) probably around A.D. 90 or even later, when he was perhaps ninety himself. The average age expectancy in his time and place was something around forty. How are these clues as to why this rumor and misunderstanding may have persisted?

This is the disciple who is bearing witness to these things, and who has written these things; and we know that his testimony is true. (21:24)

1438. The first sentence can be interpreted in two ways: (1) This disciple who is writing these words is the disciple who is bearing witness to these things; I, John, the writer of these words, witnessed these things myself; or (2) This author is someone we know; he is John, and we, his friends and/or disciples, know that his witness is true. He, as Jesus' disciple, certifies that he was an eyewitness, and we, as *his* disciples, certify that he speaks the truth. Which seems more natural to you?

H1439. Scholars are divided into four camps about the authorship of this book. Camp I says that this book as a whole was not written by John but by "the Johannine community" (that part of the early Church which consisted of John's disciples and *their* disciples), on the basis of John's oral teachings, and they used the literary device of a fictional autobiography as a kind of imaginative "thought-experiment": if we had been in John's shoes, this is what we would have seen and heard and felt. Camp II says that John wrote chapters 1–20, ending with the point of it all in 20:31; then John's friends and disciples added chapter 21 as a postscript. Camp III says that John wrote the postscript, too (21:1–23), perhaps later, after he had finished the original book with chapter 20, but that after John's death his disciples ("we") added 21:24 to certify him and his testimony. Camp IV says that John wrote all the verses. Which camp seems more likely to be right to you and why? Evaluate each of the four. Is there textual evidence for your preference for Camp I, II, III, or IV?

1440. (A) How much does this issue (question 1439) matter? (B) Which dividing line or difference between the camps is the most important? (C) Why? (D) Which is the least important? (E) Why?

H1441. (A) If the "we" in "we know that his testimony is true" refers to John's disciples and the "his" refers to John, how do these others ("we") know that John's testimony is true? (B) How do we know that anyone else's testimony is true, e.g., witnesses in court, the writers of a textbook, or newspaper reporters? For nearly all the things we think we know, we know through the testimony and teaching authority of others. How do we distinguish truth from lies with enough confidence to call it "knowing"?

1442. Is the answer to this question (1441B) any different when it refers to Christ from when it refers to a merely secular person or event?

But there are also many other things which Jesus did; were every one of them to be written, I suppose that the world itself could not contain the books that would be written. (21:25)

1443. Is this a mere exaggeration? If not, how can one person be bigger than the whole world?

We conclude with some very speculative but very practical, "existential" questions about our ultimate end, eternal life and happiness in heaven.

1444. (A) Since heaven is probably as much bigger than this world as this world is bigger than the womb, do you think that in heaven we will read these unwritten books of which John speaks, those books that this world cannot contain? (B) Are there other ways to come to know things besides books? (C) Do you think *they* will be in heaven? (D) Do you think books will be in heaven, too? (E) Why or why not?

1445. Why is this verse more important than it seems? (Hint: What would heaven be like if you one day came to the end of your knowing process and knew everything you could ever know?)

1446. Why won't heaven be boring?

1447. How big does it have to be, how much has to be there, for it never, ever to get boring?

1448. What are the only things in this world that are so inexhaustible and unpredictable and new every day that they do not ever have to get boring? (Hint: There are over seven billion of them.)

1449. Even these things get boring if we look at them wrongly. So what is the right way to look at them rightly so that they don't?

1450. (A) In light of your answer to question 1449, what should we do about that fact? (B) When should we start?